EUROPEAN STAMP ISSUES

OF THE SECOND WORLD WAR

About the Author

Formerly a Hertfordshire head teacher and then a history lecturer, Masters Programme Director and European Masters Project Manager in the University of Plymouth's Faculty of Education, Dr David Parker has published several books and many articles in scholarly and popular journals on aspects of late nineteenth- and early twentieth-century social and political history. He and his wife live in Exeter, and they have two grown-up children.

EUROPEAN STAMP ISSUES

OF THE SECOND WORLD WAR

Images of Triumph,
Deceit and Despair

DAVID PARKER

To my family

Pamela, Cheryl, Neil and Louise

with love

First published 2015
This paperback edition published 2021

The History Press
97 St George's Place, Cheltenham,
Gloucestershire, GL50 3QB
www.thehistorypress.co.uk

British Library Cataloguing in Publication Data.
A catalogue record for this book is available from the British Library.

ISBN 978 0 7509 9726 3

Typesetting and origination by The History Press.
Printed in Turkey by IMAK.

Trees for LYfe

CONTENTS

ACKNOWLEDGEMENTS

I am grateful to Guy Thomas, editor of *Stamp Magazine,* for his ready agreement to my request to include some material from three articles on Vichy France, Poland and King Peter II of Yugoslavia I wrote for the magazine between 2012 and 2014.

Note: some stamps have been enlarged and some reduced in size to ensure a balance between the images being close to their references in the text and aesthetic appearance of the page. Full descriptions of the stamps selected for illustration are given in the referenced lists at the end of each chapter. A number of stamps and covers are illustrated in colour and these can be seen in the colour section.

1

INTRODUCTION

Following the evolving fortunes of nations through their stamp issues and postal history is an absorbing study, but particularly so when associated with the thought-provoking and sometimes disturbing stories of the European countries embroiled in the Second World War. This book brings together these two elements, and uses the wide variety of carefully designed sets of stamps produced by wartime governments – whether autonomous or under enemy occupation – to follow how their leaders sought to portray their regimes, influence the people and impose their policies. Stamps were printed in hundreds of thousands, sometimes in millions. They reached every community and at every stage of the war most political leaders were keen to exploit their capacity to communicate ideas, promote events and play on emotions. As skilfully handled instruments of propaganda they were unsurpassed, not least because most people probably saw them as useful, colourful, possibly interesting, but essentially harmless little pieces of paper. This book, however, does not underestimate their considerable value to the likes of Hitler, Mussolini, Stalin and their allies, puppets and enemies, or their capacity to offer us new perspectives on the attitudes, anxieties and assumptions of the disparate warring regimes.

The 1930s were a time of great international tension, partly due to the contested legacy of the First World War, and partly because of bitter ethnic divisions going back centuries. Nazi Germany sought the return of territory in Poland, France, Belgium and Czechoslovakia taken from it by the Treaty of Versailles in 1919. Fascist Italy sought parts of newly created Yugoslavia that it had been promised as a British and French ally in the First World War but not received. Finland was forever fearful of the Soviet Union's designs as it had been a Russian province until 1918. Newly recreated Poland sought to keep both Russia and Germany at bay as much of its territory had been under their rule since the late eighteenth century.

And this was not the end of the continent's interwar troubles. The Hapsburgs' huge Austro-Hungarian domain had disintegrated after 1918 and Hungary had become a shrunken remnant of its former self, but it still viewed portions of Romania, Yugoslavia and Czechoslovakia as its rightful territory. The small Baltic states of Lithuania, Latvia and Estonia were well aware that, until 1918, they too had been Russian provinces until the Revolution provided the opportunity to break free. It was not just whole countries that had jealous neighbours. Within Czechoslovakia and Yugoslavia mutually antagonistic ethnic groups rendered both new countries internally unstable. Neither possessed an abiding sense of nationhood.

With Hitler, Mussolini and Stalin pursuing their aggressive dreams, other nations began to fear their nightmares might become realities. The potentially fatal choices before them were active opposition – as Finland rebuffed the Soviet Union – or a pragmatic alliance – as Hungary and Romania attempted with Germany – or strict neutrality – as decided upon by Norway, Belgium and the Netherlands. Nations naturally sought the alliances and treaties that best suited their prosperity and security as they perceived them at the time, and as we know with the gift of hindsight many nations made disastrous decisions.

The various spluttering conflicts finally erupted into another catastrophic world war claiming millions of lives, laying waste to great cities and huge swathes of land, and ending with the destruction of Fascist Italy and Nazi Germany and the rapid coalescing of two bitterly opposed ideological groupings – capitalist Western Europe and America and communist Eastern Europe and the Soviet Union.

Throughout the war independent nations, and nations under occupation, made great efforts to ensure their postal services operated as efficiently as possible, even under the most inauspicious circumstances. Regular postal services were taken as a sign of national efficiency and were an indication that civilian and business life possessed at least a semblance of order and normality. Postal services retained an international perspective, even though censorship was often strict and postal contact between warring nations generally banned. Countries within alliances, or occupied, received each other's mail, and they corresponded with neutral nations. These regular contacts were important for businesses and families as well as governments seeking to show they remained very much in control of affairs. All nations appreciated the vital part well-managed postal services played in maintaining and boosting the morale of service personnel, often many miles from their homes and families. Huge efforts were made to bring mail to and from distant battle zones and heavily bombed cities despite all the difficulties of collection, transport by road, rail, sea and air, sorting and delivery. Delays caused endless anxiety, and were immediately taken as evidence the war was not going well.

In these arduous conditions postal workers were highly valued and a number of states such as Germany, Romania and also war-torn Greece, Croatia and Serbia issued specially designed sets of stamps to honour their work and publicise key aspects of it, notably the use of trains, planes, motor vans and motor cycles to speed mail on its way (Fig. 1.1). It is, of course, debatable how far the sets reflected the ability of the postal service to operate successfully in these dangerous Balkan countries, where various partisan groups harassed the occupying troops and fought each other with increasing venom. Sometimes a surcharge

Fig. 1.1

raised funds for welfare charities devoted to postal staff and their families. Postal workers themselves were not entirely trusted in Axis-occupied states as their responsibilities for processing mail and freedom to move around relatively easily made them prime targets for recruitment into resistance groups. This was particularly true in Poland.

In May 1940 Great Britain issued its only wartime set (and for this reason has no chapter to itself). The stamps pictured Queen Victoria and King George VI and marked the centenary of the world's first adhesive postage stamp – the celebrated 'Penny Black'. Despite the mounting turmoil, countries as diverse as Bulgaria and Estonia remembered the anniversary too, and a number of celebratory covers, although no special stamps, appeared in Bohemia–Moravia (See Fig. 1.2a & 1.2b in colour section). The war did not stop the meeting of the European Postal Congress in Vienna in October 1942, attended by Germany and its allied and occupied countries – indeed, special stamps were issued by Germany, Slovakia, Norway and the Netherlands to mark the event (See Fig. 1.3 in colour section). It resulted in a European Postal and Telegraph Agreement, and this turned out to be the precursor of CEPT – the wider post-war Conference of European Post and Telegraph Administrations.

Fig. 1.4a

Fig. 1.4b

Most regimes appreciated that stamps were a necessary daily commodity and therefore provided a ready way of sending their own selected messages to the population. Special eye-catching postmarks were used too, sometimes ordered by the government and sometimes added for a small fee by the sender. Karl Hennig, a celebrated Hamburg dealer, pursued numerous issues, as Axis power waxed and waned across Europe, to provide his many clients with souvenir covers complete with key postmarks.

Stamp issues had the great advantage of being under the total control of the government in power – it could determine the themes, designs, production figures, dates of issue, values and surcharges. By the 1930s stamps attracted many thousands of collectors and investors, and numerous well-publicised philatelic exhibitions were staged in major cities across Europe, and it is significant that these popular events continued throughout the war in both occupied and unoccupied countries. Not surprisingly special stamps promoted the exhibitions, and a number of countries, including Nazi Germany, organised national stamp days to stimulate interest in these small but supremely important aspects of national life (Fig. 1.4a & 1.4b).

Every country, with the notable exception of Great Britain, engaged in designing a steady sequence of stamps whose images were calculated to impress upon the populace the policies and attitudes of the government or occupying power. Propaganda has become the pejorative term used to describe carefully composed messages, in words or pictures or both, intended to influence the emotions, attitudes and behaviour of the recipients. The word 'propaganda' also contains the implication that the messages twist and bend the truth, or contain less or more than the truth, or are downright lies. With regard to the wartime propaganda underpinning the philatelic issues discussed in this book, that implication is nearly but not quite always justified.

The wartime images served several purposes depending on who had authority over the country at the time. Some issues were obvious in their intended message, but many, especially in Nazi Germany, were subtle as set by set over the years built up a deceptively attractive picture of the corrupt and vicious regime. In Nazi Germany, for example, stamps constantly sought to reassure the nation that Hitler and the Nazi Party were restoring Germany's national pride, economic prosperity, welfare provision and international reputation apace. Nazi horrors were, of course, never mentioned. In Vichy France, they sought to contribute to the moral regeneration of the nation, and sometimes, as in Poland, they were part of a relentless process of Nazi humiliation. Sometimes the issues were highly optimistic, often in the face of unremitting disaster, as they attempted to unite a despairing nation, but, especially in later years, they could also hint at the suffering many families were enduring as the casualties of war soared. A theme common to most countries, and particularly so in the Soviet Union, Slovakia, Hungary and Romania, was the patriotic plea to the legacy of historic national heroes and heroines who faced persecution, betrayal and defeat until finally triumphing over their seemingly overwhelming enemies.

As this book reveals, lying behind wartime stamp issues were the infinite variations in the political, social, economic, military, ethnic and religious policies of the countries willingly or unwillingly caught up in the violent confrontations. The stamps provide invaluable insights into the diverse, and often changing, aspirations and anxieties of the regimes that commissioned them.

Illustrations

Fig. 1.1 Romania: Postal Employees' Relief Fund and Bicentenary of National Postal Service miniature sheet (March 1944). Germany: Examples from Postal Employees' and Hitler's Culture Fund sets: 3*pf*+2*pf* Postal Employees' Rally and 10*pf*+5*pf* Distributing postal employees' prizes (15 September 1939) and 6*pf*+9*pf* Postwoman at work (3 May 1944).

Fig. 1.2 Estonia: first day cover with Centenary of First Adhesive Postage Stamp set (30 July 1940). Bulgaria: Centenary stamp (19 May 1940).

Fig. 1.3 Germany: Commemorative postcard with European Postal Congress set overprinted '19.Okt.1942' marking the date of the agreement, and special postmark (19 October 1942).

Fig. 1.4 Vichy France: Commemorative cover and se-tenant stamps and label from Dijon Philatelic Exhibition (19 April 1942). The Netherlands: Stamp Day stamp (9 October 1943). Germany: National Stamp Day stamps: 6*pf*+24*pf* Philatelist (11 January 1942), 6*pf*+24*pf* Mail Coach (10 January 1943) and 6*pf*+24*pf* post horn (2 October 1944).

2

GERMANY: THE THIRD REICH 1933–45

Propaganda was central to the rise to power of Adolf Hitler and the National Socialist Party in 1933. It was, though, provided with a sound foundation by the discontent, even despair, within Germany in the aftermath of its sudden collapse in the final months of the First World War and the unexpectedly harsh terms of the Treaty of Versailles. The Allied blockade had eventually caused severe food shortages, and it was a combination of ensuing civil unrest, mutinies of disillusioned seamen, and the collapse of confidence by military leaders when their 1918 offensives faltered, which brought about the Armistice. As far as the Germans were concerned it was only an armistice, but the Allies quickly appreciated the chaotic situation within Germany and treated the cessation of hostilities as a complete victory. Kaiser Wilhelm II reluctantly abdicated, a democratic republic painfully emerged after a brief communist interlude, and in the face of Allied threats to resume the war the humiliated government had little choice but to sign the Treaty of Versailles on 28 June 1919.

By its terms Germany lost 25,000 square miles of land and 7 million people. Small areas around Eupen and Malmedy went to Belgium, and the provinces of Alsace and Lorraine reverted to France after nearly fifty years in German hands. The coal-rich Saar was placed under League of Nations authority for fifteen years, when a plebiscite would determine its future – and return it to Germany. Meanwhile, all its coal would go to France. Other historically disputed territories such as Schleswig-Holstein on the border with Denmark, and parts of Upper Silesia bordering Czechoslovakia, and southern East Prussia bordering Poland, were also earmarked for plebiscites within the next few years.

Although a separate treaty formally broke up the Austro-Hungarian Empire, Germany was forbidden to unite with the new republic of Austria. Germany also had to recognise the sovereignty of newly created Czechoslovakia, which included the remaining part of coal-rich Silesia and the largely German-speaking area of the Sudetenland that ringed its border with Germany. Poland was re-established as a sovereign nation, and was to be recognised as such by Germany. It now incorporated the old Germanic regions of Posen, Pomerania and Soldau, partly to ensure the new country had access to the sea, by what became known as the Polish Corridor that completely severed East Prussia from the rest of Germany. The important Baltic port and hinterland of Danzig, a key to Poland's prosperity, were also lost to Germany as they comprised a Free City under the League of Nations. And, although it was not part of the treaty, Germany had to withdraw from the Baltic States, Belarus and the Ukraine, all of which it had secured at the Treaty of Brest-Litovsk in March 1918 when Russia's struggling Bolshevik government decided to withdraw from the war.

Germany also lost all its colonies. The African ones were shared between France, Belgium, South Africa and Great Britain, those in China and the North Pacific went to Japan while those in the South Pacific went to Australia and New Zealand.

The Allies, but especially France, were intent upon rendering Germany incapable of future military aggression. Its army was reduced to 100,000 infantry and cavalry men, the General Staff was abolished, and new rules imposed to ensure there was no possibility of Germany building a large reserve of trained men or stockpiling heavy weapons. The Rhineland, a province running along the border with Belgium and part of France, was demilitarised and all fortifications demolished. The once mighty German navy was reduced to 15,000 men and a few elderly battleships and coastal vessels; submarines were banned. Germany was not allowed a military air force, although it could run a civilian fleet after a year or so. Particularly humiliating was the forced acceptance of a War Guilt Clause placing all the blame for the outbreak, death and destruction of the conflict upon Germany alone. As a consequence Germany was saddled with a vast reparations bill.

In the light of subsequent events, it is highly significant that the Allies had not been in complete agreement about the terms of the treaty. Georges Clemenceau, the French Prime Minister, had actually sought a Rhine border or a Rhine buffer state with Germany, and argued for the virtual commercial, military and financial emasculation of Germany. David Lloyd George, Great Britain's premier, was less obsessed with future German aggression, and felt his country could benefit from the gradual, although not immediate, restoration of Germany as a trading partner. President Woodrow Wilson of the United States was inclined to even greater leniency but was primarily concerned with creating new nations from the ancient European empires who would prosper through their new ethnic unity, self-determination and trading agreements. The Allies undoubtedly attempted to mix due punishment of Germany with vague aspirations for future European harmony, but very soon Hitler and the Nazis shrewdly perceived and exploited the weaknesses and the opportunities of Versailles to their great advantage.

The Nazis played skilfully on the anxieties and aspirations of the German people when their defeat and humiliation were compounded by the twin agonies of post-war unemployment and rampant inflation. In addition the tariffs placed by other nations on German goods impeded the country's economic recovery, and rendered the payment of reparations increasingly difficult. When the world Depression hit Germany in 1930 the nation's morale was at a low ebb and general dissatisfaction with the government at an all-time high. Hitler, however, had two significant ideas that helped him gain popular support and then seize power in 1933. By 1930 the Nazi Party (the National Socialist German Workers' Party) had evolved from a small group of fundamentally anti-capitalist agitators into a well-organised national political party vigorously promoting its ability not only to solve all Germany's economic problems but also to restore its national pride and international standing.

Despite widespread knowledge of the Nazi Party's aggressive street fighting campaign and rabid anti-Semitism, the overriding allure of achieving national stability through a combination of massive public works and heavy spending on rearmament gained Hitler wide-ranging support from all classes. In the 1932 Reichstag (Parliament) elections the Nazis secured 37.3 per cent of the vote, becoming the party with by far the largest number of seats, and although their numbers fell a little in a further election later in the year President Hindenburg had little choice but to appoint Hitler as Chancellor with effect from 30 January 1933. Crucially, the other parties failed to form an alliance to stop his appointment. In March 1933 a third election saw the party secure a dominating 43.9 per cent vote, and Hitler swiftly consolidated his power. He became dictator of Germany when Hindenburg conveniently died on 2 August 1934 and a national referendum confirmed his position as 'Führer' ('Leader').

In *Mein Kampf*, the book Hitler wrote in 1925–26, he recognised the power of propaganda. It had, he said, to appeal to the emotions rather than the intellect of the masses, and incite the imagination to envisage a better future. It had to sweep away all opposing ideas, and it had to target clear enemies of the people and provide a simple moral basis and justification for defeating them. He added, 'Propaganda must not investigate the truth objectively ... [It] must be confined to a few bare essentials and those must be expressed as far as possible in stereotyped formulas.' He scorned the ability of the masses to retain or even fully understand messages, and asserted that constant repetition was required until ideas had taken popular hold.

Although posters, speeches, films and school books hammered home the evil threat of Bolsheviks and Jews to the security and prosperity of Germany, numerous Nazi stamp issues eschewed these political and ideological campaigns and concentrated upon the celebratory and commemorative aspects of Nazi Germany. Fundamentally the philatelic images and accompanying postmarks were calculated to bring comfort, even complacency, to the millions of people using them. Until the final stages of the war their themes embraced the glories of a resurgent Germany and its recent economic achievements while not forgetting the glories of its past which Hitler was dramatically recreating for all to enjoy and admire. Women and children, homes and health, and sport and culture figured regularly in stamp issues, along with regular reminders of the all-powerful Führer and the dominant political party driving the nation forward to avenge the humiliations of 1919.

Fig. 2.1   *Fig. 2.3*

Historical links overtly intended to strengthen Hitler's legitimacy dominated early issues. Forever an admirer of the military prowess and autocracy of Frederick the Great (King of Prussia 1740–86) the first stamp of Hitler's Chancellorship, ostensibly marking the opening of the Reichstag in Potsdam, featured the monarch's portrait. In 1933 it was Frederick's devotion to national aggrandisement that caught Hitler's imagination, but a dozen years later it was his predecessor's fortitude in adversity that dominated his thoughts. Indeed, in 1945 Hitler had Frederick's coffin hidden in a salt mine to prevent its desecration (Fig. 2.1). Later that year a set of nine Welfare Fund stamps featured scenes from the operas of Hitler's favourite composer, Richard Wagner (1813–83). Wagner drew inspiration from Germanic mythology for his powerful works, notably *Der Ring des Nibelungen*, and Hitler admired the visionary figures heroically striving against misunderstanding, ignorance and evil to achieve their purpose. Wagner has been accused of anti-Semitism and a belief in superior and inferior races, but the jury remains out on any final verdict. Interestingly, many leading Nazis did not share their leader's admiration of Wagner's lengthy works (See Fig. 2.2 in colour section).

In 1933, too, the definitive set featuring the head of President Hindenburg was reprinted using paper with a swastika watermark, and all subsequent Third Reich issues followed suit. The swastika soon appeared as the key feature on the redesigned government official stamps, and was equally clear at the core of the sun bringing light to the world on the new Air set (Fig. 2.3). It was, however, sparingly used on ordinary issues, perhaps to allow people to make their own connection between the themes and the Führer. The only exceptions were issues marking Nazi Party events. A bold symbol with mythological and sacred antecedents across several cultures, the swastika was used as the national as well as the Nazi Party emblem, and so was the image of the winged eagle perched on a wreathed swastika. The eagle's head faced right when used as a party emblem and left when it became the national badge.

The most celebrated party event was the annual autumn congress or rally. Held first at Munich in 1923 and 1926, and then at Nuremberg in the heart of the Reich in 1927, 1929 and every year from 1933 to 1939, the minutely choreographed meetings became increasingly devoted to heightening the image of the Führer. The emotional speeches, martial music and colourful parades replete with hundreds of eagle standards, swastika flags and banners culminated in party members and the armed forces reaffirming their loyalty to Hitler. After the event books, pamphlets and films, notably Leni Riefenstahl's 1934 hero-worshipping *Triumph of the Will*, gave nationwide publicity to the later congresses. From 1934 onwards stamps added to the celebrations, featuring the swastika-eclipsed sun rising above Nuremberg Castle in 1934, the German eagle hovering over the city in 1935, the salute to the swastika in 1936 and, for the final three years, particularly stern and thoughtful portraits of Hitler alongside the inscription '*Reichsparteitag Nurnberg*' and the date. The miniature sheet used in 1937 possessed the cultic inscription '*Wer ein volk retten will kan nur heroisch denken*' which translates best as 'He who will save a race must think noble thoughts' (Fig. 2.4).

Fig. 2.4

Other key events and dates in the Nazi calendar merited special stamps. In March 1935 War Heroes Day featured a steel-helmeted soldier, and highlighted the sterling efforts of German soldiers during the First World War and in quelling the left-wing dissidents at home after the Armistice. The Nazis preferred to blame Germany's demise in 1918 on cowardly politicians and Jewish intrigue rather than the collapse of military morale (See Fig. 2.5 in colour section). An even more important anniversary for the Nazis was 9 November 1923, the day of their failed first attempt to seize power in the Munich '*putsch*'. Commemorative stamps in 1935, 1943 and 1944 recalled the heroism of party members in that premature and hopeless fight (See Fig. 2.6 in colour section).

Not surprisingly Hitler's birthday – 20 April – assumed national importance, and was celebrated lavishly and publicly by senior party members. It was part of the personality cult managed alongside every other aspect of propaganda by Joseph Goebbels, the head of Germany's Ministry of Public Enlightenment and Propaganda. The first celebratory stamp appeared in 1937, and each year up to 1944 a different but invariably dramatic picture appeared of the Führer in uniform looking suitably authoritative or else (as in 1940) fondly greeting a child (Fig. 2.7). The April 1945 set, the final stamps of the Third Reich, featured SA and SS storm troopers, a rare and last-minute philatelic tribute to Hitler's elite armed forces as they defended the ruins of Berlin.

Soon after the Nazis took power Goebbels skilfully exploited the 'dictated' Treaty of Versailles and blamed the malign influence of Jews for all the nation's ills. The communists were equally savagely condemned for their attempts to infiltrate Germany, and the chaos surrounding their brief seizure of power in 1918–19 lent credence to the attacks. Caricatures of manic Bolsheviks delighting in reducing families and the nation to chaos, and of money-grabbing or lustful Jews doing much the same, adorned thousands of posters and magazines, but stamps remained free from such primitive, though evidently successful, propaganda. Stamp designs were of superior quality, and their messages more subtle, for they were targeting families and businesses, both of whom, the ministry could safely assume, preferred wholesome images of prosperity and security

Fig. 2.7

Fig. 2.8   Fig. 2.9

under the Führer's charismatic leadership. Stamps and letters are very personal items of everyday life and were treated differently from the rabble-rousing propaganda against international Jewry and communism. Some indication of the success of Third Reich stamp issues was their enormous popularity with the general public, so much so that often restrictions were placed on the number of copies individuals could purchase. Virtually all commemorative issues were heavily surcharged for charities, mainly Hitler's mysterious and unaccountable Welfare Fund, but nevertheless large numbers of covers were produced as souvenirs rather than ordinary mail. Special cancellations adorned with further patriotic images and inscriptions were common, and they intensified the intended message of the stamps.

Just one set was issued, in June 1934, which harked back to Germany's overseas empire even though the Nazis had little serious interest in its restoration. Nevertheless it reminded people of the extent of the Versailles humiliation, and it was no accident that very soon afterwards sets promoted the 1934 Saar Plebiscite and the Nuremberg Rally. The four figures featured in the Colonists set had much in common with each other, and one can see why the Nazis admired them. Franz Lüderitz (1834-86) first traded in what is now Namibia, and when it was ceded to Germany, he ensured the tribes were completely subjugated and land cleared for settlers. Gustav Nachtigal (1834-85) became Consul General for West Africa and then Commissioner for West Africa and seized Togoland and Cameroon for the empire. Karl Peters (1856-1918) sought German mastery of East Africa through native treaties and the brutal use of military force, and vigorously opposed the British in the war. Hermann von Wissman (1853-1905) explored much of Central and East Africa, and then concentrated upon subjugating the tribes in the east (Fig. 2.8).

Each lost European territory Hitler restored to Germany was celebrated by a stamp issue and accompanying special cancellations. The image they created was of grateful families welcomed home, and in many cases the image was true. The first was the Saar where a plebiscite in January 1935, as laid down at Versailles, resulted in a 98 per cent turnout and a 90.8 per cent vote in favour of rejoining Germany. A tiny minority opposed the National Socialists, and they were persecuted soon afterwards. The previous year two German stamps stridently claiming ownership of the Saar had helped whip up support for reintegration, but after the plebiscite the celebratory issue featured a mother embracing a child (Fig. 2.9).

Austria was next. Hitler, and indeed many Germans, sought the union of all Germans in one sovereign nation, and the '*Heim ins Reich*' ('Home to the empire') message was widely preached. Despite the post-war ban, Nazis in both countries agitated for unification, and Austria started to succumb to severe civil unrest. Germany avidly sought Austria's mineral resources, gold reserves, hydroelectric supplies and its unemployed labour force. Under relentless pressure from the rising political and military might of Germany, and realising France and Great Britain would not intervene, Chancellor Schuschnigg of Austria first stopped actions against the Nazis, then allowed them into his government, but to Hitler's surprise finally announced a plebiscite to decide the nation's future. Sensing victory but fearing troublesome opposition, on 12 March 1938 Hitler ordered his troops into Austria well before the plebiscite. In the event overt opposition faded away, enthusiastic crowds welcomed the soldiers, the new Nazi governor Arthur Seyss-Inquart assumed control, Hitler addressed massive crowds, and on 10 April a belated overwhelming popular vote sanctioned the unification. Seyss-Inquart immediately launched actions against Austrian Jews and all those who had publicly opposed unification.

On 8 April, just before the plebiscite, Austria and Germany issued a joint stamp showing two young men from Austria and Germany with arms on each other's shoulders and banners that somehow vaunted the swastika but hid any vestige of the old Austrian flag. The border inscription read '*Ein Volk Ein Reich Ein Führer 10 April 1938*' ('One People One Nation State One Leader 10 April 1938'). Just before the plebiscite numerous Austrian stamps were cancelled with the slogan '*Am 10 April dem Führer dein "Ja"*' ('On 10 April say "Yes" to the Führer'). At the same time many covers were produced with both Austrian and German stamps, often using the celebratory (and sometimes premature) postmark from Vienna inscribed '*Tag des Grossdeutschen Reiches*' ('Greater Germany Day') (See Fig. 2.10 in colour section). That November a set of nine Winter Relief stamps featured attractive views of Austrian mountains, lakes, castles and cities. Significantly they included the statue of the great early eighteenth-century soldier, Prince Eugene, and not surprisingly the highest value stamp featured Hitler's birthplace, Braunau (See Figs 2.11 & 2.12 in colour section).

Hitler hurried on to annex the Sudetenland, the largely German-speaking part of Czechoslovakia. For some time local Nazis, with widespread support, had agitated for reunion with Germany. The deep civil unrest they caused within Czechoslovakia gave Hitler the opportunity he wanted to pressurise the Czech government into, first, agreeing to equal rights for German-Czech citizens, and then acquiescing in the celebrated Munich Agreement between Germany, Italy, France and Great Britain to cede the territory to Germany. Germany occupied the Sudetenland in early October 1938, and in March 1939 a completely isolated and demoralised Czechoslovakia was broken up. In December 1938 a smiling Sudeten miner and his wife appeared on a celebratory stamp, and in doomed Czechoslovakia a plethora of covers appeared with Czech stamps heavily over-printed with the date '1 X 1938' or *'Wir sind frei!'* ('We are free!') and cancelled with postmarks revealing the speed with which Czech place names had been replaced with German ones (see Chapter 4, Bohemia–Moravia).

On 1 September 1939 Germany invaded Poland and annexed Danzig the follow-ing day. On 18 September it issued two stamps featuring the ancient St Mary's Church and Crane Gate inscribed *'Danzig ist Deutsch'* ('Danzig is German'). The conquest of Poland as a whole received no commemorative issue, but Danzig and its hinterland was deemed thoroughly German, not least because it had been incor-porated into Prussia in 1814 and represented a particular bitter part of the Treaty of Versailles. Ever since then the vocal German population had sought reunion, and indeed on 1 September itself the Danzig Free State definitive stamps had been issued overprinted with German values (See Fig. 2.13a & 2.13b in colour section).

During the summer of 1940 the sweeping German advance through the Low Countries and France begun in May was not marked by any issue, except for two stamps featuring peaceful views of Eupen and Malmedy, two small cantons in Belgium, just 380 square miles in all, bordering Germany. Transferred from France to Prussia in 1815, they had been ceded to Belgium in 1919 and now were absorbed back into the Reich. Both cantons were largely German speaking, both had uneasy relations with other Belgian cantons, and both had sizeable and troublesome Nazi factions in the 1930s (Fig. 2.14).

On 6 April 1941 German forces invaded the Kingdom of Yugoslavia along with contingents from Italy, Hungary and Bulgaria. When the Kingdom was subsequently broken up western Slovenia was ceded to Italy, a slither in the east granted to Hungary, and northern Slovenia, formerly part of the Austro-Hungarian Empire and immediately to the south of post-war Austria, was annexed by Germany. Many Germans lived in the provinces of Steirmark and Karnten making up the newly acquired territory, and that September four

Fig. 2.14

picturesque stamps commemorated their change of nationhood. One stamp featured the ancient town hall at Marburg and its balcony from which Hitler gave his speech making 'this land German again' to mass applause (Fig. 2.15).

The sets marking the return of alienated territory had remarkably similar designs, and no doubt deliberately so. They showed picturesque rural or urban scenes, and they had no Nazi emblems. Their deliberate understatement and their comforting images pushed the more ugly aspects of Hitler's diplomatic and military triumphs into the background, and rendered the steady reversal of the Treaty of Versailles by the Führer that much more publicly impressive.

Other sets of stamps ensured Germans living within the Third Reich fully appreciated its return to its historic borders – as planned and achieved by its Führer. The Winter Relief Fund was a high profile annual Third Reich charity engaging the nation in intensive publicity and fundraising activities. In due course lengthy sets of surcharged stamps played their part not only in promoting the event but also reminding the nation of its newly restored lands with their natural and historic glories. In autumn 1939 a pictorial Winter Relief set featured views of the former Austrian cities of Graz, Klagenfurt and Salzburg, and Elbogen Castle and Schreckenstein Castle in the Sudetenland, alongside those of Drackenfels (Dragon's Rock), Goslar Castle, the ancient Romer in Frankfurt and Hohentwiel Castle in the heartland of Germany. Schreckenstein Castle had the added allure that Richard Wagner had stayed nearby when he was inspired to compose *Tannhauser,* and Drackenfels contained the cave where Wagner's hero Siegfried killed the dragon Fafnir (Fig. 2.16). Continuing this policy, the 1940 Winter Relief set included historic sites in the important cities of Torun (German Thorn) and Poznan (German Posen) which were formerly part of Poland but were now included in the German administrative regions (Gaus) of Danzig–West Prussia and Wartheland respectively. The Artus (Arthur) Court

Fig. 2.15

Fig. 2.16

Fig. 2.17

in Danzig itself was included. The post-1918 Polish corridor and free port status of Danzig so hated by Germany had been eradicated. As far as Hitler's Third Reich was concerned these cities were as much German as Kaub, Heidelberg, Trier, Bremen and Münster on the other stamps in the set (Fig. 2.17). And, just like everywhere else in the Third Reich, the ex-Polish cities were being scoured of their Jews and everyone else the Nazis considered undesirable.

The return of Alsace and Lorraine in 1940 did not merit a set. French families heavily outnumbered German ones, and many remembered the German persecution of French families during the First World War. Nevertheless the legacy of German ownership between Germany's heavy defeat of the French in 1870 and its own defeat in 1918 ensured the provinces changed hands again, although legal annexation and absorption into the Reich did not occur until 1942, after which many young men were forced into the German armed forces. In July 1940 Alsace joined Gau Baden and Lorraine Gau Westmark, and they used German definitive stamps overprinted in Gothic script with each province's name – Elsass or Lothringen – until the end of 1941 when ordinary German stamps were introduced.

Although Luxembourg was an autonomous state, it was seen as a natural possession by Germany after its occupation in 1940 and it, too, was attached to a German Gau. Up to January 1942 German definitive and Winter Relief stamps overprinted 'Luxemburg', and Luxembourg stamps overprinted with German values, were used, but after that ordinary German stamps came into general circulation.

The definitive stamps overprinted for use in Alsace, Lorraine and Luxembourg contained the portrait of the elderly German President, Marshal Paul von Beneckendorff und von Hindenburg, who had appointed Hitler chancellor in January 1933, and died the following year (Fig. 2.18). Privately Hitler scorned the First World War hero as out of touch with German needs and ambitions, but in public he strengthened his claims of legitimacy, and role in restoring Germany's former glory, by honouring the marshal while he was alive and keeping his memory alive after his death. In a dramatically staged ceremony Hindenburg's body was laid in a mausoleum added to the vast multi-towered Hohenstein Castle built at Tannenberg in East Prussia in 1924–25 on the site of the marshal's famous victory over the Russians in 1914. Black-edged Hindenburg definitive stamps added to the overall backward-looking event, which Hitler was able to use to good advantage to portray the Third Reich as essentially peace loving and trusting that the great nations of the world would recognise and respond sympathetically to its just grievances. Tannenberg became a place of national pilgrimage and, along with the great East Prussian castles at Allenstein, Königsberg and Heilsberg seized from Poland in 1772 by Frederick the Great, it was commemorated in a miniature sheet produced to celebrate the International Philatelic Exhibition in Königsberg in June 1935 (See Fig. 2.19 in colour section). The Nazis avidly promoted the thought that they were the lineal descendants of the medieval Teutonic Knights, in addition to recreating the heroic deeds of their far more distant mythical Nordic ancestors. The castles' destinies were more prosaic. In 1945 the devastated cities of Allenstein and Heilsberg were returned to Poland along with partially destroyed Tannenberg (emptied of Hindenburg's coffin by order of Hitler in January 1945). Königsberg and its empty smoke-blackened castle became part of the Soviet Union.

Fig. 2.18

It was only in August 1941 that Hitler's head replaced Hindenburg's on the definitive set. By then it looked as though Hitler would soon be master of both Western and Eastern Europe. Indeed that November Hitler was able to mark the subjugation of swathes of Soviet territory with the enforced use of these definitive stamps overprinted 'Ukraine' and 'Ostland'. The deliberately bland title 'Ostland' ('Eastland') covered Estonia, Latvia, Lithuania, north-east Poland and west Belarus; 'Ukraine' included the Crimea and parts of south Belarus as well as Soviet Ukraine. All other local post-invasion issues, usually Russian stamps with celebratory German overprints, were quickly phased out (see Chapter 18, The Baltic States). Not surprisingly the overprinted Hitler head definitive stamps proved popular with the occupying forces and relocated German families, and many covers were sent back to Germany with numerous stamps adding up to far more than the required postage rate. No other German stamps penetrated these vast regions that were earmarked for ruthless economic exploitation, the elimination of all Jews, and the gradual introduction of ethnic German communities (Fig. 2.20).

The achievements of the armed forces remained absent from philatelic issues until 1943 when the tide of war was obviously turning against Germany. Until then it had been the Nazis' domestic triumphs that contributed to ordinary families' overall sense of well-being and, at least until 1939, to the enhancement of Germany's international reputation. In 1934 the images of a sturdy blacksmith, farmer, mason and miner together with a sculptor, architect, scientist, merchant and rather paternal looking judge adorned an early Third Reich Welfare Fund set (Fig. 2.21). It reflected the regime's frequently expressed assertion that, although it could restore full employment, all able-bodied men must devote their talents to the restoration of the economy – and by that the Nazis meant obedience to the increasingly authoritarian state. No serviceman was included: the Treaty of Versailles remained in force and the military expansion programme remained surreptitious. The following year's Welfare Fund pictured ten women in highly decorative, if impractical, provincial costumes. No doubt the women represented the Nazis' ideal females – tall, blonde, blue-eyed, loyal and robust (Fig. 2.22).

Fig. 2.20

Fig. 2.21

Numerous posters and neoclassical statues promoted the ideal Aryan body. However, although Hitler and the Nazis recognised that female voters had manifestly assisted their rise to power, once in power the regime pushed the clock back to Emperor Wilhelm II's belief that women's primary concerns were '*Kinder, Kuche, Kirche*' ('Children, Kitchen, Church'). Although there were nota-

Fig. 2.22

ble exceptions, such as Leni Riefenstahl the film maker, and Hanna Reitsch the test pilot, by and large women found it increasingly difficult to enter politics or the professions, except nursing, but easier and easier to follow Nazi Party routes into organisations devoted to healthy games and exercises, motherhood classes and political indoctrination. After producing four children they were awarded the Cross of Honour of German Motherhood; if they got to eight the cross was in gold. For single German women there were largely low status jobs available as servants, clerks, farm and postal workers, and as auxiliaries in the armed forces, but in January 1943 the chronic labour shortage, despite the imported forced workers, led Hitler to order all women under the age of 50 to report for local employment. Over 14 million ended up in munitions factories.

The few stamps featuring women reinforce these trends. The allegory of a woman and child as Germany embracing a newly recovered region has already been mentioned, and a similar comforting image of a mother gathering her family within her arms adorned the 1936 set marking the International Local Government Congress (See Fig. 2.23 in colour section). The painting of a beautiful but demure Venetian girl by the celebrated artist Albrecht Dürer (1471–1528) was chosen for the stamp marking German Art Day in July 1939 (See Fig. 2.24 in colour section). The Nazis were particularly keen on Dürer whose religious paintings, especially of the Madonna, fitted in with their views, at least the ones they professed, on strict public morality and virtuous female behaviour. In 1943 the single Winter Relief stamp showed the perfect Aryan mother adoring and being adored by three children with the medal-winning fourth in a cradle (See Fig. 2.25

in colour section). The following year the set celebrating the tenth anniversary of the state's 'Mother & Child' Organisation highlighted the support offered German mothers at nurseries, in hospitals, at home by visiting nurses, and in convalescent homes (See Fig. 2.26 in colour section). In 1944, too, another smiling young Aryan girl in a headscarf publicised the Labour Corps alongside a stamp featuring a more serious looking young man. The previous year only young men had appeared in the Labour Corps set – smartly attired and armed with scythes, pick-axes, shovels and sledge-hammers (See Fig. 2.27 in colour section). The corps was founded in 1931 but reformed by the Nazis in 1935 to provide a compulsory six-month period of state service prior to military training for men, and a voluntary period of service for young women – although it became compulsory for them too in 1939. Bicycles, tools and paramilitary uniforms complete with swastika armbands were provided, the units lived together in barracks, discipline was strict, and political indoctrination accompanied regular physical training, the acquisition of various skills and long hours on farms and building sites, in army supply depots or wherever the national and local economy and war effort dictated. The unswerving commitment of young men and women to the service of the Führer was the core objective, and not surprisingly Hitler appeared in a suitably uplifting pose on the 1939 Labour Day stamp (Fig. 2.28). The same personal dedication and pride in achievement characterised the Vocational Contest for Apprentices. Stamps featuring the victor's crown on a swastika background in 1935, and behind the German eagle emblem in 1939, ensured the state's commitment to, and control of, young workers was clear to see (Fig. 2.29).

The Third Reich youth organisations embraced the Young German Folk (10–14 years) and Hitler Youth (14–18 years) for boys, and the Young Madel (10–14 years) and League of German Girls (14–18 years) for girls. Founded by the Nazis in the 1920s, membership became mandatory for boys in 1936. It was taken very seriously. For the older age group, local units were run on paramilitary lines. Their members had uniforms, took oaths of allegiance, attended regular classes, rallies and camps, and engaged in a great deal of exercise, crafts and Nazi indoctrination, including anti-Semitism and anti-communism. Membership involved

Fig. 2.28

Fig. 2.29

intense physical, mental and emotional training at a time when young people are at their most impressionable for a lifetime of devoted state service. It was also the precursor of military training, and group leaders looked out for future officer material. In 1935 stamps picturing a Hitler Youth trumpeter commemorated the World Jamboree of Hitler Youth, and in 1938 a youthful bare-chested torch-bearer was featured on stamps marking Hitler's fifth year as Führer (Fig. 2.30). In 1943 a Youth Dedication Day involving theatrical rallies replete with flags, banners, marches, martial music, speeches and oaths, featured an Aryan boy and girl against the swastika flag looking admiringly at someone, presumably Hitler, beyond the borders of the stamp (See Fig. 2.31 in colour section). The final stamp featuring a youth was issued in February 1945 to mark the People's Militia ('*Volkssturm*') and its contribution to the final stages of the war. Thousands of boys, some aged only 13, along with thousands of elderly men, were given primitive weapons, sketchy training, some semblance of uniforms and thrown into the last desperate battles in East Prussia and around Berlin. Many were brave, but they were swept aside by the Soviet armies (See Fig. 2.32 in colour section).

Fig. 2.30

Fig. 2.33

Nazi ideology preached the gospel of Nordic racial superiority, and this included physical fitness. Not surprisingly the Sports Day of the Armed Sturm Abteilung (the Panzer Division formed from the Nazi 'Brownshirts' militia) merited a stamp with a sword, swastika and laurel wreath emblem in 1942 (Fig. 2.33) The Greek ideal of a healthy mind in a healthy body lurked somewhere within Nazi ideology, and the 1936 Winter Olympic Games at Garmisch-Partenkirchen and summer Games in Berlin were planned as showpieces of Nazi organisation and German sporting prowess, and cementing the central place the nation was regaining in European affairs. In November 1935 surcharged stamps picturing skating, ski-jumping and bobsleighing advertised and raised funds for the January Winter Games, and the following May stamps in a similar style featuring a German footballer, javelin thrower, gymnast, fencer, rowers, show jumper and the torchbearer together with the only female figure, a diver, did the same for the Summer Games. Two miniature sheets were issued, each with four stamps and a clear watermark inscription reading '*XI Olympischespiele Berlin 1936*' (See Fig. 2.34a & 2.34b in colour section). Several special Olympic handstamps were available – as usual at extra cost. The great German airship, *Hindenburg*, flew over the Olympic site trailing the Olympic flag and heralded Hitler's arrival for the opening ceremony on 1 August (See Fig. 2.35 in colour section). Germany did well at both games, coming second to Norway in the Winter Games and topping the league table with eighty-nine medals in Berlin. However, controversy haunted the Summer Olympics with Hitler first wanting to ban black and Jewish competitors but later relenting in the face of mounting American opposition, and then deciding to backtrack on the heavy use of swastikas in the village and arena. Controversy arose, too, when some foreign competitors appeared to give Nazi salutes, and finally stories abounded of Hitler's anger at the black American Jesse Owens winning four gold medals. Overall, though, the Nazis considered the events fully confirmed their belief in a resurgent Germany and its swiftly rising standing in international affairs. Many overseas visitors praised the warmth of German hospitality and the smooth running of the Games.

Many domestic sports events merited stamp issues, partly as advertisements, partly to raise funds, and partly to reassure a nation increasingly accustomed to the strictures of Nazi rule that these stimulating pastimes were part and parcel of a healthy German life and culture. Indeed, despite all the traumas of war, they were perpetuated as popular and morale-boosting occasions that provided both distractions and a semblance of enduring normality as Germany began to stare defeat in the face in 1944. Horse racing was a very popular spectator sport in Germany before the war, and remained so throughout it. Each June or July from 1936 until 1944 a surcharged stamp appeared with striking pictures of horses in shades of brown to help fund and advertise the popular Brown Ribbon race meeting at Riem near Munich. In some years images of mounted Amazon warriors, Allegories of Victory and Roman charioteers linked the national event ever more closely to the heroic antecedents beloved of the Nazi hierarchy. In 1936 a miniature sheet with the watermark inscription '*München Riem 1936*' gave additional publicity, and it was used again the following year with an additional bright red overprint '1 August 1937' within an oak leaf wreath surmounted by the Third Reich's eagle clutching a swastika. No greater sign of state approval could be given (See Fig 2.36 in colour section).

More horses appeared – this time in blue – on stamps marking the annual Blue Ribbon race. Known as the German Derby since its inauguration, and inscribed as such on the stamp issued in June 1939 to mark its seventieth anniversary, the name was quickly changed when war broke out to the '*Grosser Deutschlandpreis der Dreijährigen um "Das Blaue Band"*' ('Greater Germany Prize for Three-Year-Olds in "The Blue Ribbon"'). Blue Ribbon stamps appeared in 1940, 1941 and 1942 while the race continued to be run in Hamburg, but not in 1943 and 1944 when it was transferred to Hoppegarten, the magnificent racecourse several relatively safe miles from Berlin. By the summer of 1943 Hamburg was enduring incessant bombing raids, with huge casualties and widespread devastation. In those two years stamps marked the Grand Prize of Vienna races instead (See Fig. 2.37 in colour section).

Other leisure and sporting events meriting stamp issues included the International Leisure Congress held in Hamburg in 1936 (Fig. 2.38). It was another huge event closely linked to the Olympic Games and equally welcomed by the Nazis. Over 3,000 participants from sixty-one countries attended, and over a million people were estimated to have watched the typically well-choreographed parade. Sub-titled 'Joy and Peace' the Congress was one in a line of such worldwide events, usually held in the country hosting the Olympic Games, and dedicated to promoting popular health-enhancing activities. Here, perhaps, the Nazis overplayed their hand, as there was much subsequent criticism of the Third Reich's authoritarian approach to what would now be called state sport and leisure management. No doubt indicative of the Nazi trend was the 1938 set picturing the ancient cathedral, town hall, Centenary Hall and also the new Hermann Göring Stadium in Breslau, the city about to host the sixteenth German Sports Tournament (Fig. 2.39).

Hitler displayed an abiding interest in the ability of architecture to transform Nazi ideology into, literally, concrete form for all to see and admire. Huge arenas such as those at Nuremberg, Berlin and Breslau were perfectly suited to his desire to cloak events with awe-inspiring emotional overtones calculated to enhance the image of the Third Reich, and in particular its Führer, with participants and onlookers alike. Hitler dwelt not so much upon one architectural style as upon the style most likely to achieve his purpose in a particular setting. Fundamentally he desired monumental structures that transmitted a sense of the authority and confidence of the Third Reich, while at the same time enveloping its people in the security it bestowed. The Winter Relief stamp set in 1936 featured nine of them, ranging from the multi-arched Heroes Memorial at the Nuremberg Rally complex, the colonnaded Museum of (officially recognised) German Art in Munich, the grand Führerhaus of the Nazi Party also in Munich, the multistoried Air Ministry in Berlin, and the slab-like glass-plated Berlin Deutschlandhalle used in the Olympic Games, to the wide and sweeping roads through the Alps and soaring bridges across the Rivers Salle and Mangfall (See Fig. 2.40 in colour section). In 1938 stamps featured the new theatre funded by the state and opened by Hitler in another grand ceremony full of flags, bands, soldiers and speeches in Saarbrücken. By 1939 a vast quarry in Stuttgart had been turned into the large public Killesberg Park complete with a grand hall that held the National Horticultural Exhibition that year. Its colonnaded entrance hall, so typical of Third Reich state-funded buildings, featured on the stamps marking the event. The massive portals of the late eighteenth-century Brandenburg Gate in Berlin became a key Nazi symbol, and dwarfed the torchlight parade beneath it in the stamp marking the tenth anniversary of the Third Reich in January 1943 (Fig. 2.41).

Fig. 2.38

Fig. 2.39

Fig. 2.41

No opportunity was lost to enhance the Third Reich's manufacturing reputation and trading contacts either worldwide before the war or with its satellite states during it. The annual trade fair held in the great city of Leipzig had existed since the Middle Ages, and attracted merchants from across Europe. From 1895 it was known as *Muster-Messe* (Pattern Fair) and the stamps promoting it included the double MM logo created in 1917. The fair was huge, with several dozen 'fair-houses' or pavilions, and between the wars a new technical fairground was built. In 1940 stamps featured historic sites in the city along with a view of the fair, and the following year a set inscribed '*Reichmesse Leipzig 1941*' pictured the ancient cloth and exhibition halls, the grand railway station and the House of Nations. Ironically, just as the fair had reached its height under the Nazis, the whole site was given over to armament production, and not surprisingly in due course it attracted heavy bombing (Fig. 2.42).

Fig. 2.42

Since 1921 Vienna had staged a trade fair and attention switched there with two promotional sets in 1941 containing pictures of the city and striking items from the arts that characterised this event (See Fig. 2.43 in colour section). The arts in Vienna, as elsewhere in Greater Germany, were subject to the dictates of the Reichkulturkammer (the Reich Chamber of Culture), a department within the Ministry of Propaganda, which controlled all aspects of cultural life, notably literature, music, the theatre and fine arts. Most modern art and music were deemed 'decadent' and banned, and the work of Jewish artists and composers stood little chance of reaching the general public. Stamp issues reinforced Nazi preferences. In 1942, 1943 and 1944 stamps featured exquisite examples of the goldsmiths' craft in sets marking the tenth and subsequent anniversaries of the German Goldsmiths' Institution (See Fig. 2.44 in colour section).

In 1934 a stamp marked the 150th anniversary of the poet, playwright and philosopher Friedrich von Schiller (1759–1805) whose essays arguing that human beings could exercise reason to control their emotions to such an extent that their sense of duty and personal inclinations could be in perfect harmony no doubt gratified Hitler, who believed he had achieved such an elevated state of being. In 1943 two stamps commemorated the Styrian poet Peter Rosegger (1843–1918) whose works attained great popularity as well as the favour of both the German and Austro-Hungarian emperors for their love of the countryside and a shrewd but largely favourable analysis of the social impact of modernisation (Fig. 2.45).

In 1935 three stamps featured approved composers of suitable birth, vintage and style – Heinrich Schütz (1585–1672), whose work influenced Johann Sebastian Bach (1685–1750), the composer of the celebrated Brandenburg Concertos, and his Baroque contemporary George Frederick Handel (1685–1759). Mozart (1756–91) was another favourite Nazi composer, and a stamp in 1941 marked the 150th anniversary of his death. Keen to claim him as a German genius, the Nazis ordered 'Mozart weeks' and numerous concerts to be held across German-occupied Europe that year. Ironically Mozart was born in the archbishopric of Salzburg, a virtually independent state within the loosely federated Hapsburg Holy Roman Empire, but it seems he preferred to think of himself as German rather than Austrian (See Fig. 2.46 in colour section).

Several Third Reich stamps marked the work of German scientists. Common features were the closeness of their work with state institutions and the practical value of their research to the nation. Otto von Guericke (1602–86) conducted key experiments into vacuums, pistons and the nature of space, and he was also the long-serving burgo-master of Magdeburg and friend of the Elector of Brandenburg, who was a great patron of science. Two others, both Nobel prize-winners, made remarkable contributions to the health of the nation, and indeed the world. Emil von Behring (1854–1917) created antitoxins for the treatment

Fig. 2.47

Fig. 2.45

of diphtheria and tetanus, the latter a great killer of wounded soldiers. Robert Koch (1843–1910) was a bacteriologist who identified the causes of tuberculosis, cholera and anthrax (Fig. 2.47). Long before 1914 Imperial Germany had established a national health service, and in the 1920s the republic had revitalised and modernised it. The Nazis both promoted and controlled the work of medical practitioners, many of whom joined the Nazi Party. The nation enjoyed a range of state subsidised health services, but at the same time as the wartime issues appeared commemorating Behring (1940) and Koch (1944) a number of doctors were conducting their researches into eugenics, deformities and the effects of high altitude and frozen seas on the helpless inmates of concentration camps.

German technology was encouraged by Hitler, and not least in the manufacture of racing cars and also cheap cars for the masses. The Berlin Motor Show had been staged each year, and occasionally twice a year, since 1897, and returned in 1921 after a break during the war and the civil chaos that followed it. Its popularity had faded, though, and the event struggled to keep going until the powerful new breed of German racing cars produced during the Third Reich seized the public imagination. In 1931 just under 300,000 visitors attended, but in 1936 Motor Show stamps featuring the pioneering manufacturers Gottleib Daimler and Carl Benz reflected the renewed interest stimulated by national success. 825,000 flocked to the event in 1939 when the new 'Volkswagen' (people's car) was on show. Not surprisingly a set of stamps appeared that February featuring the first Daimler and Mercedes-Benz cars, the world speed record-breaking Mercedes-Benz and Auto-Union racing cars, and the new '*Kraft durch Freude*' ('strength through joy') Volkswagen ordered by the Führer soon after he took office (See Fig. 2.48 in colour section). Difficulties linked to satisfying Hitler's demand for mass producing a family car capable of 100km an hour for just 990 Reichmarks meant that Hitler was the only German who actually received a 'VW Beetle' before the start of the Second World War. In May 1939 the set was reissued overprinted 'Nürburgring – Rennen' to commemorate the international German Grand Prix (See Fig. 2.49 in colour section). It was widely believed to be the most demanding and dangerous race in the world when it was held on this famous circuit between Cologne and Frankfurt with its narrow track and 174 bends. An Auto-Union car won in 1934 and then either Auto-Union or Mercedes-Benz won each year between 1936 and 1939, the last race before the war. In 1935 the senior Nazis in attendance were incensed when an Alfa Romeo just beat the favourite, Manfred von Brauchitsch in a Mercedes-Benz, to the flag.

Other German technical achievements commemorated in stamps included the great airships – the LZ127 *Graf Zeppelin* and the LZ129 *Hindenburg* – that sailed sedately to and fro across the Atlantic Ocean. Although all commemorative stamps attracted special cancellations and cachets, the airship voyages were probably the most popular. German airships had carried mail from 1908 until they were requisitioned for military use in 1914, but it was the *Graf Zeppelin* that caught the public imagination with its flights between Germany and the

USA from September 1928 onwards. In 1929 it circled the globe, and made 590 flights before it was taken out of service in 1937. Each flight carried about 12 tons of mail. In 1933 a set of Zeppelin stamps originally issued in 1928 reappeared overprinted '*Chicagofaht Weltausstellung 1933*' ('Chicago World Fair Flight 1933') (Fig. 2.50). The huge Century of Progress International Exposition in Chicago was seen as a perfect opportunity for the new Nazi government to impress the world as the legitimate and confident successor of a faltering and discredited republic. The Nazis envisaged a swastika-adorned German pavilion and airship flying slowly overhead sealing the image of a resurgent nation in the eyes of the world. Unfortunately even many German-Americans opposed the Nazi regime, although others were avid supporters, and amidst great controversy the old red, yellow and blue German flag was used. Nevertheless the arrival of the *Graf Zeppelin* over Chicago was a highlight of the fair, watched by excited crowds.

A year later a portrait of Count Ferdinand von Zeppelin and the *Graf Zeppelin* appeared on the highest value of the new Airmail set, and in March 1936 the new *Hindenburg* was celebrated in two airmail stamps as it began its spectacular but short career (See Fig. 2.51 in colour section). Both airships took time out from their civil voyages to act as propaganda agents of the Third Reich, flying over the Rhineland, the Saar and the Sudetenland at critical times dropping publicity leaflets, and visiting the Olympic Games and Leipzig Fair. Although the very public devastation of the *Hindenburg* as it approached its mooring mast at Lakehurst in the United States on 6 May 1937 ended the awesome era of the Zeppelins, in July 1938 two stamps picturing the pioneering count and the *Graf Zeppelin* marked the centenary of his birth. In 1940 the surviving parts of airships were broken up as scrap metal to be used in aircraft production.

Ships, trains and aeroplanes also received attention. The centenary of the German railways in 1935 saw a set picturing ancient and modern locomotives culminating in the impressive new streamlined expresses. The first steam-hauled train ran from Nuremberg to Furth in Bavaria in 1835 – when Germany was still a cluster of independent states. In 1944 the Focke-Wulf Condor, Dornier Do-26 Flying Boat and Junkers Ju-90B appeared on a set marking the twenty-fifth anniversary of the German Airmail Service – a service that endured all perils up to the final days of the war (Fig. 2.52). In 1937 a Winter Relief set

Fig. 2.50   Fig. 2.52

pictured nine German vessels from fishing smacks and train ferries to great ocean liners. One was the new 25,000 ton *Wilhelm Gustloff*, named by Hitler in memory of the assassinated Swiss Nazi Party leader. On 30 January 1945 the liner was in the Baltic Sea and crowded with soldiers and civilians escaping the Russians advancing across East Prussia. It sank within minutes of being hit by three torpedoes from a Soviet submarine and 9,400 lives were lost. The liners *Tannenberg* and *Hamburg* sank after hitting mines in the war, and *Europa* was captured by the Allies in 1945 (See Fig. 2.53 in colour section).

Very few military figures appeared on stamps before 1943; the exceptions were the steel-helmeted veteran and the 'Brownshirt' in 1935 and a Civil Defence Union officer in 1937 (Fig. 2.54). Eight years later, though, Soviet armies were pushing the Germans westwards, and huge casualties were being incurred. In addition, the new generation of Allied bombers was reaching far into Germany, even Berlin itself. There were savage penalties imposed for defeatist talk, but the drafting of women into employment, the shift in propaganda to persuading the nation it was the only European bulwark against communism, and the tacit admission that this would be a long war were clear signs that things were not going well, even if people preferred to believe Hitler's vision of ultimate victory. By then Goebbels' well-honed skills in controlling the media had ensured the concepts of the *Führerprinzip* (the leader principle or cult), the *Volksgemeinschaft* (the people's community or socialist state) and the *Herrenvolk* (the master race) had been firmly driven home. Now the final concept, that of *Blut und Boden* (blood and soil) would rise to the surface as even greater sacrifices were called upon. Suddenly in March 1943 a set of twelve stamps marking Heroes' Day featured the fearsome weaponry of the modern

armed forces in dramatic action. A U-boat had just attacked a merchant ship, an SS unit was firing a heavy machine gun, an advancing infantryman was about to hurl a grenade, and searchlights were piercing the sky, anti-aircraft guns were firing, parachutists were landing, and Stuka aircraft were releasing their bombs. It is a moot point whether families found the images stimulating, alarming or comforting (Fig. 2.55).

Fig. 2.54

Fig. 2.55

Fig. 2.57

Fig. 2.58

A similar set issued a year later coincided with the intensification of Allied bombing against civilian as much as industrial targets, and the obvious retreat of German and satellite armies in the face of overwhelming Soviet forces. Goebbels minimised the scale of the setbacks and eulogised German courage and fortitude, and perhaps the difference between the 1943 and 1944 sets lies in the later set's overall lack of aggressive attacking drama. The thirteen stamps covered a large range of weaponry from submarines and motor torpedo boats to armoured trains and tanks, and seaplanes and rockets, but a key special postmark contained the revealing inscription *'Deutschland Wird Siegen!'* ('Germany will triumph') implicitly acknowledging that determination and defiance in defence – until the tide turns – is the set's desperate message (See Fig. 2.56 in colour section).

Historical German cities were honoured in 1944 and 1945, notably Königsberg, Innsbruck, Fulda and Oldenburg, to inspire the beleaguered nation with the enduring legacy of German traditions and culture, but the Third Reich's final stamps featured the remnants of its shattered armed forces (Fig. 2.57). In February 1944 three determined infantrymen are seen advancing with rifles and bayonets at the ready but on closer inspection one is an old man and another a young lad (see Fig. 2.32). They are members of the Volksturm, the ill-trained and ill-armed militia wasted in the Third Reich's last desperate battles. The stamp's inscription *'Ein Volk Steht Auf'* ('the people arise') hardly masks the military bankruptcy. As Soviet troops neared the heart of Berlin, the very last stamps appeared on Hitler's birthday, 20 April 1945. They pictured the determined faces of an SA trooper and an SS trooper, members of the Führer's most fanatical units. The fact that the stamps were designed, printed and officially released signifies their importance as instruments of propaganda – or the surviving Nazis final succumbing to their own propaganda – but in the prevailing chaos very few were used for postage (Fig. 2.58).

Illustrations

Fig. 2.1 25*pf* Frederick the Great from the Opening of the Reichstag set (12 April 1933).

Fig. 2.2 40*pf* Parsifal from the Wagner-themed Welfare Fund set (1 November 1933).

Fig. 2.3 15*pf* from State Official Series (18 January 1934), 25*pf* from Air set (21 January 1934) and 16*pf* from Party Official set (2 March 1942).

Fig. 2.4 Nuremberg Rally stamps (29 August 1934, 7 September 1935, 3 September 1936, 3 September 1937 miniature sheet, 25 August 1939).

Fig. 2.5 6*pf* 'Steel Helmet' from the War Heroes Day set (15 March 1935), and Heroes Remembrance Day stamp (10 March 1942).

Fig. 2.6 Twentieth Anniversary of Munich Rising stamp (5 November 1943).

Fig. 2.7 Hitler's Birthday stamps (13 April 1939, 10 April 1940, 14 April 1944).

Fig. 2.8 25*pf* Hermann von Wissman from German Colonisers' Jubilee set (30 June 1934).

Fig. 2.9 Saar plebiscite and restoration stamps (the 6*pf* from 26 August 1934 and 12*pf* from 16 January 1935).

Fig. 2.10 Illustrated cover inscribed with the '1850–1938' dates of the Austrian Post Office, the Joint Austrian Plebiscite stamps (the larger Berlin issue on the left, the smaller whiter Vienna issue on the right) and the last set of Austrian stamps marking Christmas 1937 (8 April 1938).

Figs 2.11 and 2.12 Cover with 3*pf*+2*pf* Forchtenstein Castle and 12*pf*+6*pf* Prince Eugene statue in Vienna from the 18 November 1938 Winter Relief set. The cover also has the two German stamps (2 December 1938) featuring miners marking the creation of the Sudetenland Gau, together with a commemorative postmark from Brux, the German name for the former Czech city of Most.

Fig. 2.13 8*pf* and 1 *RM* overprinted Danzig stamps (1 September 1939) and cover with the German '*Danzig ist Deutsch*' set and commemorative postmark (18 September 1939).

Fig. 2.14 Eupen and Malmedy set (15 July 1940).

Fig. 2.15 12*pf*+13*pf* Steirmark and 6*pf*+9*pf* Karnten from the Northern Slovenia set (29 September 1941).

Fig. 2.16 4*pf*+3*pf* Drachenfels and 5*pf*+3*pf* Goslar Castle stamps from the Winter Relief set (October–December 1939).

Fig. 2.17 3*pf*+2*pf* Danzig Artushof and 15*pf*+10*pf* Prague New Theatre from the Winter Relief set (November–December 1940).

Fig. 2.18 Single examples of ordinary, and Osten, Alsace, Lorraine and Luxembourg overprinted, and black-edged mourning President Hindenburg definitive stamps.

Fig. 2.19 Königsberg International Philatelic Exhibition miniature sheet (23 June 1935).

Fig. 2.20 Single examples of ordinary, and Ukraine and Ostland overprinted, Hitler head definitive stamps.

Fig. 2.21 25*pf*+15*pf* Sculptor and 40*pf*+35*pf* Judge from the Welfare Fund set
(5 November 1934).

Fig. 2.22 5*pf* +3*pf* Rhineland and 6*pf*+4*pf* Lower Saxony costumes from the Welfare
Fund set (4 October 1935).

Fig. 2.23 3*pf* from the International Local Government Congress set (3 June 1936).

Fig. 2.24 German Art Day stamp (12 July 1939).

Fig. 2.25 Winter Relief stamp (1 September 1943).

Fig. 2.26 3*pf*+2*pf* Day Nursery from the 'Mother and Child' Organisation set
(2 March 1944).

Fig. 2.27 12*pf*+18*pf* 'Pick and Shovel' Fatigues and 6*pf*+4*pf* Girl Worker from the
Labour Corps sets (June 1943 and June 1944 respectively).

Fig. 2.28 Labour Day stamp (28 April 1939).

Fig. 2.29 12*pf* Victor's Crown and 6*pf* Eagle and Laurel Wreath from the Vocational
Contest for Apprentices sets (26 April 1935 and 4 April 1939 respectively).

Fig. 2.30 6*pf* Trumpeter from the World Jamboree of Hitler Youth set (26 July 1935)
and 12*pf*+8*pf* Hitler Youth from the Fifth Anniversary of Hitler's Leadership set
(28 January 1938).

Fig. 2.31 Youth Dedication Day stamp (26 March 1943).

Fig. 2.32 Mobilisation of People's Militia stamp (6 February 1945).

Fig. 2.33 SA Sports Day stamp (12 August 1942).

Fig. 2.34 12*pf*+6*pf* Ski-jumping from the Winter Games set (25 November 1935)
and one of the two Summer Games miniature sheets (1 August 1936).

Fig. 2.35 Commemorative postcard, with cachet, flown in the airship *Hindenburg* on
1 August 1936 over the Olympic Stadium.

Fig. 2.36 'Brown Ribbon' Horse Race overprinted miniature sheet (1 August 1937).

Fig. 2.37 25*pf*+5*pf* German Derby (18 June 1939), 25*pf*+100*pf* 'Blue Ribbon'
(22 June 1940) and 12*pf*+88*pf* Vienna Grand Prix (August 1944).

Fig. 2.38 6*pf* 'Leisure Time' International Recreational Congress stamp (30 June
1936).

Fig. 2.39 6*pf* Hermann Goring Stadium from the sixteenth German Sports
Tournament set (21 June 1938).

Fig. 2.40 Se-tenant 5*pf*+3*pf* Heroes Memorial, Nuremberg and 6*pf*+4*pf* Bridge
across the Saale, and se-tenant 12*pf*+6*pf* Alpine Road and 3*pf*+2*pf* Frontier
Autobahn from the Winter Relief set (September–November 1936).

Fig. 2.41 12*pf*+18*pf* Theatre from the Saarpfalz Gautheater (9 October 1938) and
15*pf*+5*pf* Columned Entrance from the Stuttgart Horticultural Exhibition (22 April
1939) sets, and the 54*pf*+96*pf* Brandenburg Gate commemorating the Tenth
Anniversary of the Third Reich (26 January 1943) stamp.

Fig. 2.42 12*pf* Exhibition Building from the Leipzig Fair set (1 March 1941).

Fig. 2.43 3*pf* Dancer (8 March 1941) and 12*pf*+8*pf* Belvedere Palace (16 September
1941) from the Vienna Fair sets.

Fig. 2.44 12*pf*+88*pf* Cream Jug and Loving Cup from the tenth anniversary of the National Goldsmiths' Institution set (8 August 1942).

Fig. 2.45 6*pf* Friedrich von Schiller (5 November 1934) and 12*pf*+8*pf* Peter Rosegger (27 July 1943).

Fig. 2.46 Cover with the Composers' Anniversaries set (21 June 1935).

Fig. 2.47 6*pf* Otto von Guericke (4 May 1936), 25*pf*+10*pf* Emil von Behring (26 November 1940) and 12*pf*+38*pf* Robert Koch (25 January 1944).

Fig. 2.48 Illustrated cover with the Berlin Motor Show set and special postmark (17 February 1939).

Fig. 2.49 6*pf*+4*pf* Berlin Motor Show stamp with Grand Prix overprint (18 May 1939).

Fig. 2.50 2RM 1928 Zeppelin stamp overprinted '*Chicagofaht Weltaussteliung* 1933' (10 October 1933).

Fig. 2.51 Cover, and cachets, with the two Hindenburg airmail stamps (16 March 1936) flown on the airship's first North American flight.

Fig. 2.52 12*pf* Modern Locomotive from the Railway Centenary set (10 July 1935) and 12*pf*+8*pf* Dornier Do26 Flyting Boat from the twenty-fifth Anniversary of Airmail Services set (11 February 1944).

Fig. 2.53 The ill-fated liners *Wilhelm Gustloff* (6*pf*+4*pf*), *Tannenberg* (12*pf*+6*pf*) and *Hamburg* (25*pf*+15*pf*) from the Winter Relief set (4 November 1937).

Fig. 2.54 3*pf* from the Reichs Luftschutz Bund (National Civil Defence Union) set (3 March 1937).

Fig. 2.55 4*pf*+3*pf* Machine-Gunners, 12*pf*+8*pf* Grenade Throwers and 25*pf*+15*pf* Junkers Ju87B Dive Bombers from the Armed Forces and Heroes' Day set (21 March 1943).

Fig. 2.56 15*pf*+10*pf* Tank, 24*pf*+10*pf* Armoured Train and 30*pf*+20*pf* Alpine Trooper from the Armed Forces and Heroes' Day set (11 March 1944).

Fig. 2.57 Single stamps commemorating the 1,200th anniversary of Fulda (11 March 1944) and 600th anniversary of Oldenburg (6 January 1945).

Fig. 2.58 Berlin cancelled-to-order set marking Hitler's 56th birthday (20 April 1945).

3

FINLAND

Finland spent the war years attempting to steer a difficult course, both politically and militarily, that allowed it to preserve its hard-won independence from the aggressive policies of its giant neighbour, Soviet Russia, and from too close an entanglement with Nazi Germany as its forces thundered into Denmark and Norway and then across the Baltic States of Lithuania, Latvia and Estonia towards Leningrad. Its stamp issues directly reflect its military actions, domestic hardships and attempts to bolster national pride at a time of potentially lethal alliances.

Between 1809 and 1918 Finland had been under Russian sovereignty. A Grand Duchy within the Tsarist Empire, Finland remained largely peaceful until Russia's attempts to tighten central control of its sprawling western provinces in the early twentieth century caused increasing resentment. During the 1917 revolution in Russia Finland seized the moment to declare its independence, and after a brief but bloody civil war a capitalist democracy was established and the first Finnish president elected in 1919.

In the 1920s there were several potentially explosive incidents along the sensitive border with the Soviet Union, and in the 1930s the Soviet Union limited and then completely blocked Finnish access to the shipping lanes between Lake Ladoga and the Gulf of Finland. Conversely, some in Finland dreamed of reoccupying Karelia that had been ceded to the Soviet Union in 1920 in return for the northern port of Petsamo and its hinterland. Stalin remained deeply concerned that the Finnish border was only 32km from Leningrad and that Finnish islands straddled the sea approaches to the city through the Gulf of Finland.

Under the infamous German–Soviet Union pact of 1939 Finland, along with the three Baltic States, was deemed within the Soviet sphere of influence. Soon afterwards the Baltic States accepted Soviet demands for military bases, and subsequently lost their independence in 1940. Finland refused similar pressures, and vigorously opposed a Soviet invasion in November 1939. The famous Winter War was a humiliation for the Soviet Union whose over-confident commanders were outwitted, and their ill-trained troops slaughtered by the hugely outnumbered but highly mobile Finnish army. Skilfully commanded by Marshal Carl Mannerheim, and well camouflaged and fast-moving through the deep forests, the Finns outflanked and destroyed two complete Soviet divisions at

Tolvajarvi, and another two at Suomussalmi. But Soviet reinforcements were endless. By March 1940 Finland was exhausted, even though its 25,000 casualties were a tenth of the Soviet Union's. By the Treaty of Moscow Finland agreed to cede the Karelian Isthmus, including the important city of Viipuri bordering Lake Ladoga, to the Soviet Union.

Later in 1940 Finland accepted a deal with Nazi Germany under which weapons were supplied in return for permission for German troops to pass through Finnish territory on their way to Norway. In June 1941, days after Hitler invaded the Soviet Union, Stalin launched strikes against several Finnish cities, and the Continuation War began, lasting until September 1944. Initially Finnish forces under Marshal Mannerheim did well, retaking the Karelian Isthmus, advancing towards Leningrad, occupying swathes of new territory in Eastern Karelia, and finally cutting Leningrad off from the north. With the Soviet Union engaged in a life or death struggle with Germany, the Finns held their new front line until June 1944 when its army was surprised by a massive Soviet assault and was pushed back to its March 1940 borders. The Finns were fortunate that Stalin concentrated on racing to Berlin rather than crushing Finland, and an armistice in September 1944 merely ratified the 1940 frontier.

Fig. 3.1

Fig. 3.2

Finnish stamps reflected the conflict in distinctive ways. Masking the nation's exhaustion, in February 1940 the Lion of Finland was proudly publicised on a stamp raising funds for the National Defence League (Fig. 3.1). A regular series of surcharged stamps sought to raise funds for the Red Cross, a dire necessity in such times of crisis. In 1940 a Red Cross set pictured ancient and modern Finnish soldiers, in 1941 and 1945 sets portrayed civilian workmen and families, in 1942 and 1943 they focused on arms of Finnish provinces, but in 1944 they were harder hitting and pictured Red Cross ambulances, trains, airplanes and hospitals in action (Fig. 3.2).

On 30 August 1941 a set picturing Viipuri Castle celebrated the reconquest – the previous day – of the strategically important city on the Gulf of Finland north of Leningrad (See Fig. 3.3 in colour section). Clearly the event had been eagerly anticipated. The city had been Finnish until it was evacuated and ceded to the Soviet Union at the end of the Winter War, and now it was hurriedly resettled with Finns. The war dominated stamp issues in 1941. A number of Military Field Post stamps and overprints began in that year, and both the wartime president, Risto Ryti, and the military commander-in-chief, Marshal Mannerheim, had sets of six stamps devoted to their portraits (See Fig. 3.4 in colour section & 3.5 below left).

Fig. 3.5

Risto Ryti (1889–1956) was prime minister during the Winter War, and became president in December 1940. Although an Anglophile at heart, the trading links with Germany and the threats from the Soviet Union led to his military cooperation with Germany, although Finland was careful never to sign the Tripartite Pact with Germany, Italy and Japan. Nevertheless he believed Germany would overrun the Soviet Union, and certainly he allowed concentration camps to be built in Eastern Karelia as part of an ethnic cleansing policy. Hard pressed in 1944, he promised Germany, in return for supplies, that he would not seek a separate peace with Stalin. Nevertheless not long afterwards he was forced to resign (or renege on his promise) and his successor, Marshal Mannerheim, secured an armistice, as a result of which Finnish and German troops in Lapland turned from allies into foes. In 1946 Ryti was tried and imprisoned as a war criminal, although many saw him as a scapegoat for striving to keep his country autonomous and democratic in extremely perilous circumstances. In such sensitive international circumstances, it is not surprising that there were no stamps marking Finland's alliance with Nazi Germany.

Nevertheless the new, if temporary, province of Eastern Karelia was deemed significant enough to merit several issues to itself. Some were pre-war sets reissued in new colours and overprinted '*Ita-Karjala Sot.hallinto*' ('East Karelia Military Administration') but others were the December 1941 Risto Ryti and Carl Mannerheim sets, reissued a couple of months later, also in new colours and overprinted (See Fig. 3.6a & 3.6b in colour section). The plethora of covers with sets of '*Ita-Karjala*' stamps and Eastern Karelian postmarks, especially from its capital Aanislinna, formerly the Russian iron and timber producing city of Petrozavodsk, reveals the popularity of the occupation. In November 1943 the Finnish provincial arms set of stamps was extended to include Eastern Karelia (Fig. 3.7).

In contrast to Ryti, Marshall Mannerheim (1867–1951) became, and remains, a national hero. A Russian general before the Bolshevik Revolution and Finland's independence, he crushed the Finnish Bolsheviks in the civil war, and later led the Finnish army to stunning victories and equally skilful defensive actions. However he was careful to avoid all German offers of any personal authority over German forces, of formal military alliances and of participation in other German campaigns. He retained popularity as an essentially Finnish patriot, and during a brief but important spell as president (August 1944–March 1946) he distanced Finland from Germany, negotiated peace with Stalin, avoided charges of 'crimes against peace' and ensured the Allies came to respect the nation's autonomy.

Fig. 3.7

Fig. 3.8

Fig. 3.9

Fig. 3.10

Fig. 3.11

Other issues celebrated the nation's specific culture and, thereby, its autonomy. In 1940 a stamp marked the tercentenary of Helsinki University, in 1942 the tercentenary of the introduction of printing into Finland was celebrated, and in 1944 a stamp commemorated the centenary of the birth of the popular writer Minna Canth (1844–97), whose plays highlighted the plight of women and workers (Fig. 3.8). One of a pair of stamps issued in May 1942 pictured Helsinki's soaring cathedral and classical city hall that contrasted, no doubt deliberately, with the other's view of Tampere's smoking chimneys and factories. Together they showed a confident and productive nation, and it was probably no accident that the battles at Tampere and Helsinki had been the decisive ones in the defeat of the Bolsheviks in the brief but bitter Civil War of 1918 (Fig. 3.9).

Major political figures in Finland's short and perilous independent existence were not forgotten either. In May 1941 a mourning stamp was issued picturing President Kyosti Kallio's (1873–1940) farewell review of troops on his retirement – which was in fact the day he died, 19 December 1940 (Fig. 3.10). President from 1937 to 1940, his reputation as a consolidator of Finnish political stability and advocate of social reform had been highlighted recently to sustain national morale in the war. The death of another staunch defender of Finnish independence and culture, Pehr Svinhufvud (1861–1944), the former regent, prime minister and president, was marked by a second mourning stamp in

August 1944 (Fig. 3.11). President from 1931 to 1937, he had triumphed over the troublesome fascist movement within the country, and also ensured the extreme socialists had not taken advantage of the situation. European mourning stamps were unusual, although not unknown, and these were clearly calculated to link Finland's current military and political campaigns with those of the young nation's fragile but determined past.

Finland was deemed an ally of Nazi Germany in the Paris Peace Treaty, and ordered to pay huge reparations to the Soviet Union – which it accomplished by 1952. Nevertheless it retained its 1940 borders and independence intact – the only European country bordering the Soviet Union to do so.

Illustrations

Fig. 3.1 2m+2m Lion of Finland National Defence Fund (15 February 1940) stamp.

Fig. 3.2 Red Cross sets: the 50p+5p Crossbowman from the Military Figures set (26 January 1940), the 50p+5p Lapland from a Provincial Arms set (2 January 1943), 2.75m+25p Brothers in Arms Welfare Fund (15 May 1941) stamps, the 3.50m+35p Karelia from a similar set (2 January 1942), the 4.50m+1m Red Cross aeroplane from the Transport & Hospital set (2 January 1944) and the 3.50m+75p Mother and Child from a Families & Workers set (2 May 1945).

Fig. 3.3 Censored commercial cover with the 1.75m from the Reconquest of Viipuri set (30 August 1941) and the 1.75m+15p Farmer from a Red Cross Families and Workers set (2 January 1941).

Fig. 3.4 1943 Military Field Post stamps.

Fig. 3.5 1.75m President Risto Ryti and 5m Marshal Carl Mannerheim (31 December 1941).

Fig. 3.6 Illustrated first day cover from Aanislinna with the set of overprinted definitive and commemorated stamps (1 November 1941) for use in Eastern Karelia. Two similarly overprinted stamps from sets in new colours portraying President Ryti and Marshal Mannerheim (20 February 1942).

Fig. 3.7 First day cover with the Eastern Karelia arms stamp surcharged for the National Relief Fund (1 March 1943).

Fig. 3.8 2m University Building marking the 300th anniversary of Helsinki University (1 May 1940), 3.50m Medieval Press from the Tercentenary of the Introduction of Printing in Finland set (10 October 1942) and 3.50m Portrait marking the birth centenary of Minna Canth (20 March 1944).

Fig. 3.9 50m Tampere and 100m Helsinki (2 May 1942).

Fig. 3.10 President Kallio mourning stamp (15 May 1941).

Fig. 3.11 President Svinhufvud mourning stamp (1 August 1944).

4

BOHEMIA–MORAVIA

After his successful dealings with Austria, a triumphant Hitler turned his attention to neighbouring Czechoslovakia, a country wracked by political and ethnic instability. The eastern half, Slovakia, disliked the post-1918 forced marriage with the western half, Bohemia–Moravia, feeling its largely pastoral economy and eastern-looking culture had little in common with its domineering, more highly industrialised, western-looking partner. Bohemia–Moravia was not only surrounded on three sides by Germany but German-speaking families dominated large swathes of Czech land (the Sudetenland) along those three sides – and had little in common with the Czechs or the newly created Czechoslovakia. The situation was ripe for exploitation by Hitler, especially when a strongly nationalist political party akin to the Nazis, and ultimately indistinguishable from it, came into being in the Sudetenland.

The situation in the late 1930s owed much to the complex ethnic and border issues facing the peacemakers at Versailles after the First World War. The Czechs had arrived in Bohemia shortly after the collapse of the western Roman Empire, and the Germans had arrived around its edges much later – mainly in the thirteenth century. A principality by the ninth century and a kingdom in the twelfth, Bohemia grew to become a leading state in Medieval Europe, notably under King Premysl Otaker II (1253–78), whose lands stretched to the Adriatic, King John the Blind (1310–46), whose pro-French alliances led to his death at the Battle of Crécy, and King Karel (1346–78) who made Prague a great city to match his election as Holy Roman Emperor. The Catholic Hapsburgs started to rule Bohemia in 1526, and consolidated their grip in 1620 after the defeat of the Protestant rebellion in 1620. Gradually the old kingdom of Bohemia faded away, except as the Hapsburg Emperor's subsidiary title, and became absorbed into the overall Austrian Empire.

Although ancient borders changed dramatically from time to time, the history of Slovakia followed a different route. In the eleventh century it became part of the Polish state to the north, in the thirteenth century it was ravaged by the Mongols from the east, and after a couple of centuries of regional autonomy wracked by internal disputes it became the uncomfortable northern borderland of the Ottoman Empire near where it met the Hapsburg Empire. As Ottoman power waned Slovakia fell under Hungarian domination, although Hungary itself was agitating for great autonomy within the overall Hapsburg Empire. In 1867 the Hapsburg Empire finally split into two distinct parts and Franz Ioseph became King of Hungary while remaining Emperor of Austria. Slovakia lay within Hungary, whereas Bohemia–Moravia lay within Austrian territory. In the later nineteenth-century atmosphere of cultural and political nationalism both Slovakia and Bohemia–Moravia found their lowly provincial status increasingly unacceptable. It was the shared aspiration for independence, but not a desire for unification, that brought the Czech and Slovak leaders together in the 1890s to discuss the means of achieving their dream.

In the First World War some Czechs and Slovaks fought in the Austro-Hungarian armies but many others – up to 90,000 it has been estimated – enlisted in the Czechoslovak Legions which fought on the Allied side in France and Italy, and later against the Bolsheviks in Russia. The legions' goal was to raise the international profile of the independence movement, and especially the new Czechoslovak National Council founded by the Czech leaders Tomas Masaryk and Edvard Benes and the Slovak war hero General Milan Stefanik. The more Austria–Hungary threatened to execute captured legionaries as traitors, the more their exploits – notably in the Ukraine against Austro-Hungarian forces at Zborov in 1917 and against the encircling Germans at Bachmac the following year – acquired heroic status at home and abroad.

The plan succeeded. Faced with mounting ethnic tensions and internal disputes, and by pressure from US President Woodrow Wilson, who sought self-determination for the major ethnic groups within Austria–Hungary, the new Emperor Karl's last ditch attempt to create a federal union of semi-autonomous imperial states collapsed as nation after nation announced its independence – the Czechs doing so in Prague on 28 October 1918 and Slovakia agreeing two days later. Two Allied treaties in 1919 and 1920 finally established their official borders with defeated Germany and Hungary and newly independent Poland – although all them were bitterly disputed and became the source of Czechoslovakia's increasing isolation. Sizeable minorities of Hungarians and Germans now lived in the new Republic of Czechoslovakia; the former were in the majority in southern Slovakia and the latter in the Sudetenland. In addition the Czechs outnumbered the Slovaks, Slovakia was much less developed than Bohemia–Moravia, and Slovaks resented what it perceived as the Czechs' domineering attitude towards them politically, economically, socially and culturally. It soon seemed that as many groups sought the country's demise as had recently worked for its creation.

The government strove to hold the country together, and stamp issues played their part. In March 1938 a set and miniature sheet commemorated the birthday of ex-President Masaryk, one of the key figures in the founding of the state, who had died in September 1937 (Fig. 4.1). Significantly, Masaryk was portrayed holding a young child dressed in the Slovak national costume. Soon afterwards a set marked the battles fought by the Czech – and Slovak – legionaries in Italy,

Fig. 4.1

Fig. 4.2

Fig. 4.3

France and Russia. Each stamp had a label attached inscribed with the victories in one of those countries (Fig. 4.2). A third set in June 1938 accompanied the huge Sokol Games held that year (Fig. 4.3). The Sokol movement had started in 1862 and held games every five to eight years embracing exercises, sporting competitions, shows and displays, all of which had strong cultural and nationalist elements. President Benes was among the 350,000 who attended, and the Games were considered particularly important in the face of Nazi threats.

It counted for nothing. Czechoslovakia's disintegration and humiliation by Germany, and indeed other major European nations, began with the Sudetenland. Encouraged by Hitler, Konrad Heinlein, the Fascist leader in the Sudetenland, demanded its union with Germany. Threatening war, Hitler frightened his appeasers in France and Great Britain into agreeing with him, and Mussolini, that Heinlein's demands should be met. The Czech government was ignored, and the famous agreement was signed at Munich in 29 September 1938. A month later Poland took advantage of Czechoslovakia's turmoil and isolation to annex the disputed Czech part of the mineral rich Cieszyn Silesia region that had been divided between them in 1920. And that November Germany and Italy forced Czechoslovakia (or rather the increasingly autonomous Slovakia) to cede the southern third of Slovakia to Hungary. Stamps in each country celebrated their new acquisitions, and in early October 1938 joyous towns across the Sudetenland overprinted numerous Czechoslovak stamps – including those of President Masaryk, the Czech Legion and the Sokol Games – with the slogan '*Wir sind frei*' ('we are free') or a swastika-adorned postmark, and in many cases both (See Fig. 4.4 in colour section). Henlein became its Reich governor.

Czechoslovakia continued to disintegrate internally. In early October, as German troops entered the Sudetenland, Slovakia declared itself autonomous under an administration headed by Monsignor Jozef Tiso, the Roman Catholic priest who led the Slovak People's Party. At the same time Carpathian Ruthenia, a small province at the far eastern end of Slovakia, declared itself autonomous as well. In November the fatally wounded state renamed itself Czecho-Slovakia in acknowledgement of its new unhappy federal status. It rendered rather pointless the dignified miniature sheet issued by the struggling government in December 1938 featuring an Allegory of Peace to mark the twentieth anniversary of Czechoslovakia (Fig. 4.5).

Fig. 4.5

Fig. 4.7

Fig. 4.9

On 18 January 1939 a Czecho-Slovak stamp that pictured Bratislava, the capital of Slovakia, was issued with an overprint announcing the inauguration of the Slovak Parliament within the new federal state (See Fig. 4.6 in colour section). On 23 April two brand-new stamps were belatedly issued with the country's name amended to 'Cesko-Slovensko', but already they had been overtaken by events (Fig. 4.7). On 14 March Slovakia took its next step, and on Hitler's prompting declared itself a completely independent state, although under German protection – and de facto authority. Carpathian Ruthenia was less fortunate. Its brief period of autonomy, marked with a carefully designed special stamp issued on 15 March, ended abruptly the following day when Hungarian troops, with Hitler's agreement, marched into Chust, its major city (See Fig. 4.8 in colour section). Ironically, the stamp pictured the wooden church at Jasina on the River Tisa where in 1918–19 Ruthenian insurgents opposing Hungarian rule had established a tiny, and equally short-lived, republic.

On 15 March 1939, too, the besieged but basically compliant President Hácha was bullied by Hitler into signing away to Germany full authority over the remaining part of Czechoslovakia – the Czech-inhabited regions of Bohemia–Moravia. His choice was cooperation or invasion. A plethora of covers arrayed with Czechoslovakian stamps but adorned with celebratory cachets and cancelled with special German postmarks, usually bright red, marking the occupation were produced for German domestic delectation, often dated 20 April to mark Hitler's birthday. In July a range of current Czechoslovak stamps picturing its arms, President Masaryk and views of the country's cities, castles and cathedrals was reissued overprinted '*Böhmen u. Mähren*' (German) and '*Cechy a Morava*' (Czech) to reinforce the final demise of the old republic and the creation of the new German protectorate (See Fig. 4.10 in colour section). In due course the stamps with regional views were reprinted with the twin titles in the basic design, but those values featuring the national arms or heroes were soon replaced by new ones picturing innocuous linden leaves (See Fig. 4.9 & 4.11 in colour section).

Hácha remained as president but power lay with the Reichsprotektor, and Germans controlled every ministry and regional office. Political parties and trade unions were banned, the press and wireless strictly censored, and Jews placed outside the law and dismissed from all public posts. The massive Czech iron and steel works, and munitions and automobile factories, were redirected to reinforcing the Nazi war effort, and as much agricultural produce as possible was transported to Germany. The Czechs were soon subject to strict rationing. Every effort was made to minimise and ultimately wipe out Czech nationalist culture, and increasingly harsh strategies evolved for eliminating the intelligentsia through arrests, deportation and execution, and selecting others who might be amenable to assimilation into the Greater Reich as citizens while exploiting the rest as an ultimately disposable labour force. Most Czechs were considered *untermenschen* (subhuman) just like the Poles, Romani, Serbs, Russians and Jews. In September 1941 Hitler became convinced that his first protector, Konstantin von Neurath, was not radical enough in exploiting Bohemia–Moravia and appointed SS Obergruppenführer Reinhard Heydrich as his deputy but with full executive powers that effectively rendered von Neurath superfluous. Arrests, deportations and executions intensified, especially of Jews and Romani, all the remaining cultural institutions were shut down, and large batches of forced labourers were transported to Germany. Heydrich's efficient State Minister, the Sudeten-born SS Gruppenführer Karl Frank, handled much of the detailed implementation of Nazi policy.

Most stamp issues carried essentially German themes, even if it did not seem so at first sight. In fact the only stamps commemorating a purely Czech achievement were the pair issued in August 1941 for the centenary of the birth of the composer Anton Dvorak (1841–1904) (Fig. 4.12). Even then the Nazis probably believed, or at least claimed, that Richard Wagner and Johannes Brahms were

Fig. 4.11

Fig. 4.12

Fig. 4.14

Fig. 4.15

the seminal influences on the Czech composer. In September 1941 a set pictured a peaceful rural harvest and a huge blast furnace at Pilsen, but the exhibits, techniques and processes on display at the Prague Fair the stamps were promoting were entirely for the benefit of Germany (See Fig. 4.13 in colour section). And it was specifically the German Red Cross Fund that was supported by special issues each year (Fig. 4.14). The 1940 and 1941 stamps showing German soldiers tended by devoted nurses were attached to labels adorned with the German eagle and swastika, the date and an inscription in German and Czech ensuring everyone knew which country's Red Cross Fund was paramount. The 1942 stamp had the eagle and swastika hovering over the soldier's bed, and in 1943 just the eagle clutching a red cross was deemed sufficient as the words '*Grossdeutsches Reich*' were in the top margin and the twin titles for Bohemia–Moravia relegated to minute print at the bottom. The words '*Deutsches Reich*' or '*Grossdeutsches Reich*' (Greater German State) dominated the stamps on Hitler's birthday issue on 20 April 1942 and also the long series of definitive stamps that summer featuring Hitler's portrait for use in the protectorate. The annual stamps issued for the Führer's birthday always portrayed him to maximum effect as the country's overlord watching it from a balcony or addressing a mass rally (Fig. 4.15). In common with the General Government in the central rump of Poland where birthday stamps were also issued, the protectorate was considered part of the expanding Greater Germany only for the purpose of settling Aryan families as the conquered people's numbers were ruthlessly reduced.

Over 10,000 'Volksdeutsche' came to live in the protectorate, largely in areas abutting the Sudetenland.

Particularly humiliating were the spread eagle and swastika overprint marking Germany's third anniversary of occupation and the Nazi emblems on the fifth anniversary set (See Fig. 4.16a & 4.16b in colour section). And the set issued in October 1941 to mark the 150th anniversary of the death of Wolfgang Mozart (1756–91) was not so much a sop to Prague, where *Don Giovanni* was first performed, as a glorification of a composer whose birth at Salzburg, employment by Emperor Joseph II, and work in German and Austrian cities such as Mannheim, Munich,

Fig. 4.17

Augsberg, Vienna and Berlin was deemed to place him at the heart of Austro-German culture (Fig. 4.17). In Vienna his anniversary was celebrated in an 'Imperial German Mozart Week' during which Dr Goebbels made an anniversary speech, in Paris the Nazis arranged a Mozart festival, and throughout the Reich he was hailed – or hi-jacked – as a German composer of genius.

In January 1943 another set of stamps appeared seeming to feature famous Czechs from the great days of the fourteenth-century kings of Bohemia (See Fig. 4.18 in colour section). One was the celebrated mason, Peter Parler (c.1330–90), who built Prague's magnificent Charles Bridge across the River Vltava and All Saints Chapel in Prague Castle, designed part of the city centre, and undertook substantial work on St Vitus Cathedral. He was, though, German, and a member, probably the most renowned one, of a Cologne family that secured commissions all over Europe. He also built the Church of Our Lady in Nuremberg.

A second stamp featured Count John of Luxembourg (1296–1346), son of the Holy Roman Emperor Henry VI. Born and raised in France, John became Count of Luxembourg in 1309 and King of Bohemia in 1310. Although he stabilised the state by calming the warring factions, the Czech nobility hated him as an alien intruder. Secure in his imperial status, and as a prince-elector of the Holy Roman Empire, he decided to leave Bohemia to be ruled by his chief barons and he spent the rest of his life actively supporting the Teutonic Knights against Poland, seeking and then selling his rights to the Polish throne, and dying fighting for France against the English at the Battle of Crécy. His fame rested largely on his courage fighting at Crécy even though he was blind, but Bohemia best remembered him as an absentee monarch who imposed heavy taxes to pay for international ventures of minimal benefit to Bohemia. In the nineteenth century the Prussian royal family considered him to be a revered ancestor and reburied him in a grand tomb at Kastel-Staadt. In 1945, however, Luxembourg reclaimed his body.

The final stamp featured John's son, Charles (1316–78), who succeeded his father as Count of Luxembourg and King of Bohemia and was subsequently elected King of Italy and Holy Roman Emperor. His lasting fame in Czechoslovakia stems from his strengthening and adornment of Prague with its famous university, bridge, cathedral and castle, and making Bohemia the power-base of an extensive kingdom stretching into Moravia, Silesia, Lusatia and Brandenburg. The Germans, though, sought to honour him as the Holy Roman Emperor, whose lands stretched far beyond Bohemia. And, of course, any reminder of Bohemia's fine past, however misconceived in the eyes of the Nazis, contrasted pitifully with its present annexation and humiliation.

Richard Wagner (1813–83) was a German-born composer beloved by Hitler and the Nazis, and the 130th anniversary of his birth in 1943 prompted a set of commemorative stamps featuring his portrait and scenes from *The Mastersingers of Nuremberg* and *Siegfried* (Fig. 4.19). Although the trials and tribulations of his mythical heroes attracted nationalists from all countries after his death, it was Adolf Hitler who began the appropriation of Wagner and his music to the Nazi cause. Wagner's own views on Aryan racial supremacy and the place of Jews in society are complex and still hotly debated, but certainly under the Nazis the influential Wagner Society promoted his music as the purest representation of the glory of the German race. The stories and settings helped. Siegfrid was raised to kill the fearsome dragon, and his journey embraces the conquest of his foes, his final understanding of fear and his daunting passage through the magic fire. *The Mastersingers of Nuremberg* recreates the hard yet appealingly simple lives of the craftsmen of old Germany, and was interpreted as a supremely patriotic work. Part of a prelude accompanied Leni Riefenstahl's celebrated film of the 1934 Nuremberg Rally as her camera 'floated' above the old city. In May 1944 the composer Bedrich Smetana (1824–84) merited a pair of stamps. Always now associated with the rising Czech nationalism of the nineteenth century, Smetana was perhaps more associated in German minds with his strong links with Wagner (Fig. 4.20). Indeed Smetana's time as composer and conductor in Prague were blighted by persistent criticism that he was too strongly

Fig. 4.19

Fig. 4.20

influenced by Wagner, and also by the Hungarian composer Franz Liszt, to develop a recognisable Czech style of opera.

On 28 May 1943 an unusual black stamp was issued featuring the name and death mask of Reinhard Heydrich, the Deputy Protector, his dates '7.III.04 – 4.VI.42' and the SS lightning emblem (Fig. 4.21). It had been a year and a day since he had been severely wounded in an attack by a British-trained team of Czech and Slovak soldiers

Fig. 4.21

sent by the Czech government-in-exile to assassinate him. His deliberate policy of terror had badly weakened the resistance, destroyed the remaining cultural groups, and cowed the people by the savage reprisals that followed every hostile act. However, he had increased production, and begun to pacify the workforce with better rations and free clothing. Choosing a hairpin bend in a suburb of Prague on Heydrich's daily route into the city centre, Jan Kubis and Jozef Gabcik waited for his open-top car. They knew the over-confident Heydrich rarely bothered with an armed escort. Gabcik's Sten gun jammed at the crucial moment, but Kubis threw a bomb that struck the almost stationary car. Although losing blood, Heydrich tried to chase Kubis, while his driver followed Gabcik and shot him as he fled. Local people took Heydrich to hospital but probably sepsis set in and he died on 4 June. An elaborate funeral ceremony was held in Prague, and another in Berlin. Inaccurate information reached the investigators that the small towns of Lidice and Lezaky not far from Prague had hid the assassins. On 10 June all men over the age of 16 were killed in both places, and all the women in Lezaky too. The women in Lidice were deported to Ravensbrück concentration camp, and eighty-one children were killed in gas vans and others forcibly deported for Germanisation. Both towns were burned and Lidice's ruins levelled. Karel Curda, an associate of Kubis and Gabcik, was among the thousands arrested and in return for payment gave his interrogators the names of local contacts. The trail led to the Church of Saints Cyril and Methodius in Prague where after a fierce gun battle Curda identified the mortally wounded Kubis and the dead body of Gabcik. The church's bishop, senior priests and several lay members were later shot by firing squads. Curda was hanged for high treason in 1947. The savagery of Nazi reprisals led the Allies to formally dissolve the 1938 Munich Agreement and decide that the Sudetenland would be returned to a restored Czechoslovakia at the end of the war.

During the autumn of 1944 Soviet troops entered Slovakia, and in May 1945 American troops liberated Pilsen in west Bohemia. However, the Americans proceeded no further, as it had been agreed that Soviet armies would be allowed to liberate Prague as well as Berlin. As a result, the Americans did not reply or respond to the pleas for help from the Czech resistance fighters who rose against the German forces in Prague on 5 May, four days before the arrival of the

Soviet army and the formal German surrender the following day. As the towns and cities across the country were liberated numerous local overprints celebrating the event were plastered across Hitler's portrait on the surviving stocks of German definitive stamps, and then cancelled with postmarks that ensured the dates were clearly legible (See Fig. 4.22a & 4.22b in colour section).

In accordance with the Allied agreement a reunited Czechoslovakia was immediately created, the wartime Czech puppet President Hácha was imprisoned, and American and Soviet troops withdrew. Throughout 1945 various stamps bearing the title 'Ceskoslovensko' were designed and issued from major cities. Kosice in south-east Slovakia was the first, no doubt because it had just been transferred back from Hungarian control. Starting in March 1945 three Kosice stamps and a miniature sheet featured the restored country's arms and a Soviet soldier in profile, and four more stamps showed hands, perhaps Czech and Slovak ones, firmly clasped over a sunlit map of the reunited nation. However, the hammer and sickle near one hand seems to suggest that it was a Soviet hand clasping a Czechoslovak one (Fig. 4.23). Between April and October 1945 a less politicised set from Bratislava in west Slovakia pictured the rampant lion Czech coat of arms over a spray of linden leaves (Fig. 4.24). During the same months the restored Czechoslovak government of Edvard Benes issued the linden leaves series in new colours and several new values, and these were followed shortly by more obviously celebratory sets portraying national heroes such as President Masaryk, General Stefanik, eight of the most courageous wartime resistance fighters (including Gabcik, but not for some reason Kubis), and the partisans fighting in the Slovak uprising of August 1944 against the Nazis and their ally, Slovakia's President Tiso (Fig. 4.25a & 4.25b and see also Chapter 5, Slovakia, where the Slovak Uprising set is illustrated).

Alongside the series of stamps featuring General Stefanik and President Masaryk there were ones featuring the restored President Benes. Under his decrees citizens of German and Hungarian extraction had their property expropriated and were then expelled from the country. Although not a communist, Benes had established friendly links with Stalin during the war, not least

Fig. 4.23

Fig. 4.24

because France and Great Britain had deserted him before it. His hopes that the new Czechoslovakia would remain a free democracy were dashed, though, in 1947 when mounting communist pressure obliged him to appoint the communist leader Klement Gottwald as prime minister. Ministries were packed with communists, and then Gottwald threatened strikes, and even civil war, unless a completely pro-communist administration was appointed. In February 1948 the sick Benes gave way, and a general election followed in which electors were presented with a single list of communist-approved candidates. Gottwald succeeded Benes in June, and his portrait duly appeared on stamps in October.

Illustrations

Fig. 4.1 1k+50h Masaryk and Child + label from the Child Welfare and Birthday of the Late President Masaryk set (7 March 1938).

Fig. 4.2 50h Battle of Bachmac (against the Germans in Ukraine) + label from the 20th Anniversary of the Czech Legion set (11 March 1938).

Fig. 4.3 2k Jindrich Fügner (a founder) + label from the 10th Sokol Games set (18 June 1938).

Fig. 4.4 Celebratory cover with Czechoslovak stamps overprinted '*Wir sind frei*' with a local handstamp, and the new Deutsche Reichspost special postmark including the swastika and slogan '*Heil Hitler*' from Reichenberg (Liberec in Czech) in north Sudetenland dated 8 October 1938.

Fig. 4.5 20th anniversary of Czechoslovakia miniature sheet (19 December 1938).

Fig. 4.6 First day cover (18 January 1939) with the Czech 10k Bratislava stamp overprinted with new value and inauguration of Slovak Parliament inscription and special postmark.

Fig. 4.7 30h and 1k stamps inscribed '*Cesko-Slovensko*' (23 April 1939).

Fig. 4.8 Illustrated first day cover with the Carpathian Ruthenia Parliament stamp and Chust postmark issued on 15 March 1939. The stamp was on sale for one day in Prague and Chust.

Fig. 4.9 Celebratory cover with Czechoslovak stamps cancelled with special German postmarks and cachets on Hitler's birthday, 20 April 1939.

Fig. 4.10 1k President Masaryk, 20h heraldic arms, and 2.50k pictorial stamps overprinted by the German Protectorate of Bohemia−Moravia (15 July 1939).

Fig. 4.11 New 25h Linden Leaf and 1.20k Brno Cathedral stamps from the set designed with German Protectorate title (from autumn 1939).

Fig. 4.12 60h Portrait + label from the Centenary of Anton Dvorak's Birth set (25 August 1941).

Fig. 4.13 Cover with the Prague Fair set of stamps issued on 7 September 1941 with special fair postmark showing the Exhibition Hall. The red cachet saying 'Victory! Germany fights for Europe on all fronts' emanates from Dr Goebbels' short-lived challenge to Winston Churchill's 'V' sign. '*Sieg*' rather than '*Viktoria*' is the German word for 'Victory' but Goebbels asserted '*Viktoria*' had a special use as the battle-cry against the Bolsheviks. See also Chapter 8, Norway.

Fig. 4.14 1.20*k*+80*h* Red Cross stamps (29 June 1940 + label, 20 April 1941 + label).

Fig. 4.15 3*k* Hitler head definitive stamps (July 1942) and 1.20*k*+3.80*k* Hitler overlooking Prague from Birthday set (20 April 1943).

Fig. 4.16 First day cover with the Third Anniversary of German Occupation set + special postmark (15 March 1942) and 4.20*k*+10.80*k* Nazi eagle over Bohemian and Moravian Arms and 10*k*+20*k* National Costumes from the Fifth Anniversary set (15 March 1944).

Fig. 4.17 60*h*+60*h* Standetheater, Prague, and 1.20*k*+1.20*k* Portrait + labels from the Mozart set (26 October 1941).

Fig. 4.18 Winter Relief set featuring 60*h*+40*h* Charles IV, 1*k*20+80*h* Peter Parler, 2*k*50+1*k*50 John of Luxembourg (29 January 1943).

Fig. 4.19 1.20*k* Portrait from the 130th anniversary of birth of Richard Wagner (22 May 1943).

Fig. 4.20 60*h*+1.20*k* Portrait from the 60th anniversary of the death of Bedrich Smetana (12 May 1944).

Fig. 4.21 60*h*+4.40*k* Death Mask commemorating the 1st anniversary of the death of Reinhard Heydrich (28 May 1943).

Fig. 4.22 Covers with local overprints of protectorate stamps marking the liberation of Zamberk on the northern border (5 May 1945) and Hradec Králové to its south (7 May 1945).

Fig. 4.23 1.50*k* Map and clasped Czech and Russian hands and 6*k* Czech Arms and Soviet soldier (from the set issued in Kosice March–May 1945).

Fig. 4.24 3*k* Arms and Linden Leaves (from the set issued in Bratislava) (April–December 1945.

Fig. 4.25 3.00*k* Linden Leaves (from set issued in Prague, May–October 1945). 40*h* J. Gabrik (one of the agents sent to assassinate Heydrich) from the War Heroes set (18 August 1945). 7*k* President Benes from the National Figures set (1945–47). Theresienstadt Concentration Camp commemorative cover with the President Masaryk set (July 1945–March 1946).

5

SLOVAKIA

The unhappy marriage of the Czechs and Slovaks dating from 1945 was finally brought to an end in a peaceful divorce in December 1992 when Czechoslovakia was divided into two independent nations – Slovakia and the Czech Republic. It was no surprise; historically the country's two parts were very different.

A similar split had occurred just over fifty years earlier. Persistent pressures for Slovak autonomy had wracked the new republic of Czechoslovakia soon after its creation at the end of the First World War. Squashed between the openly hostile nations of Germany and Hungary, and an enigmatic Soviet Union whose intentions always unsettled the minds of Czech politicians, Czechoslovakia had struggled to preserve its borders and independence while at the same time trying to quell the rising tide of nationalism across Slovakia. Slovakia was predominantly pastoral, Roman Catholic and eastward-looking in its trade and culture, while the dominant Czechs in the north-western half, Bohemia–Moravia, were largely Protestant, more industrially centred and more westward-looking. While still under Hungarian rule before 1914, the Slovaks had agitated for greater autonomy. Their movement possessed strong mystical, conservative and Roman Catholic elements, and indeed their most famous leader was a Roman Catholic priest, Father Andrej Hlinka, who helped found the Slovak People's Party in 1913 and was its chairman until his death in August 1938. Resenting the inclusion of Slovakia within Czechoslovakia, Hlinka was a permanent political thorn in the sides of Tomas Masaryk, the new country's first president, and his successor Edvard Benes.

Hlinka became a controversial figure not only as the leader of a major political party aimed at disrupting the new country but also as the founder of a burgeoning Slovak nationalist and Roman Catholic youth movement strongly reminiscent of the Nazis' Hitler Youth. Hlinka died before the final fragmentation of Czechoslovakia in 1938 and 1939 but was replaced as party leader by his deputy, Father Jozef Tiso. Tiso was able to take speedy advantage of the increasingly menacing pressure on Czechoslovakia exerted by Hitler to manoeuvre political autonomy for Slovakia – or, more accurately, a degree of independence subject strictly to keeping in favour with the Führer. Tiso, and initially most Slovaks, thought the price worth paying, not least because

Fig. 5.3

Fig. 5.2

Slovakia's own rising fascism created a marked degree of sympathy with German authoritarianism, and with Germany's own hostility towards the Poles and Russians as well as the Czechs. Germany, Tiso believed, would keep Slovakia free from further outside aggression.

Isolated internationally, Czechoslovakia had little option but to acquiesce when Germany occupied the Sudetenland after the Munich Agreement, followed by Poland annexing the largely Polish-speaking part of Cieszyn Silesia awarded to Czechoslovakia after the First World War, and by Hungary seizing the southern third of Slovakia and Carpathian Ruthenia further to the east.

Soon Slovakia broke away completely. First Tiso and Hitler forced the Czech government to rename the country Czecho-Slovakia to signal Slovakia's autonomy within the decaying state, and on 18 January 1939 the overprinted Czecho-Slovak stamp picturing Bratislava, Slovakia's capital city, announced the inauguration of the Slovak Parliament (See Figs 4.6 & 5.1 in colour section). Two months later, on 14 March 1939, Tiso seceded from Czecho-Slovakia, secure in Hitler's agreement to be the country's protector. Tiso became prime minister, and then president, with considerable domestic powers, unlike Bohemia–Moravia which fell under direct German control.

The Slovak issues were very different to those of Bohemia–Moravia. They highlighted the presidency of Jozef Tiso, key events and achievements in Slovakian history, and the importance of preserving Slovak culture. The contribution stamps made to the identity of the new state was considered vital, as shown by the wartime philatelic exhibition held in Bratislava in 1942 and the accompanying special exhibition set (Fig. 5.2). There was, of course, no hint of the regime's subjection to Nazi authority. Indeed, although Tiso suppressed other political parties and agreed to the deportation of Jews from Slovakia, he represented the less fascist and more nationalist faction within the dominant Hlinka People's Party. And the largely Roman Catholic population of peasants and urban workers remained satisfied with Tiso's elevation of Slovak culture, his hostility towards the Soviet Union, and his efforts to create and maintain economic prosperity. Careful of its image, the regime did not miss the opportunity in September 1943 to publicise the opening of the new rail link between Strazke and Presov in eastern Slovakia with a set of stamps (Fig. 5.3).

The first issue after the declaration of Slovak independence took the form of Czecho-Slovakian stamps proudly, if hurriedly, overprinted '*Slovensky stat 1939*' (See Fig. 5.4 in colour section). Some of them were from the Czechoslovak arms series of 1929–37, others were Slovak castles and landscapes selected from the 1936 Czechoslovak 'National Views' set, and there were a few more portraying former presidents Masaryk and Benes, and the renowned seventeenth-century Czech promoter of universal education, Jan Komensky (Comenius). Three of the overprinted stamps, though, pictured the Slovak national hero General Milan Stefanik (1880–1919). Early in his life Stefanik had been inspired by Masaryk and Benes to campaign for a united Czech-Slovak state free from Austro-Hungarian domination. He became a founder member and active leader of the Czech Legion, the large army of volunteers dedicated to the defeat of Austria–Hungary, and his diplomatic skills helped ensure the Allies recognised the Czechoslavak National Council as the post-war government in waiting. In the chaos of 1918–19 he worked to rid the emerging country of foreign troops but, significantly, he fell out with Masaryk over the exact position of Slovakia vis-à-vis Bohemia and Moravia. In May 1919 he was killed when his plane crashed in mysterious circumstances near Bratislava airport, raising long-lasting Slovak suspicions of Czech duplicity.

A purely Slovak set honouring Stefanik was prepared in May 1939, twenty years after he died, but remained unissued, probably because the Germans disliked marking the career of a recent high-profile enemy. A few sets, however, escaped to be cancelled to order (Fig. 5.5). Soon afterwards a long-serving series was introduced picturing Father Hlinka, the revered founder of the nationalist political party and youth movement that kept Tiso in power (Fig. 5.6). The first issues were the 50*h* and 1*k* stamps from the short-lived Cesko-Slovensko (Czecho-Slovakia) state overprinted '*Slovensky stat*', but in the summer of 1939 the 5*h*, 10*h*, 20*h*, 30*h*, 50*h*, 1*k*, 2*k* and 3*k* values followed with the new inscription '*Slovenska Posta*'. Newspaper and postage-due stamps followed the same changes, and were soon issued with the new state's name.

Fig. 5.5

Fig. 5.6

A set issued at intervals in 1939 and 1940, with several reprinted in 1943, portrayed selected Slovak mountain views and local costumes. They were closely associated with the rise of cultural nationalism (Fig. 5.7). The 5*h* green showed the picturesque Tatra valley of Zelene Pleso, which had developed fifty years earlier as a domestic tourist site, and the 10*h* chocolate portrayed the Tatra peak of Krivan, which had long been a symbol of Slovakian ethnic and nationalist pride. The 30*h* chestnut pictured the celebrated wooden church of Javorina. This was on the northern border area claimed by Poland, and indeed briefly occupied by it after the Munich Agreement before it was returned when Poland was crushed and divided by Germany and the Soviet Union in 1939. The set included stamps showing the Orange Hawkweed (*Kvety Tatier*) and the Tatra chamois deer (*Kamzik*) that were also used as symbols of Slovakian nationhood. Two large stamps were added profiling President Tiso to ensure his personal connection with the historic movement, and similarly designed Tiso stamps appeared right up to the dying months of the regime in March 1945. In November 1939 an airmail set showed aeroplanes ascending over Lake Csorba and flying over the Tatra mountains (Fig. 5.8). Both pictures represented modern aeronautical technology but also the popularity of the numerous health spas and mountain pathways of this stunning region. They defined the essentially emotional, romantic and cultural aspects of Slovakian nationalism.

Fig. 5.8

Fig. 5.7

Two important sets were dedicated to marking key historic moments in recent Slovakian history. On 26 May 1941 a set of three stamps commemorated the eightieth anniversary of the presentation of the Slovak Memorandum to the Austrian Emperor Franz Joseph seeking equality for the Slovak nation within the empire, especially from the Hungarians who dominated the region and actively sought to suppress minority rights and culture (See Fig. 5.9 in colour section). It was to little avail, as the repressive Hungarian policy of 'Magyarisation' denying minority interests and imposing a Hungarian-based education system remained firmly in place. This policy intensified after the Austrian Empire gave way to Hungarian pressure and created the Dual Monarchy in 1867 allowing a new Kingdom of Hungary, albeit ruled by Franz Joseph, far greater autonomy. The stamps portray two key delegates, Stefan Marko Daxner and Bishop Stefan Moyses. Moyses had been a deputy in the Hungarian Parliament in Bratislava in 1847−48, and in 1851 he became bishop in Banska Bystrica, where he had created several Slovak-centred schools. In 1863 he was elected chairman of the Matica Slovenska, a centre dedicated to research into, and the promotion of, Slovak history, literature and culture. After a few years Hungary closed down the Matica and also several Slovak high schools, and by 1914 only the clergy − such as Andrej Hlinka and Josef Tiso − and a few wealthy families possessing independent means were in social or educational positions that enabled them to promote Slovak national interests. Significantly a number of covers, as here, were postmarked Turciansky Svaty Martin. This is the northern Slovak city that became a cultural and political centre of Slovak nationalism in the nineteenth century, and was the seat of the Matica.

The second set, issued on 14 December 1942, celebrated the 150th anniversary of the foundation of the National Literary Society (See Fig. 5.10 in colour section). Although fervent Slovak nationalism only grew as a political force in the nineteenth century, earlier patriots had striven to create an identifiable Slovak culture. The Jesuits had been key figures. In 1787 the priest Anton Bernolak published a Slovak grammar and in 1792 he founded the Slovak Literary Society in Trnava in western Slovakia − where the cover displayed here was postmarked. He based the grammar on the dialect in the Trnava region, and later the Jesuits founded schools there and also a printing press and monastery. Father Bernolak is the central figure in the cassock standing behind the table in the illustration of the inaugural meeting. Among others active around this time, Jan Holly wrote historical epics to provide Slovaks with a literary heritage.

In 1943 stamps commemorated the lives of two other leaders of the nationalist movement alongside Father Hlinka (Fig. 5.11). The first was Ludovit Stur (1815−56), a poet, philosopher and politician who had led the Slovak national revival in the middle of the nineteenth century. He was the author of the present-day standard Slovak language, the organiser of the Slovak volunteer movement during the 1848 uprising against the Hapsburgs, a leader of a very briefly independent Slovakia during that uprising, and, afterwards, a much criticised and frequently persecuted member of the Hungarian Diet. This legislative assembly strove for Hungarian autonomy within the Hapsburg Empire but was utterly opposed to Slovakia freeing itself. His life was cut short by a fatal riding accident. The second was Martin Razus (1888–1937), a Lutheran pastor, poet and novelist who constantly evoked Slovak history and culture in his writings. A prolific author and major Slovak publicist between the two world wars, Razus became the ideologue of the Slovak National Party and was for a time its chairman. Throughout this time the Hlinka portrait stamps remained widely available, and in 1942 a surcharged set picturing a Hlinka Youth member standing proudly alongside a Slovak soldier ensured the military as well as party ambitions of the youth movement were not forgotten (Fig. 5.12). Nevertheless, as surcharged sets raising money for Red Cross, Winter Relief and Armed Forces Funds also appeared from 1941 onwards, these stamps inevitably sent a different message to families about the casualties and hardships associated with fighting the war (See Figs 5.13 & 5.14 & 5.15).

The Tiso regime actively promoted Slovak culture and education despite all the wartime pressures. In October 1943 a set of stamps in aid of the Culture Fund included one emotively inscribed 'The Slovak language is our life', and others that pictured the National Museum, the revised Matica Slovenska College and an agricultural student (See Fig. 5.16 in colour section). Interestingly the registered cover shown here included a pair of recently issued Hlinka stamps, quite possibly to emphasise the nationalist element. As we have seen in earlier issues, Slovakian nationalism was rooted in the mystical benefits of the natural landscape and rural life, and healthy life-supporting country occupations were admired and encouraged. Health was encouraged with a Sports set in 1944 picturing a footballer, skier, diver and runner (Fig. 5.17). Surcharged stamps on behalf of Child Welfare appeared in 1939, 1941 and 1944. However, the later relief fund sets were as much concerned with families decimated by the casualties of war as the promotion of healthy living (Fig. 5.18). It was probably no accident that the December 1944 stamp illustrated here shows children by themselves.

Fig. 5.11

Fig. 5.12

Fig. 5.13

Slovak units fought in German armies on the Eastern Front, and as the death toll mounted so did disillusionment with the Axis alliance and nagging thoughts of changing sides. In March 1944, with the war on the Eastern Front turning sharply against Hitler and his East European allies, Slovakia issued a set of eight stamps with fearsome, if largely imaginary, portraits of early medieval warlords of Slovakia and Moravia (See Fig. 5.19 in colour section). All of them had three highly desirable characteristics in common: they embraced and furthered Christianity; they were constantly assailed by aggressive neighbours; and while they were not always victorious they never hesitated to challenge their enemies or missed an opportunity to extend their domain. The 50*h* green commemorated Prince Pribina Okolo, an early ninth-century Christian ruler of Nitra in south-west Slovakia. The 70*h* scarlet pictured Prince Mojmir and the 2*k* turquoise his son Prince Kocel, who successively seized and held lands extend-

Fig. 5.14

Fig. 5.15

Fig. 5.17

ing from Nitra to Lake Balaton in the mid-eighth
century and established a Christian principality. In
846 Mojmir lost part of his mineral rich territory to
the Franks under Louis II, who entrusted it to his
son Prince Ratislav, pictured on the 80*h* red-brown
stamp. Ratislav's future reputation was enhanced
by an aggressive extension of his territory combined with an invitation to Christian missionaries
and the development of a medieval Slovak language. In 871 Prince Svatopluk, pictured on the
1*k* 30 ultramarine stamp, succeeded to the throne,

Fig. 5.18

was crowned king by the Pope in 880, and by his death in 894 he had conquered
all Bohemia, Pannonia (lands embracing modern western Hungary and Slovakia
and northern Serbia, Croatia and Bosnia) and the Vistula Basin. However, soon
afterwards civil war broke out between Mojmir II and his brother Svatopluk II,
pictured on the 3*k* brown and 5*k* purple stamps, which ended in Mojmir's brief
ascendancy, followed by reconciliation, but both brothers were killed in battle
against the invading Magyars in 906, heralding the imminent demise of the
independent Slav state. Throughout the Second World War Slovakia engaged in
constant quarrels with Hungary over its treatment of Slovaks living there, notably in the southern borderland Hungary had annexed in 1939.

The eighth stamp, the 10*k* black, featured Prince Braslav, the last prince of
Pannonia who faced the final onslaught of the victorious Magyars. His name

is linked with the twenty-fifth anniversary badge and special Bratislava post-mark on the cover featuring the 1944 Sports stamps. The ancient name for Bratislava's castle was 'Braslava', possibly based on Prince Braslav, but in the Middle Ages the city was known as Pressburg, and later it was renamed Pozsony by the Hungarians after one of their local heroes. In the nineteenth-century rising Slav nationalists created a movement to bring back the name Bratislava, but it was unsuccessful until 1919 when the Slovaks fought off a largely Czech campaign to impose the alternative name 'Wilson City' after the American president.

The Slovak Republic ceased to exist on 4 April 1945, when Soviet forces advancing westwards finally captured Bratislava. In August 1944 the German army had seized control of the country when it arrived in force to suppress a major uprising against Tiso's regime by dissident units of the Slovak Army and Air Force and a variety of nationalist and communist resistance movements acting in concert with the government-in-exile. Ostensibly the uprising aimed at recreating Czechoslovakia and restoring Edvard Benes to power. The initial plan was to occupy the Dukla Pass connecting Slovakia and Poland through the Carpathian Mountains, and hold it long enough for a Soviet army to pour through from Poland. Unfortunately premature strikes by some resistance groups led the Germans to strengthen their forces and virtually usurp the Tiso regime. After initial success, the uprising found-ered in a welter of uncoordinated initiatives and constant disagreements between its leaders combined with aggressive and well-managed German counter-attacks. It was not helped by the Soviet Union's politically motivated decision to limit its promised support to communist guerrilla groups rather than the far better trained Slovak military units. Dukla Pass was not held, Tiso survived a little longer, thousands of Slovaks died and thousands of com-munists insurgents had been well-armed. A year later, in August 1945 the reunited Czechoslovakia issued a set of stamps commemorating the uprising. They revealed that it had already passed into national mythology. One showed all the Allied flags flying together, another a Soviet soldier and partisan clasp-ing hands, and a third the sun shining on Banska Bystrica, the centre of the uprising seized and destroyed by the Germans (Fig. 5.20).

The German victory was short-lived, but the persistent efforts of guerrilla groups meant that German retaliation destroyed many Slovak com-munities. An unconvincing stamp issue in October 1944 entitled 'Protection' showed a Slovak mother and children sheltering behind a shield inscribed with the Slovak arms and holding off

Fig. 5.20

advancing flames – but to most people it must
have seemed unclear who was the enemy
being kept at bay. It was the final flurry of a
fast fading clerical–fascist regime (Fig. 5.21).
In 1945 most of Slovakia was absorbed back
into a restored Czechoslovakia as very much
the junior member, but Carpathian Ruthenia
was lost to the Soviet Union. In 1947 Father
Tiso was executed as a war criminal, and

Fig. 5.21

by 1948 the communists controlled the whole country. Slovak nationalism,
so proudly upheld despite its reliance upon Nazi support, was ruthlessly suppressed.

Illustrations

Fig. 5.1 (see Fig. 4.6).

Fig. 5.2 40*h* Stamp Collector and 80*h* Postmaster General from the Bratislava
Philatelic Exhibition set (23 May 1942).

Fig. 5.3 2*ks* Viaduct stamp from the Opening of the Strazke to Presov Railway set
(5 September 1943).

Fig. 5.4 Celebratory postcard with Czechoslovak arms, views and portrait stamps
overprinted '*Slovensky Stat 1939*'. It was posted in Krompachy in south-east Slovakia
which witnessed a bloody revolt in 1921 against unification with the Czechs.

Fig. 5.5 2*k* General Stefanik and tomb from the Stefanik set (May 1939).

Fig. 5.6 50*h* overprinted 'Cesko-Slovensko' Father Hlinka stamp (April 1939) and 3*k*
from the redesigned Slovenska Posta set (April–June 1939).

Fig. 5.7 10*h* Krivan, 30*h* Javorina, 50*h* Tiso and 4*ks* Rural Sawyer from the Mixed
Views, Costumes and Tiso set (1939–1942).

Fig. 5.8 30*h* Heinkel He 111C over Lake Csorba and 3*ks* Heinkel He 116A Over the
Tatra Mountains from the Air set (20 November 1939).

Fig. 5.9 Cover with the set (26 May 1941) marking the 80th Anniversary of the
Presentation of the Slovak Memorandum to the Emperor Franz Joseph, postmarked
Turciansky Svaty Martin, the seat of the Slovak Matica.

Fig. 5.10 Cover with the set (14 December 1942) commemorating the 150th anniversary
of the founding of the National Literary Society in Trnava, postmarked Trnava.

Fig. 5.11 Set (1943) featuring Ludovit Stur (80*h*), Martin Razus (1*k*) and Father
Hlinka (1*k*30).

Fig. 5.12 70*h*+1*ks* Soldier and Youth from the Hinkla Youth set (14 March 1942).

Fig. 5.13 50*h*+50*h* Wounded Soldier and Orderly from the Red Cross Fund set
(10 November 1941).

Fig. 5.14 Winter Relief Fund set (1943).

Fig. 5.15 Cover with the set of three stamps in aid of Slovak fighting forces (28 July 1943). Hlinka and Tiso stamps have been added to enhance the message.

Fig. 5.16 Censored cover with the National Culture Fund set (14 October 1943) postmarked Presov and sent to Vsetin, across the border in Bohemia–Moravia. In 1919 a short-lived Slovak Soviet Republic was created in Presov, and Vsetin was a centre of Czech resistance to the Nazis and contributed to the 1944 Slovak Uprising.

Fig. 5.17 Illustrated cover for the 25th anniversary of the naming of Bratislava with the set of Sports stamps (30 April 1944) postmarked Bratislava.

Fig. 5.18 Child Welfare Fund stamp (18 December 1944).

Fig. 5.19 70*h* Prince Mojmir, 80*h* Prince Ratislav and 1.30*k* Prince Svatopluk from the Fifth Anniversary of Independence set (14 March 1944).

Fig. 5.20 2*k* Banska Bystrica and 4*k* Soviet soldier and Slovak partisan from the Anniversary of the Slovak Uprising set (29 August 1945).

Fig. 5.21 70*h*+4*k* from the 'Symbol of Protection' set (6 October 1944).

6

POLAND

Throughout the centuries Poland's borders have shifted dramatically in the wake of wars and shifting alliances. The country has few easily defended borders, and always contained a hotchpotch of nationalities whose race, religion and traditions were often at variance with the dominant Polish regime. By the late eighteenth century the vast lands of the once vibrant and prosperous Polish–Lithuanian commonwealth were wracked by constant wars and internal political conflicts, and as a result the rapacious autocracies of Russia, Austria and Prussia partitioned the territory: between 1772 and 1795 Poland was systematically wiped from the map. After the defeat of Napoleon in 1815 a small kingdom of Poland was recreated but subject to Russian authority. Inevitably several Polish revolts occurred throughout the nineteenth century as rampant nationalism swept the continent, but each one collapsed and was followed by increasingly rigorous Tsarist control. Many of the revolutionaries became folk heroes as a new generation of Poles fought for their freedom against twentieth-century aggressors (See map on p. 251).

After the defeat of Germany and Austria in 1918 the victorious Allies recognised the right of an independent Poland to exist, not least to check future Bolshevik aggression. However, the reconstituted country was surrounded by enemies, each one furious at the newly drawn Polish borders. Lithuania resented its occupation of the Vilna region, the Soviet Union wanted back the 150-mile strip of territory it had lost to Poland, and Czechoslovakia sought the whole of the coal-rich border area of Cieszyn Silesia which had been divided between them. On top of this Germany seethed at the new corridor of former German territory giving Poland access to the Baltic and now separating East Prussia from Germany, and also at the creation of the Free State of Danzig with its predominantly German population and trade agreement favouring Poland.

Throughout the 1920s and 1930s Poland boldly defied all diplomatic and military challenges to its borders, but it remained isolated. It defeated Soviet forces in a bitter war between 1919 and 1921, and steadily built up, and flaunted, its armed forces. However, it assumed, erroneously and fatally, that its allies France and Great Britain would come to its aid if attacked, and never envisaged invasion from both the west and the east. In September 1939, though, the country disappeared again, swallowed up in ruthless invasions by Germany and the

Soviet Union working together in temporary harmony – and the Second World War began. Russia got back all the 'Polish' land east of the River Bug – Galizien, western Belorussia and western Ukraine – only to lose it again in the summer of 1941 when Germany suddenly turned on its Bolshevik ally. All Belorussia and the Ukraine were incorporated into the administrative Reich Commissariats Ostland and Ukraine respectively, while Galizien, which bordered Hungary and Romania in the south, was absorbed into the newly created General Government, the bland name for the central part of Poland extending to Warsaw in its furthest north, Cracow in the south-west, Przemysl in the south-east and Lublin in the east. It recreated the First World War nomenclature of the Government General of Warsaw set up by the German Empire. All the provinces west of Warsaw, Lodz and Cracow that were formerly part of the pre-1918 German Empire were absorbed into the German Reich and became part of the administrative Gau Wartheland. Land around Danzig joined the Gau Danzig–East Prussia.

The Gaus, or regions within the Reich, used ordinary German stamps, and the Reich Commissariats Ostland and Ukraine used German definitive stamps overprinted Ostland or Ukraine. However, the rump of pre-war Poland – the General Government – saw a plethora of philatelic issues, all of them promoting Nazi dominance and contributing to the eradication of Polish culture and nationalism.

The General Government became the dumping ground for thousands of Poles evicted from the Gau Wartheland to make way for a new wave of German settlers, and was seen as little more than a territory the Germans could ransack for produce and forced labour. Ill-serviced and overcrowded Jewish ghettoes were created in several cities, and thousands of Polish Jews were killed in four huge concentration camps. Savage reprisals, including the taking and shooting of civilian hostages, followed every attempt by the Polish underground resistance movement to disrupt the occupying forces.

The initial stamp issue, in December 1939, was the German definitive set portraying President Hindenburg and blandly overprinted '*Deutsche Post Osten*' ('German Post East') with Polish values in groschen and zloty (Fig. 6.1). In February and March 1940 they were replaced by a lengthy set of recent Polish stamps, most commemorating famous medieval kings, later revolutionaries and recent presidents, heavily overprinted to the point of obliteration with the German eagle and swastika, the inscription 'General Government', and large new values (See Fig. 6.2 in colour section). There could be no mistaking the complete humiliation. Indeed, the spread eagle clasping a swastika was the region's new coat of arms. From October 1941 onwards these stamps were replaced by a long set of large stamps featuring Hitler's head in profile (Fig. 6.3). By then the inscription included '*Deutsche Reich*' indicating that the territory had been annexed by Greater Germany. And, in common with Germany and Bohemia–Moravia, the General Government celebrated Hitler's birthday with special issues (Fig. 6.4). Although the Nazis discussed various uses for the occupied region, the key policy was

Fig. 6.1

Fig. 6.3

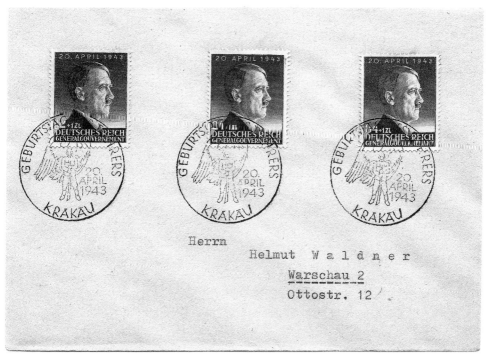

Fig. 6.4

its 'Nazification' by the eradication of Polish culture, and, indeed, many Poles, and gradual resettlement with German families.

Alongside the definitive series punching home Poland's degradation, a number of pictorial sets were issued. Numerous philatelic covers with full sets of stamps were produced, often with first day of issue special postmarks. Many were sent back to Germany by the occupying forces. Cracow became the seat of the governor-general, the hard line Nazi Hans Frank, and many covers possessed Cracow cancellations. It was viewed as a German city, not Polish, not least because it had been fought over by Prussia, Austria and Russia in the eighteenth century and spent from 1846 until 1918 as part of the Austro-Hungarian Empire, the close First World War ally of Germany. Between August 1940 and September 1941 a set of eleven stamps were issued picturing historic sites such as Cracow's Castle, Florian Gate, Cloth and Town Halls, the Dominican and St Mary's Churches, and Copernicus Memorial, and also Lublin's Cracow Gate and Old Church (See Fig. 6.5 in colour section). Significantly, each stamp included the German eagle and swastika 'flying' above the site, marking the historic city's new – or restored – ownership. Poland had ceased to exist. Its cultural institutions and higher schools were shut down, numerous factories, farms and estates confiscated, and few Poles were employed in government departments, except at a local level. Auschwitz extermination camp was not far from Cracow. The increasing German presence in the countryside was celebrated in October and December 1940 with two sets of stamps portraying healthy, handsome and happy Aryan country folk (Fig. 6.6).

Fig. 6.6

Cracow and Lublin were planned to become purely German residential and economic centres, with an increasing eviction rate of all Poles, except necessary labourers, and Warsaw was condemned to be a rigorously controlled reception area for Jews and other undesirable groups such as gypsies and criminals. Warsaw appeared only once on a German stamp, and that was to mark the anniversary of the Nazi Party in occupied Poland in August–September 1943. It was one in an unusual set of stamps featuring an embossed white shield incorporating the German eagle and swastika superimposed on pictures of the cities of Lublin, Cracow, Radom, Warsaw and Lemburg (See Fig. 6.7 in colour section).

In contrast, Cracow and Lublin appeared frequently. In August 1942 a set marked the 600th anniversary of Lublin, with two stamps featuring an old engraving of the city under its ancient coat of arms, and two more picturing the modern city under the German eagle and swastika (Fig. 6.8). Lublin had been founded long before 1342, but that was approximately the date King Casimir the Great fortified the city and built the castle. In 1943 and 1944 stamps pictured Cracow's historic Barbican and medieval castle, and also the impressive Tyniec

Fig. 6.8

Fig. 6.9

Monastery sited on a cliff 40m above the River Vistula and guarding entry
to the city (Fig. 6.9). After repeated destruction at the hands of invaders, the
Benedictine monastery had been closed by the Hapsburgs in 1816 and remained
neglected and empty until July 1939, when a few monks returned – and survived the German occupation. In October 1944 a large high-value stamp marked
the fifth anniversary of German occupation with a picture of Cracow Castle –
which Poles knew only too well was the seat of German government (Fig. 6.10).

Two colourful sets were issued in November 1942 and July 1944 picturing between them what appeared to be ten major figures in Polish history. Indeed, it is likely that many Poles assumed the portraits to be just that, but their intended purpose was to highlight each person's essentially German origins. And no doubt Germans purchased the vast majority of these commemorative stamps (See Fig. 6.11 in colour section). The 1942 set included:

Fig. 6.10

- ❖ 12g+8g violet: Veit Stoss (1445/50–1533). Born in Nuremberg in southern Germany, Veit Stoss was a sculptor who settled in Cracow for twenty years where he carved magnificent wooden altars and stone tombs, complete with elaborate figures. In later life he returned to live and work in Nuremberg, where he was buried.
- ❖ 24g+26g lake: Hans Dürer (1490–1535/8). Also born in Nuremberg, Hans was the younger brother of the renowned Albrecht Dürer and also a talented artist. He became court painter to King Sigismund I, and his works adorned several Polish churches and mausoleums.
- ❖ 30g+30g purple: Johann Christian Schuch (1752–1813). Born in Dresden, Schuch studied in its Academy of Fine Arts and was then employed as the superintendent of the royal gardens in Warsaw and later as a landscape gardener for many Polish noble families.
- ❖ 50g+50g blue: Jozef Elsner (1769–1854). Born in Grottkau, near Breslau in Prussia, Elsner worked mainly in Warsaw as a composer, conductor and teacher. His most famous pupil was Chopin. He retired from work in the theatre after criticism that he was too German for local tastes.
- ❖ 1z+1z green: Nicolaus Copernicus (1473–1543). Born in Torun, a city in royal Prussia ruled by Poland at the time, Copernicus was a celebrated mathematician, canon lawyer, economist, physician and astronomer (who placed the sun rather than the earth at the centre of the universe). He studied in Cracow, and lived and worked mainly in Warmia, Frauenberg and Allenstein, places constantly fought over before, during and after his lifetime, and later dominated by Prussia.

The Germans took great pains to claim Copernicus as their own. In May 1943 the 400th anniversary of Copernicus's death was marked by a special Deutsche Post Osten sheetlet of ten stamps with his portrait, anniversary dates, swastikas in each corner and an inscription stating clearly that he was a German astronomer (See Fig. 6.12 in colour section).

The July 1944 set (See Fig. 6.13 in colour section) included:

❖ 12*g*+18*g* green: Konrad Celtis (1459–1508). Born in Würzburg, Bavaria, Celtis was a major Renaissance figure who taught at several German universities, wrote plays and poetry, rediscovered early German literary works, edited Latin texts and established learned societies, including one in Cracow.

❖ 24*g*+26*g* red: Andreas Schlüter (1660–1714). Born in Danzig, Schluter was a baroque sculptor and painter who created statues for the Polish King Jan III Sobieski's palaces, and then became court sculptor and architect for the Elector Frederick III of Brandenburg (1688–1701), later King in Prussia (1701–13).

❖ 30*g*+30*g* purple: Hans Boner (*c.*1463–1523). Born in Landau, in the Rhine Palatinate, Boner settled in Cracow as an increasingly wealthy merchant in spices, metals, timber and livestock. In due course he became governor of Cracow and a royal banker, securing vast estates in return for rescuing the royal treasury from bankruptcy. He was a great patron of German artists.

❖ 50*g*+50*g* blue: Frederick Augustus (1670–1733). Born in Dresden, Frederick Augustus was Elector of Saxony (1694–1733) and also secured the throne of Poland in 1697 through bribery and conversion to Roman Catholicism. In 1704 he lost his throne in a disastrous war when he allied with Peter the Great of Russia against Sweden, but regained it when Peter eventually proved victorious in 1709 – only to find that Russia was now able to exercise increasing influence over Polish affairs.

❖ 1*z*+1*z* brown: Gottlieb Pusch (1799–1837). Born in Leipzig, Pusch became a famous teacher, chemist, mineralogist and geologist in Warsaw University.

The sets were an all-embracing effort to exert the political and cultural dominance of German culture at Polish expense. However, when the July 1944 set was issued, German forces were already losing control of Polish territory, and Stalin was putting into motion plans for reconstituting Poland, and indeed resiting it significantly to the west, as a communist-controlled satellite state. New Polish stamps began to oust German ones, and they spread across the liberated eastern provinces until they covered the whole country in early 1945. In Lublin, on 22 July 1944, a communist-backed Committee for National Liberation was declared to be the new Polish provisional government, and immediately signed a friendship pact with the Soviet Union. Officially Stalin was just within his rights as established at the Allied Teheran Conference, where Churchill and President Roosevelt had reluctantly agreed to Stalin's request to keep his share of Poland as divided in the 1939 Nazi–Soviet Pact. In the face of the Soviet onslaught there was little the older established independent Polish government-in-exile in London could do. And there was nothing at all it could do after it encouraged the Polish resistance to launch a major uprising in Warsaw that August, largely to forestall Russian occupation, only for it to be savagely repressed by the Germans, and the remainder of the war-torn city destroyed. It cost 200,000 Polish lives, including ordinary citizens as well as partisans.

Polish ministers fleeing the Germans had formed a government-in-exile in France and then London. The horrifying evidence of the Soviet massacre of Polish officers at Katyn during the Soviet–German occupation in 1939–40, together with total opposition to Stalin's demands that the eastern provinces should revert to the Soviet Union after Hitler's defeat, ensured the exiled government remained marginalised while the Western Allies reached a pragmatic accommodation with Stalin over post-war Poland. During the war the government-in-exile issued two sets of stamps that were permitted on Polish naval and merchant vessels and troops in Polish camps across Great Britain. Few are found today outside commemorative covers. They pictured wrecked Polish cities, Polish warships, Polish-manned bombers, soldiers in action and saboteurs. They reflected the thousands of Poles serving in Allied units on land, sea and in the air. On 27 June 1944 four of the stamps were overprinted 'Monte Cassino 18.V.1944' to commemorate the heroism of Polish units who were the first to successfully scale the heights of the well-defended monastery blocking the Allied advance up mainland Italy. A single stamp followed on 3 February 1945 to raise funds for the survivors of the premature 1944 Warsaw uprising (See Fig. 6.14a & 6.14b in colour section).

In Poland itself, the communist-inspired stamps of late 1944 and 1945 tell the story of the country's liberation. Some issues harked back to key events in Polish history, usually revolts, and the lives of celebrated Polish patriots – most of whom failed to achieve the national independence they so bravely sought. Nevertheless they inspired the regeneration of national pride, and created an enticing myth of future independence. In September 1944 three national heroes, long remembered in Polish literature and culture, were portrayed in rather crudely produced stamps (Fig. 6.15). One (25g) was Romuald Traugutt (1826–64), an inspiring leader of the 1863 uprising against Tsarist rule and hanged after Russian armies crushed the rebel forces. Another (50g) was the celebrated general, Tadeusz Kosciuszko (1746–1817), whose adventurous life embraced dashing exploits as an officer fighting the British in Washington's army during the American Revolutionary War, winning victories in the Polish–Russian War of 1792 (although not stopping further partition

Fig. 6.15

Fig. 6.16

Fig. 6.17

of the country) and leading the ill-fated 1794 Polish uprising against Russia. Although a Polish Legion later fought for Napoleon, Kosciuszko refused to join it, realising with bitter disappointment that France would make little effort to establish an independent Poland. The third romantic figure was Jan Henry Dabrowski (1755–1818) (1z) who fought in the 1794 uprising, and was a general in the Polish Legion fighting for Napoleon with high hopes of national liberty until the Emperor's final defeat. In January 1945 the Romuald Traugutt stamp from the National Heroes set was reissued overprinted with the date '22.I.1863' which, it was assumed, most Poles knew as the starting date of his tenacious uprising against the Tsarist regime (Fig. 6.16).

In September 1944 a stamp reproduced the national White Eagle, and another pictured the celebrated Grunwald Monument near Cracow marking the site where, in 1410, the combined forces of Poland, Lithuania and Russia defeated the feared Teutonic Knights of Germany in one of the greatest medieval battles (Fig. 6.17). Right up to the Second World War Germans attributed their defeat at Grunwald to the treachery of a commander within their ranks who was sympathetic to the Poles – a 'stab in the back' argument much like the one attributing the German army's defeat in 1918 to civilian and republican plots aimed at overthrowing the emperor and military leadership.

In February 1945 the White Eagle stamp was reissued as a set of ten stamps, each one overprinted with the date in January 1945 when key places within the General Government had been liberated by Soviet armies – albeit with significant help from Polish forces fighting alongside them (See Fig. 6.18 in colour section). The stamps gave the popular impression that Poland was fast becoming free and independent. Other stamps in March, April and September 1945 celebrated the liberation of Warsaw, Lodz, Cracow and Gdansk (Danzig) (Fig. 6.19).

Fig. 6.19

That autumn, after the final defeat of Germany, a succession of stamps was issued which centred on three themes:

❖ First, there were the constant reminders of the savagery of Nazi Germany. On 1 September a stamp vividly portrayed the steadfast Polish resistance to the German naval attack on the garrison of Westerplatte at Danzig, exactly six years earlier, which opened the Second World War. Straddling late 1945 and early 1946 a set of six stamps portrayed significant buildings in Warsaw as they were before and after German bombardment (See Fig. 6.20a & 6.20b in colour section).

❖ Second, there were reminders of Polish history, with stamps in September 1945 once again marking the Battle of Grunwald, and others in November 1945 and January 1946 commemorating the 1830 and 1863 revolts against Tsarist Russia (Fig. 6.21).

❖ Third, there were the issues heralding the advent of communism as the key factor in Polish affairs. These had been presaged by a series of three overprinted White Eagle stamps (See Fig. 6.22 in colour section). The first, issued on 31 December 1944 marked the first anniversary of the creation of the K.R.N. (*Krajowa Rada Narodowa* or

Fig. 6.21

State National Council) – a puppet parliament of Polish communists dedicated to the creation of a Soviet-controlled Polish government after the war. The second, issued on 15 January 1945, announced the winding up, on 31 December 1944, of the PKWN (*Polski Komitet Wyzwolenia Narodowego* or Polish Committee of National Liberation), which had had temporary authority within liberated Polish territory. The third marked its replacement by the RTRP (*Rzad Tymczasowy Rzeczypospolitej Polskiej* or Provisional Government of the Republic of Poland).

Great Britain and the USA protested, but Stalin had got his way. A stamp in June 1945 marked the Postal Workers' Congress in Poznan and another in November portrayed workers from different fields shaking hands at the Trades Union Congress (Fig. 6.23). The heroic images of determined workers are reminiscent of similar Soviet stamps. Indeed, by the end of 1945 it was all over. The hard-line Stalinist, Bolesaw Bierut, was firmly established as president, and thousands of German settlers trekked westwards as refugees.

Fig. 6.23

Illustrations

Fig. 6.1 Germany's Hindenburg definitive stamp overprinted '*2 Zloty 2 Deutsche Post Osten*' (December 1939).

Fig. 6.2 Souvenir cover sent from Warsaw to Hamburg with Polish stamps heavily overprinted with the German eagle and swastika, the inscription 'General Government' and new values (February–March 1940).

Fig. 6.3 Souvenir first day cover with Hitler portrait definitive stamps (26 October 1941) and Cracow postmark commemorating two years of German occupation.

Fig. 6.4 First day cover with Hitler's 54th Birthday set (20 April 1943).

Fig. 6.5 12*g* Copernicus Memorial, Cracow, 30*g* Old Church, Lublin, 48*g* Town Hall, Sandomir, and 1*z* Bruhl Palace, Warsaw, from the Historic Cities set (5 August 1940–8 September 1941).

Fig. 6.6 12*g*+8*g* Peasant from the Winter Relief Fund set (1 December 1940).

Fig. 6.7 30*g*+70*g* Radom from the Third Anniversary of the Nazi Party in German Occupied Poland set (August–September 1943).

Fig. 6.8 Cover with the set commemorating the 600th anniversary of Lublin (15 August 1942).

Fig. 6.9 Cover with 2*z* Cracow Barbican and 4*z* Tyniec Monastery stamps (10 April 1944).

Fig. 6.10 10z+10z Cracow Castle marking the fifth anniversary of German occupation (26 October 1944).

Fig. 6.11 First day cover with the set of notable figures linked to the commemoration of the third anniversary of German occupation (20 November 1942).

Fig. 6.12 Inscribed miniature sheet commemorating the 400th anniversary of the death of Nicolaus Copernicus (24 May 1943).

Fig. 6.13 Cover with the second set of notable figures (15 July 1944).

Fig. 6.14 Cover with part of the Polish Government in Exile in London set issued 15 December 1941. 75g Machine-Gunners from the Monte Casino overprinted set (27 June 1944). Warsaw Uprising Relief Fund stamp (3 February 1945).

Fig. 6.15 25g Romuald Traugutt, 50g Tadeusz Kosciuszko and 1z Jan Henry Dabrowski from the National Heroes set (7 September 1944).

Fig. 6.16 Overprinted Romuald Traugutt stamp marking 82nd Anniversary of the 1863 Polish Revolt (22 January 1945).

Fig. 6.17 50g Grunwald Memorial stamp (13 September 1944).

Fig. 6.18 3z Warsaw from the White Eagle stamps overprinted with surcharges and dates cities were liberated (12 February 1945).

Fig. 6.19 5z Liberation of Warsaw (9 March 1945), 1z Lodz (15 March 1945), 2z Cracow (10 April 1945), and 3z imperforate Gdansk (Danzig) (15 September 1945).

Fig. 6.20 Cover featuring major Warsaw buildings before and after the German occupation (1945–46). Cover with the stamp marking the sixth anniversary of the Defence of Westerplatte (1 September 1945).

Fig. 6.21 10z Historic Polish Soldiers commemorating the 115th anniversary of the 1830 revolt stamp (29 November 1945).

Fig. 6.22 Overprinted White Eagle stamps (December 1944 and January 1945) announcing steps in the communist takeover of Polish civil government.

Fig. 6.23 First day card marking the Trades Union Congress in Warsaw (18 November 1945).

7

DENMARK

It was Denmark's misfortune that it lay directly in the path of German ambitions in the far larger country of Norway to the north whose lengthy coastline could harbour British ships and whose neighbour Sweden possessed valuable mineral deposits. Jutland, the northern part of Denmark, was seen as a useful base for the invasion of Norway, and Denmark possessed further strategic value as the gateway to the Baltic Sea. As elsewhere, Hitler signed a non-aggression treaty with Denmark in 1939, but on 9 April 1940 his forces burst across the border by land, sea and air. The flat land was impossible to defend and, because Denmark had failed to modernise its army for fear of antagonising Hitler, its forces were too small and inadequately armed to offer much resistance. Within hours the Danish cabinet surrendered 'under protest', hoping to come to an advantageous peace.

Their hopes were founded on the ethnic similarities between the two countries, the long period of mutually beneficial commerce between them, and the Germans appearing to bear no grudge against Denmark for securing the return of northern Schleswig after the First World War. The Germans were, indeed, prepared to act leniently. Their main wartime interests were not primarily strategic or hostile ideologically, but the securing of Danish agricultural produce at advantageous prices and the creation of a model German protectorate where the 'Nordic Aryan' people responded positively to Nazi ideas on government, race and culture.

The Germans were fortunate that Danish government ministers remained in post, and that Parliament agreed to function 'normally' because it was allowed to retain much of its power over domestic policy. The Danish police and judiciary stayed largely untouched, and King Christian X decided not to flee – indeed there was hardly time – and remained head of state. Completely unguarded, each day the king rode through Copenhagen on his horse to the cheers of the crowd. The pre-war definitive stamps featuring the Danish crown, a Danish caravel and the king's head and be-medalled torso stayed in circulation until they were replaced from 1942 onwards with a full-faced portrait of Christian, still in military uniform (Fig. 7.1). Unusually, the various Danish political parties, except the communists, stayed in being and agreed to cooperate with each other and with the government to ensure minimal upset to the Germans and minimal intervention by them in Danish affairs. The German Reich was represented officially in Denmark through a Reich plenipotentiary accredited to the royal court.

Fig. 7.1

Acting pragmatically, the majority of Danes supported the new enforced partnership as it seemed the best way to preserve domestic peace and reasonable
prosperity. And, of course, until the Soviet Union started to push back the German
advances on the Eastern Front in 1942 it looked as though the Nazis would rule
most of continental Europe indefinitely. However, the Danish government and
people were faced with never-ending German demands for greater concessions
and cooperation backed up whenever the Germans were frustrated by threats of
direct rule. Inevitably as time passed the Danes found their domestic policies
were getting dangerously close to those of Nazi Germany. The government, for
example, agreed to ban news reports prejudicial to German–Danish relations,
to outlaw the Communist Party and arrest all communists, and to join the Anti-
Comintern Pact alongside Finland, although it refused to send its troops to fight
the Soviet Union. Nevertheless, in 1942 the Danes rejected demands to discrim-
inate against Danish Jews, and many families helped hundreds of Jews to escape
by sea to neutral Sweden, and the government consistently refused to enter into
a customs and currency union with Germany, fearing the economic and political
repercussions. The Germans did not push these issues further, deciding that
the high degree of cooperation already achieved was worth preserving.

New stamp issues were few. Unlike Poland, for example, there were none
aimed at humiliating the country, and unlike Belgium, the Netherlands,
Hungary, Romania and Bulgaria there were none glorifying the nation's past,
and, of course, unlike the Soviet Union there were none rallying the country in its hour of crisis. Perhaps the wartime emphasis upon the new King
Christian stamps, with his daily morale-boosting presence among his subjects, was sufficient in the extremely delicate circumstances. Significantly,
other members of the royal family appeared on wartime stamps. In November
1939 King Christian's wife, Queen Alexandrine had featured on a surcharged Red Cross set, and a new value on an identical portrait was issued
in December 1940 (See Fig. 7.2 in colour section). Interestingly, her sister
Princess Cecilie had married the kaiser's son, Crown Prince Wilhelm of
Germany (1882–1951), who for a time in the 1930s was a strong supporter
of Adolf Hitler. In 1941, and again in 1943, a surcharged Child Welfare stamp
was issued featuring Princess Ingrid, the wife of Crown Prince Frederick,
holding their baby daughter, Princess Margrethe (Fig. 7.3).

Just two issues commemorated famous figures in Danish history. The bicentenary of the death of the Danish-born explorer Vitus Bering on 19 December 1941 occurred during the early German advances into the Soviet Union under Operation Barbarossa. The Russians often claimed him as a hero themselves, and belatedly issued a set of stamps commemorating the bicentenary in 1943, but the Danish government was far nearer the date with its issue on 27 November 1941 featuring Bering's storm-tossed ship *Sv Pyotr*. Born in Jutland in 1681, Bering enlisted in the newly formed Russian navy in 1703. He distinguished himself in Russia's long war with Sweden, and in 1725 Tsar Peter I (Peter the Great) commissioned him to explore unknown north-east Siberia and seek a route to the East Indies. In 1728 he sailed through the straits now named after him, but the American coast was invisible in thick fog. He believed Asia and North America to be unconnected, and that he had found the elusive North-East Passage, but his assumption was greatly criticised on his return. In 1733 he led the largest scientific expedition the world had seen during which 10,000 men in groups surveyed the Russian Siberian coast and the west coast of North America as far as modern Mexico. As part of this long expedition, in 1741 Bering sighted the northern shore of the Gulf of Alaska and some of the Aleutian Islands, but fell ill and died just before the end of the year (Fig. 7.4).

The second famous figure was the renowned mathematician and astronomer Ole Romer (1644–1710) commemorated in September 1944, the tercentenary of his birth in Arhus. He was a particularly notable benefactor of Danish commerce and civilian life, which, more than his international fame, was perhaps why this

anniversary was deemed particularly noteworthy at this time. As a young man Romer was tutor to the French Dauphin, and helped construct the celebrated fountains at Louis XIV's new Palace of Versailles. Returning to Copenhagen in 1681 he became professor of astronomy and established his observatory in the Round Tower of Trinity Church, which had received its own celebratory stamp in 1942 (Fig. 7.5). Through his observation of eclipses he pioneered ways to calculate the speed of light, and he sought to

Fig. 7.3

Fig. 7.4

Fig. 7.5

Fig. 7.7

Fig. 7.6

measure temperature accurately and to calculate longitude. As royal mathematician he introduced the first national system of weights and measures, including the definition of a mile as four minutes of arc latitude. As an inventor he introduced the first oil street lamps in Copenhagen, and as a senior city official he concerned himself with easing the problems of the city's poor and unemployed, and modernising the fire service, water supply and system of sewers.

Another commemoration, this time the twenty-fifth anniversary of Danish Airlines, revealed a close commercial connection with Germany by picturing one of the Focke-Wulf Fw 200 Condors the airline had purchased just before the war – the only European airline to do so outside Germany (Fig. 7.6). The only other wartime set comprised views of three early medieval rural churches at Ejby on the island of Zeeland, Osterlars on the island of Bornholm, and Hvidbjerg in western Jutland. Interestingly, and it may or may not be surreptitiously connected with the issue, Osterlars church possesses a famous pillar adorned with Bible scenes including the Day of Judgement showing naked figures sent to hell, which is represented by a hideous dragon (Fig. 7.7).

Unlike pro-Nazi Vichy France, and tightly controlled Norway and the Netherlands, the Danish government never sanctioned any stamps promoting and funding 'home-grown' pro-Nazi military units recruiting its citizens. Nevertheless, they existed, and were well-known. Southern Denmark possessed a large German-speaking minority, especially after northern Schleswig was annexed after the First World War. In 1941 some readily joined the newly created Free Corps Denmark to fight on the Eastern Front, and eventually several thousand other Danes joined them. The government made little protest and even allowed members of its own armed forces to enlist. In the summer of 1942 the Free Corps fought in the Battle of Demyansk where Axis forces narrowly escaped encirclement by Soviet armies. The following winter they fought in the defence of Velikiye Luki, an important communication centre between Leningrad and the south, and again just escaped capture when the Soviets retook the city. On their return home the men's reception was cold, and often hostile. In 1943 the legion was disbanded. Most legionaries then joined the new 24th SS Panzergrenadier Regiment Danmark alongside a

Norwegian one within the 11th SS Panzergrenadier Division Nordland. The division was engaged in a series of brutal battles, first against Tito's partisans in Croatia, and then in the bitterly contested retreat of Axis forces from the Soviet Union, through Estonia and Latvia, to East Prussia, the Oder River and finally the defence of Berlin. The few survivors either surrendered to the Russians or escaped to the West – in both cases to face imprisonment and, for some, execution.

Some other active collaborators, including ex-soldiers, joined the notorious Hilspolizei, the Danish auxiliary police corps attached to the German Gestapo. The Hilspolizei came into being in 1944 after mounting civil unrest and cases of active resistance the previous year led the Germans to remove the Danish government, suspend Parliament, and run the country under martial law through tightly controlled Danish ministries. Later on the Germans disbanded the ordinary police force as untrustworthy and deported over 1,900 of its officers. King Christian's deliberately curt reply – '*Spreche Meinen besten Dank aus. Chr.Rex*' ('Sending my best thanks, Christian Rex') – to the Führer's effusive telegram celebrating his 72nd birthday in 1942 had enraged Hitler, and done little to help relationships.

In the final months of the war both German terror tactics and Danish active resistance intensified. Nevertheless, although Denmark was a small country, the estimated 850 resistance members, 360 concentration camp inmates and 900 other civilians killed in air raids, disturbances and reprisals were not nearly as high a percentage of the population compared with other occupied nations. However another 100 soldiers and 1,850 sailors died serving the Allies.

On 5 May 1945 Denmark became free again. Later 40,000 people were arrested as suspected collaborators, and 13,500 convicted, of whom forty-six were executed. There was, though, much talk about the politicians and businessmen who remained untouched by the investigations and had been enriched by their collaboration. There were also worries about how the victorious Allies would perceive Denmark as a result of its overall policy of peaceful, if reluctant, co-existence.

The first post war issue in September 1945 celebrated King Christian's 75th birthday.

Illustrations

Fig. 7.1 Pre-war 4*o* crown and waves, 30*o* caravel, and 2*f* King Christian definitive stamps remaining in wartime circulation, and the 75*o* King Christian definitive stamp from the set issued on various dates from 26 September 1942.

Fig. 7.2 Red Cross + Odense Philatelic Society first day cover with the booklet pane of two Queen Alexandrine 10+5*o* Red Cross Fund stamps and two ordinary 10*o* definitive stamps (7 September 1940) with a special Odense cancellation.

Fig. 7.3 20+5*o* Princess Ingrid and infant Princess Margrethe from the Child Welfare set (8 September 1943).

Fig. 7.4 10*o* Bering's ship *Sv Pytor* from Bicentenary of the Death of Vitus Bering set (27 November 1941).

Fig. 7.5 Tercententry of the Birth of Ole Romer (25 September 1944) and Trinity Church Round Tower (27 November 1942) stamps.

Fig. 7.6 Twenty-fifth Anniversary of Danish Airlines (29 October 1943).

Fig. 7.7 15*o* Osterlars (7 September 1944) and 20*o* Hvidbjerg (14 July 1944) from the Danish churches set.

8

NORWAY

Norway was the country most heavily occupied by German forces, with 300,000 service personnel stationed there soon after the invasion in April 1940 right up to their surrender in May 1945. Yet overall Norway's occupation was less severe than in most other countries, and far less brutal than in the primarily Slavic regions of Poland and the Ukraine. Civil rule was determined by the Reich Commissariat for Norway and largely administered by a pro-German Norwegian puppet government. The legitimate Norwegian government headed by King Haakon VII continued in existence in exile in London, which effectively denied the Germans and their local fascist supporters any claim to be their lawful successors. Delays caused by the sinking of several German warships, and determined resistance by several Norwegian army units, were long enough for Haakon, his family, and senior government ministers to escape from Oslo and eventually reach Tromso where they boarded the British cruiser HMS *Glasgow*. The Germans had hoped to capture the king and pressurise him to give their occupancy some cloak of legitimacy, as had occurred in Denmark and Belgium. Vidkun Quisling, the leader of the *Nasjonal Samling* (National Gathering), Norway's small and peripheral fascist party, had high hopes of attaining power and thrust himself forward the moment the invasion began, but was first rejected by the king and Parliament, and then pushed aside by the Germans who realised he possessed far too little support.

From 1933, when Hitler assumed power, Norway had followed a policy of neutrality, stemming partly from economic necessity at a time of world recession, partly from widespread pacifism, and partly from a feeling that a European war posed no particular threat to it. Gradually, however, the country realised that both Germany and Great Britain had a strategic interest in opposing each other's mastery of Norway's coastline, airfields and routes to Swedish iron ore mines. Norway started to rearm, but it was too late. Great Britain sought the use of Norway's huge merchant fleet, and wanted cooperation in blockading trade to Germany. In German eyes, Norway seemed to favour the Allies rather than abiding by strict neutrality, especially when it only half-heartedly tried to stop the British destroyer HMS *Cossack* boarding the German tanker *Altmark* in Jossingford in February 1940 to rescue 299 sailors seized after their ships had been sunk by the pocket battleship *Graf Spee*. In British eyes, though, Norway's attempts at obstruction, and general lack of support, rendered it untrustworthy, and Great Britain planned its own invasion of Norway for April 1940. It was too late – by a day or so. On 8 April, while Norway was protesting about imminent British mine-laying, German ships and troops were already closing in on Oslo and other Norwegian ports.

The sudden and determined attack shocked and paralysed the Norwegian government as well as the nation as a whole. The major ports and airfields were occupied quickly and although a number of Norwegian units resisted fiercely, the British and French counterattack by sea, notably at Narvik, succumbed to inferior numbers but superior battle tactics and was forced to withdraw. By 10 June Norway was conquered. Henceforth German ships could roam the North Sea and more easily access the Atlantic, German bombers could reach Great Britain, and access to Scandinavia was denied to the Allies. By 22 June France had succumbed too, and Great Britain was isolated. Initially the German Reichskommissar Josef Terboven assumed power in Norway, with some Nasjonal Samling politicians actively collaborating. Later on Quisling himself formed a puppet cabinet in a tense and uncomfortable relationship with Terboven.

At first sight Norwegian stamp issues ignored the German occupation, with the country's name and essentially Norwegian themes looming large in each one. In common with several pre-war issues, ordinary definitive stamps consistently featured the curled post horn symbol – including the crown – and the rampant Norwegian lion clutching its axe (Fig. 8.1a & 8.1b). Nevertheless the regular commemorative designs had two clear-cut wartime purposes. One

Fig. 8.1a

Fig. 8.1b

Fig. 8.2

was to maintain the semblance of normality and continuity with pre-war issues by highlighting key features and personalities of Norwegian history and culture, as long as they were acceptable to the Nazis, and the other was to strengthen Norway's existing if rather tenuous links with right-wing nationalism and fascism. The Nazis perceived the classic Nordic statuesque physique, especially when accompanied by blue eyes and blonde hair, as racially akin, even identical, to the pure Aryan Germanic people, and therefore entirely susceptible to Nazi propaganda and ideology. Indeed the birth of 'pure-bred' babies fathered by German personnel, especially members of the SS whose Aryan ancestry had been recorded, by Norwegian women was actually encouraged. At least 8,000 such births were officially registered – the only ones outside Germany itself. Quisling himself thought Norwegians were a law-abiding and rational people much like the Germans, and therefore would rally to his well-reasoned arguments supporting and justifying the prosperity, confidence and European leadership of Nazi Germany.

The first commemorative stamps of the occupation featured Dr Fridtjof Nansen (1861–1930), the distinguished Norwegian explorer, scientist and statesman (Fig. 8.2). In 1895 he reached, on foot, the furthest north then attained, and later as professor at Kristiana University he was a founder of the neuron theory and did pioneering work on ocean currents. Originally a republican he changed his views and was instrumental in persuading Prince Charles of Denmark to become king of Norway when Norway separated from Sweden in 1905. He was awarded the Nobel Peace Prize in 1922 for his work on behalf of refugees after the First World War. There was no anniversary behind the issue, but the new regime may well have thought it apposite to remind everyone that in 1925 this uniquely prominent Norwegian had founded the Fatherland Society, a strongly anti-social-ist political organisation. Like Quisling, Nansen had come to believe in strong centralised government placing due emphasis upon race and heredity. It outlived him, although it faded away with the outbreak of the Second World War.

Not surprisingly the heroic legacy of the Vikings was to the fore in many issues. In May 1941 a Fishermen's Families' Relief Fund stamp pictured a Femboring – a small, shallow, wooden planked, rudder-steered boat akin to ancient Viking ships – sailing in the shadow of a vast iceberg. It was pictured off the coast of Haalogaland where an exhibition was being held celebrating this rugged north-ernmost province of Norway steeped in national legends of powerful chieftains uniting their unruly tribes and facing equally unruly neighbours (Fig. 8.3). Soon afterwards another issue brought the Viking legacy into modern times. Colin

Fig. 8.3   Fig. 8.4

Archer (1832–1921) was a Norwegian boat builder of Scottish descent who designed the *Fram*, the ship used by both Nansen and Roald Amundsen on their polar expeditions. Immensely strong, unusually wide and shallow, well insulated, fitted with an electric generator, and equipped with engines as well as sails, the *Fram* was well suited to exploration in freezing conditions. The stamps featured the bearded Archer and his other equally famous vessels, the highly durable rescue boats *Oslokoyta* and *Colin Archer* that he designed and built for the Norwegian Lifeboat Institution (Fig. 8.4).

During the latter part of 1940 and first half of 1941 Vidkun Quisling gradually established himself within the Nazi government. The key factors were his willingness to create a volunteer regiment to train and fight alongside the German army, hopefully alongside the Finns, and to support German policies regarding the Jews. It seems he was deluded enough to think that such pro-German actions would lead to greater internal autonomy for the country. In the event Josif Terboven tightened his grip, crushing the milk strike in Oslo, rounding up Communist Party leaders, silencing the trade unions, carrying out several executions, creating a domestic Gestapo-style state police force and confiscating wireless sets. Oslo University was placed under a Nasjonal Samling director and later a very public strike and arson attack by students led to its closure and further arrests. Ironically in September 1941 a stamp had celebrated the centenary of the university building (See Fig. 8.5 in colour section). Quisling had no choice but to agree to all this, and endure the public obloquy. All other political parties had been banned.

Several stamp issues revealed the new turn of events. In August 1941 a stamp emblazoned with the Norwegian flag and an advancing soldier urging on his unseen colleagues sought funds for a Norwegian Legion to fight against the Soviet Union (See Fig. 8.6 in colour section). A Finnish flag flies beneath the Norwegian one, the soldier wears a Norwegian, not German, helmet and uniform, and the Nasjonal Samling badge (the Cross of St Olaf) adorns his raised arm. A large rally in Oslo got recruiting under way, and eventually about 6,000 Norwegians enlisted. From the outset, however, the volunteers were issued German uniforms, with merely a collar tab and cuff band signifying their nationality. The Germans never intended the force to be Norwegian except in name, and on campaigns its senior officers were German. In February 1942 it fought in fierce battles around Leningrad and suffered many casualties. In May 1943 the Legion was dissolved and many of its survivors joined the Waffen-SS Panzergrenadier Regiment Norge and participated in battles along the Finnish–Soviet front line – where some trained on skis. In June a stamp emblazoned with the Quisling sponsored army 'Frontier Guard' emblem was issued on behalf of the Soldiers' Families' Relief Fund (See Fig. 8.7 in colour section). Any funds it raised were sorely needed, although no doubt the stamp was spurned by many. In 1944, as Axis armies were being destroyed, Norwegian units were dispatched to support several other hard-pressed Waffen-SS regiments in Latvia and Croatia, and finally in Berlin as Soviet armies took the city. Thousands of other Norwegians had joined labour battalions, and several hundred enlisted in Luftwaffe and Kriegsmarine support units.

In August 1941 an issue appeared comprising the Post Horn and Lion definitive stamps overprinted with a large black 'V'. At the same time coils of specially printed 10 *ore* Lion stamps with a white 'V' as part of the design were placed in coin-operated stamp machines (Fig. 8.8). That summer Winston Churchill had started to use his hand 'V' sign in the morale boosting 'V for Victory' campaign,

and Joseph Goebbels, Germany's Propaganda Minister, had sought to hijack the 'V' claiming it stood for 'Viktoria', the symbol of imminent German triumph over the Bolsheviks. The German word for victory was '*Sieg*' but nevertheless the Germans ordered 'V' to be painted on thousands of buildings

Fig. 8.8

across Europe as well as appearing on the Norwegian stamps. Surreptitiously, though, some Norwegians managed to add two more 'Vs' to the daubed signs and sometimes they added the whole of the new catchphrase 'Vi Vil Vinne' (We Will Win). Confounded, Goebbels aborted his 'Viktoria' campaign, and the 'V' stamps were withdrawn on 29 November the same year. However anyone daubing a 'V' or its Morse equivalent (...–) on buildings was liable to deportation or even execution. And, as we shall see, the episode was not forgotten.

Despite Terboven's loathing of Quisling, on 1 January 1942 the Germans transferred the civil administration of the country to the Nasjonal Samling with Quisling as minister-president. Two stamps portraying the head of Quisling in quasi-regal pose marked the occasion, although celebrations were largely limited to Nasjonal Samling members. A new set of official stamps for government business was created, with the Quisling emblem its central feature (Fig. 8.9). And in 1942 the inauguration of the European Postal Union provided the opportunity to create the illusion of seamless administrative continuity and independence through the issue of a commemorative stamp picturing the recent Quisling stamp alongside the country's first postage stamp in 1855 (Fig. 8.10).

Fig. 8.9

Fig. 8.10   *Fig. 8.11*   *Fig. 8.12*

In reality, however, the German garrisons remained at full strength, Norway remained under the overall control of its Reichskommisariat, and Quisling's efforts to adopt increasingly pro-Nazi policies failed to secure any German interest in giving Norway greater independence, let alone treat it as an ally. His efforts to make membership of a quasi-Hitler Youth organisation compulsory only served to arouse bitter protest and the resignation of hundreds of teachers and parish priests. Another futile initiative was marked by a reissuing of the Quisling portrait stamp in August 1942, this time overprinted '*Rikstinget 1942*' – the name he gave to a hopelessly unpopular National Assembly with advisory powers that fell far short of the old Parliament (Fig. 8.11). It was surcharged to aid war orphans. By then the Norwegian Legion had suffered significant losses.

The Nasjonal Samling's attempts to associate itself closely with the nation's folk culture and Viking legacy continued throughout these years. In the autumn of 1941 a striking set commemorated the 700th anniversary of the death of Snorre Sturlason (1178–1241), an Icelandic poet, historian and politician at a time when his country was independent but very much part of the Scandinavian social, economic and cultural world (Fig. 8.12). He was twice law-speaker at the Icelandic Parliament, the Althing, and is pictured on the 20 *ore* red stamp. He wrote a history of Norse mythology (the *Prose Edda*), and of the Norse kings (the *Heimskringla*) that begins in legend and ends in early medieval fact. Episodes are featured on the other five stamps. He believed that the gods began as heroic human beings – chieftains and kings – whose subsequent burial sites became places of veneration and centres of cults. As new generations go into battle or fall on hard times their dead leaders are remembered, called upon for help, and thereby deified. As tribes defeat other tribes, the victor's gods grow stronger. Although the German National Socialist Programme formally linked itself to Christianity, many Nazis were deeply attracted to Norse myths about powerful leaders achieving god-like qualities and powers, instilling and drawing upon the devotion of followers, and fulfilling the long-awaited destiny of the nation and race. In 1218 Sturlason sailed to Norway where the royal family helped with his stories, but eventually he joined a plot against King Haakon IV and was murdered at Reykholt, his home in western Iceland.

In June 1942 the opportunity was taken to celebrate the centenary of the birth of composer Rikard Nordraak (1842–66) (Fig. 8.13). Devoted to Norwegian folk music and an ardent nationalist he composed the Norwegian National Anthem, first performed on 17 May 1864. He was a friend of Edvard Grieg (1843–1907), another composer who promoted and popularised Norwegian culture and folk tales, and was featured in stamps in June 1943 (Fig. 8.14). The satirical poet, Johan Wessel (1742–85), was also commemorated, but probably as much for his active involvement in the *Norske Selskab* (the Norwegian Society) which did much to promote a national identity through its members' writings, as for his own witty tales of human frailties (Fig. 8.15).

After the occupation many Norwegian servicemen found their way to the United Kingdom, although it was hardest for soldiers to escape the country. Over 100 Norwegian ships and over 7,000 sailors served among the Allies, two Norwegian Spitfire squadrons – 331 and 332 – were created, and Norwegian soldiers served

Fig. 8.13

Fig. 8.14   *Fig. 8.15*

in Iceland, South Georgia and in late 1944 in the retaking of Finnmark, the bitterly contested northernmost province bordering Finland and the Soviet Union. Within Norway itself, resistance groups smuggled people out of the country, sabotaged shipping and supply depots, and gathered intelligence to send to London. Perhaps the most famous episode was the blowing up of the Vemork heavy water plant. In 1942 the government-in-exile successfully petitioned the British government for its own stamps (rather than British ones) to be available to various Norwegian military units. On 1 January a set of six (a 10 *ore* value and above) went on sale at the Norwegian Embassy in London and various consular offices, and later they were allowed on mail aboard Norwegian ships and in army camps on important days in the Norwegian calendar (See Fig. 8.16 in colour section). The 5 *ore* and 7 *ore* stamps were added when the whole series went on general sale in Norway on 22 June 1945. The 5 *ore* and 10 *ore* featured the new destroyer *Sleipnir* (the swift grey eight-legged horse of Norse mythology) that escaped the Nazis, the 15 *ore* pictured a pilot, the 7 *ore* and 30 *ore* a Norwegian merchant convoy, the 40 *ore* mountain troops on patrol, and the 60 *ore* King Haakon VII. The most famous stamp, though, was the 20 *ore* that celebrated the powerful image of 'Vi Vil Vinne' painted on a country road. The stamps, although welcome to Free Norwegian Forces, had little or no impact upon wartime life within the country itself.

The Quisling government made an unusual attempt to portray normality in April 1943 when it reissued the pre-war stamps promoting the Norwegian Tourist Association (Fig. 8.17). They featured the Norwegian–American liner *Bergensfjord* sailing beneath a vast cliff face. Ironically, by then the ship was safely in British hands, having docked in New York on a routine voyage two days before the German invasion. It was converted into a troop ship and spent the rest of the war sailing 300,000 miles and transporting 165,000 troops to various war zones. A Winter Relief Fund set in November 1943 also portrayed a deceptively peaceful normality with comforting picture book scenes of snow-covered mountains, fir trees and wooden cottages. A year later, as food and materials continued to be in short supply with so much transported to Germany, the Winter Relief Fund set once again celebrated rural life with scenes of healthy-looking peasants chopping trees, ploughing fields, spinning wool and feeding children (Fig. 8.18).

Fig. 8.17   Fig. 8.18

In contrast, a brutally realistic set issued in May 1944 raised money for ship-wrecked mariners but also charged the British with killing dozens of Norwegians in ruthless attacks on unarmed Norwegian vessels (See Fig. 8.19 in colour section). The 10 *ore* stamp showed the small freighter *Baroy* sinking off Narvik on 13 September 1941 after being struck by a torpedo from a patrolling plane attached to the carrier HMS *Victorious*. Only eighteen were saved from the twenty-six crew, fifty-nine civilians and thirty-five German soldiers on board. The 15 *ore* stamp shows the mixed cargo and passenger liner *Sanct Svithun* during the moments it was strafed, bombed and sunk by six Canadian Bristol Blenheim aircraft just off Ervik on 30 September 1943 while on a routine voyage from Bergen to north Norway. Between fifty and sixty crew and Norwegian and German passengers were lost, although local people rescued seventy-eight survivors who managed to beach the ship after the attack. The 20 *ore* stamp pictured the small passenger ship *Irma* plunging stern first to the bottom of the North Sea near Kristiansund on 13 February 1944 after attacks by a British motor torpedo boat belonging to the Royal Norwegian Navy. Sixty-one Norwegians died, and only twenty-five survived the attack. Another torpedo boat sank the freighter *Henry* in the same area soon afterwards. All the incidents were widely publicised and fervently condemned by the Quisling regime. It blamed the exiled King Haakon for seeking the destruction of civilian ships and lives. Indeed, controversy surrounded the sinking of the *Irma* and *Henry* as the torpedo boats had orders not to attack lone passenger ships, but contrary to Quisling denials the torpedo boats' captains claimed the ships were in convoy and accompanied by a German naval trawler.

An unusual single stamp appeared in June 1944 to mark the thirtieth anniversary of the first flight across the North Sea by Tryggve Gran from Cruden Bay near Peterhead in Scotland to Stavanger in southern Norway (See Fig. 8.20 in colour section). His achievement in a flimsy Blériot monoplane was stunning but as it took place on 30 July 1914 his fame was immediately overshadowed by the outbreak of the First World War. In a crowded life Gran, an expert skier, had accompanied Captain Scott to Antarctica in 1911–12 on the recommendation of Nansen, and after his epic North Sea flight he had masqueraded as Captain Teddy Grant to join the British Royal Flying Corps. Fighting on the Western Front and then against the Bolsheviks in 1919, he had won both the Distinguished Flying Cross and Military Cross. More significantly for this stamp issue, though, between the wars Gran had become acquainted with Göring and then become closely associated with Quisling's Nasjonal Samling that made much of both his political leanings and heroic status in its wartime propaganda. After the war he was convicted of treason, and briefly imprisoned.

Fig. 8.21

Reichskommissar Joseph Terboven killed himself on 8 May 1945, the German forces in Norway surrendered on 11 May, and a few days later Crown Prince Olav and several government ministers arrived from London, and were followed by King Haakon on 7 June. Olav appeared on a stamp in March 1946 and King Haakon in June, both in uniform. Another stamp honoured the Norwegian Air Force and the training camps in Canada, and re-established the Allied cause and the Norwegian monarchy as the true inheritors of the Viking tradition by featuring a ghostly Norse warrior standing behind the figures of the airmen (Fig. 8.21). In the end several thousand Norwegians – some estimates claim as many as 20,000 – were given prison sentences, and twenty-five were executed, including Vidkun Quisling.

Illustrations

Fig. 8.1 2*o* Post Horn and 5*k* Lion Rampant definitive stamps issued from 4 October 1940. Cover with a Lion Rampant stamp and the Quisling Norwegian Legion's 'Norsk Front' 'patriotic' postmark used in March and April 1945.

Fig. 8.2 10+10*o* Portrait from the Fridtjof Nansen National Relief Fund set (21 October 1940).

Fig. 8.3 Femboring stamp (16 May 1941).

Fig. 8.4 10*o*+10*o* Colin Archer and 30*o*+10*o* lifeboat stamps from the Fiftieth Anniversary of the National Lifeboat Institution set (9 July 1941).

Fig. 8.5 Centenary of Oslo University Building stamp (2 September 1941).

Fig. 8.6 Norwegian Legion Support Fund stamp (1 August 1941).

Fig. 8.7 Soldiers' Families' Relief Fund stamp (2 August 1943).

Fig. 8.8 10*o* white 'V' machine stamp and 12*o* Post Horn and 30*o* Lion definitive stamps overprinted 'V' (August 1941).

Fig. 8.9 20+30*o* Vidkun Quisling portrait stamps, one overprinted '1–2–1942' (both issued 1 February 1942) and 60*o* Eagle emblem from the Quisling administration's Official series (1942–44).

Fig. 8.10 Inauguration of the European Postal Union stamp (12 October 1942) .

Fig. 8.11 Vidkun Quisling portrait stamp overprinted '*Rikstinget 1942*' (26 September 1942).

Fig. 8.12 20*o* Snorre Sturlason from the 700th Anniversary of the Death of Snorre Sturlason set (September and October 1941).

Fig. 8.13 10*o* Rikhard Nordraak, 15*o* Viking Embarkation and 30*o* sea and mountains with the national anthem from the Birth Centenary of Nordraak set (12 June 1942).

Fig. 8.14 20*o* Portrait from the Centenary of the Birth of Edvard Grieg set (15 June 1943).

Fig. 8.15 15*o* Portrait from the Bicentenary of the Birth of Johan Wessel set (6 October 1942).

Fig. 8.16 Cover with the initial set of Government-in-Exile stamps (1 January 1943).

Fig. 8.17 15*o* Cliffs and liner *Bergensfjord* from Norwegian Tourist Association set reissued 1 April 1943.

Fig. 8.18 40+10*o* Landscape (10 November 1943) and 15+10*o* Tree Felling (1 December 1944) from the Winter Relief Fund sets.

Fig. 8.19 Shipwrecked Mariners' Relief Fund set (20 May 1944).

Fig. 8.20 30th Anniversary of the first North Sea flight by Tryggve Gran (30 June 1944).

Fig. 8.21 Norwegian Air Force and Canadian training stamp (28 March 1946).

9

THE NETHERLANDS

In his book *Hitler 1936–1945: Nemesis*, Ian Kershaw reminds the reader how often Hitler spoke during the period of relative quiet of autumn and winter 1939–40 – the period dubbed the 'Phoney War' – about the inevitability of war with the Soviet Union, but the need, first, to have secured victory against Great Britain and France. He saw the industrial might of the Ruhr as an Achilles heel. It was the largest armaments complex in Europe, but vulnerable to attack by France, possibly supported by Great Britain, through Belgium and the Netherlands. He had little interest in the fervent attempts of the weak Low Countries on his north-western borders to remain neutral in any future European conflagration. Kershaw quotes him as telling army leaders in November 1939, 'I shall attack France and England at the most favourable and earliest moment. Breach of the neutrality of Belgium and Holland is of no importance. No one will question that when we have won.'

The Netherlands had remained neutral during the First World War, with the horrors of war limited to neighbouring Belgium as the German armies hastened through it on their way to defeat France. When that sweeping movement was halted short of Paris, the resulting war of attrition in the trenches took place far enough away to leave the Netherlands untouched by German aggression and strategically of little interest to the Allies except to bar the great port of Rotterdam as far as possible to German sea-going trade.

During the economic recession of the early 1930s various fascist groups emerged in the Netherlands but, despite their great efforts, and encouragement by Germany, they never attracted mass support. Until 1938 the Dutch government spent little on national defence, believing that the greater European powers, notably France and Germany, would respect its long-standing neutrality and that one of them would come to its aid if attacked by the other. Only in 1938 and 1939 did expenditure increase on army training, on creating fortified positions around major cities such as Amsterdam, Dordrecht and Utrecht, and on enabling vast swathes of low-lying land east of Amsterdam to be flooded in the event of attack. The country was mollified to some extent, though, by Hitler's guarantee of neutrality to Queen Wilhelmina in

Fig. 9.1

October 1939 just a month before he made his real views clear to his generals. A new set of definitive stamps featuring the queen was introduced on 1 April 1940 – but it was soon to be withdrawn (Fig. 9.1).

There was no formal declaration of war when German troops invaded the Netherlands, Belgium and Luxembourg on 10 May 1940 as a prelude to the major task of crushing France. Hitler worried about a possible British advance into the Netherlands, and one major German strike sought to occupy the south of the Netherlands and then seize Rotterdam and Antwerp. The offensive caught the Dutch largely unprepared, and certainly without comparable armoured vehicles and aircraft. However, some units put up a spirited defence, shooting down many transport planes and destroying a parachute attack, but within a few days the Germans had crossed the River Maas and overrun the west of the country. The civilian areas of Rotterdam were heavily bombed, and soon afterwards the city surrendered to the German army commander who was waiting outside. With other cities threatened with similar raids, army supplies running low and German military superiority only too obvious, General Winkelman, the Dutch commander-in-chief, surrendered on 15 May although some units fighting alongside the French held out a few days longer. The Germans, however, successfully cut the Allied forces in two, pinning over 350,000 British and French soldiers between them and the Channel coast, with Dunkirk being the only port remaining in Allied hands.

A carefully prepared exodus on a British destroyer enabled Queen Wilhelmina and the Dutch government to escape to Great Britain and form a government-in-exile. A hard working and popular monarch, Wilhelmina broadcast regularly to her subjects, although they were forced to listen in secret for fear of German reprisals. When her prime minister, Dirk Jan de Geer, was convinced the Allies would lose the war and insisted on returning home to negotiate a peace settlement with the Germans along the lines of Vichy France, she abruptly dismissed him. He was replaced by the far more aggressive Pieter Gerbrandy, who exercised considerable authority over the exiled Dutch war effort, including the domestic resistance movement and also the Dutch colonial empire that remained loyal to the Crown, thereby enabling the Allies to retain control of the Aruba and Curacao oil refineries.

The Netherlands was ruled by a German civilian government headed by the Austrian-born Nazi, Arthur Seyss-Inquart, and members of the 100,000 strong Dutch National Socialist Party were appointed to most provincial and local government posts This was in marked contrast to Belgium, which remained under German military control, and to Denmark and Vichy France which were allowed their own governments, although under German supervision. The Nazis ultimately aimed to incorporate the Netherlands into Greater Germany as Hitler saw the Dutch people as Aryan and therefore worthy of German citizenship. Nevertheless, despite such slight sympathy and kinship, and the absence of consistent brutality as practised in Eastern Europe, Seyss-Inquart decided upon a strict policy of *Gleichschaltung*, meaning 'enforced conformity', which included the suppression of all non-Nazi social and cultural organisations and the elimination of all socialist and communist parties. Much agricultural produce was sent from the Netherlands to Germany and its armed forces, and rationing became increasingly strict. Many thousands of men aged between 18 and 45 were dispatched to German factories in the Ruhr as forced labourers, where Allied bombing increasingly added to their sufferings. And 25,000 houses near the coast were cleared of inhabitants and many of them demolished when the Germans, or rather thousands of forced labourers, built the massive 'Atlantic Wall' to counter any Allied invasion across the Channel. Other Dutch workers, and ordinary commercial contractors, built ten massive Luftwaffe bases so that the Netherlands could become the front line in the aerial attacks on Great Britain.

After an initial period of German inaction, the Jews were ejected from coastal towns, dismissed from public service, and then ruthlessly persecuted. The very intensity of this seriously compromised Seyss-Inquart's heavy-handed attempts to win over the Dutch to Nazi attitudes and ambitions. When, first, a strike and then a public letter from the Dutch Roman Catholic Church condemned the early deportations, the Nazis reacted violently, executing strike leaders and arresting key clergy. Only about 30,000 of the 140,000 Jews living in the Netherlands before the invasion – some of whom had fled there from Germany – survived the war. Although many Dutch families sheltered Jews, many others collaborated with the Germans and hunted down the evaders. Anne Frank and her family are the most famous example. And a unique event in recent Dutch history inadvertently made the situation worse. In 1917 the Dutch government had resolved the mutual hostility between the churches, and between them and secular political parties, by adopting universal suffrage, proportional representation and equal funding for state and church schools. Effectively this 'pillarised' Dutch society inasmuch as everyone became part of a 'pillar' based upon religious or political affiliations, with each grouping having its own schools, sports and social clubs, newspapers and trades unions. This meant many families possessed little knowledge of other 'pillars', and looked largely within their own communities for aid and support. It also meant that Jewish 'pillars' were relatively easy to track down.

When the Queen Wilhelmina stamps were withdrawn, they were replaced by an earlier Dutch definitive series featuring a flying dove. On 1 October 1940 these long-standing national stamps were reissued again with the design completely obliterated by new value overprints. In 1941 further values were added with the 'flying dove' design allowed back in public view (See Fig. 9.2 in colour section). Other than banning the queen's portrait, little attempt was made to crush Dutch culture and national history through stamp issues. On 11 May, just as the Germans were advancing into the country, a pictorial set on behalf of the national Cultural and Social Relief Fund commemorated five Dutch cultural figures (Fig. 9.3). These were Vincent van Gogh (1853–90), the troubled artist whose reputation was belatedly beginning to soar, Everhardus Johannes Potgieter (1808–75), a popular playwright, Petrus Camper (1722–89), an anatomist and anthropologist whose religious and scientific studies centred on the demarcation of humans from animals, Jan Steen (c.1626–79, a renowned painter of daily life, and Joseph Scaliger (1540–1609), a Classical scholar and historian much vilified by the Jesuits for raising the status of other races, such as the

Fig. 9.3

Jews, Persians and Egyptians, as worthy of serious study. In September 1940 the Germans contented themselves with merely changing the colour of the Jan Steen stamp and overprinting a higher value and surcharge. Another Relief Fund set of national, but entirely uncontroversial, figures was allowed in May 1941, featuring the medical pioneers Doctor A. Mathusen (1805–78) and Jan Ingenhousz (1730–99), the early female novelist Aagje Deken (1741–1804), the painter Johan Bosboom (1817–91) and the poet A.C.W. Staring (1767–1840) (Fig. 9.4).

Fig. 9.4

The Dutch series of Child Welfare stamps continued with a set in December 1940 featuring a young girl picking a dandelion, and another in December 1941 featuring Rembrandt's painting of his young son, Titus (See Fig. 9.5 in colour section). Interestingly, in 1655, when the picture was painted, Rembrandt and his family lived in fashionable Breestraat in Amsterdam. It was, though, becoming a wealthy Jewish quarter (later known as Jodenbreestraat) and Rembrandt's Jewish neighbours were sometimes asked to sit as models for his religious paintings. Nevertheless Hitler and many Nazis perceived his powerful portrayal of noble historical figures as symbolising the wider German spirit and the sombre 'blood and soil' myth of the Nazi's Aryan mythology. Rembrandt's paintings entered many Nazi collections. The Dutch Nazi movement enthusiastically promoted this association, seeing Dutch and German unity as the ultimate end result. The Nazis went so far as to promote an opera and film of Rembrandt's life, award a 'Rembrandt Prize' for works promoting National Socialist culture, and (unsuccessfully) replace Queen Wilhelmina's birthday by Rembrandt's on 15 July as a Dutch national holiday.

In November 1942 a surcharged pair of stamps picturing a steel-helmeted Dutch Waffen-SS trooper raised funds for the Netherlands Legion, and thereby raised the profile of the Dutch National Socialist Party and the significant degree of active collaboration (See Fig. 9.6 in colour section). Already by the summer of 1941 there had been enough Dutch volunteers to form the SS Volunteer Legion Niederlande, and by the end of the war over 20,000 Dutchmen had joined various units of the German armed forces. As in Vichy France, Norway and Belgium the Dutch legionaries believed they were an independent Dutch military force, and part of a resurgent Netherlands fighting alongside its German allies, but in reality they were part of the German army, and under its firm authority. The Legion Niederlande was engaged in heavy fighting around Leningrad and Lake Ladoga in 1942 and early 1943. Later that year the legion was subsumed into a new Netherlands Brigade comprising two panzer regiments with a total strength of just over 9,300 officers and men. It fought brutal battles against partisan forces in Croatia, and then returned to the Leningrad area where along-side German armies the two regiments were gradually forced back by repeated Soviet attacks to the River Narva in Estonia. Stubborn fighting held up the Soviet advance until one of the regiments was caught in the open and massacred by Soviet aircraft and encircling ground forces. The surviving regiment was pushed towards Courland and narrowly escaped being completely trapped by a risky evacuation by sea along the Baltic coast. The two regiments were reformed early in 1945, although greatly under strength. One was annihilated by the Russians during the Battle of Halbe south-east of Berlin, and the remnants of the other surrendered to advancing American forces near Parchim in the north. Several of the survivors were executed after the war.

One of the Dutch regiments had been named General Seyffardt after a senior figure on the Dutch General Staff who became an enthusiastic collaborator, and the other was named de Ruyter after a seventeenth-century naval hero. During 1943 and 1944 a series of pictorial stamps featured famous naval figures, most of whom were connected with Dutch victories over the English or the French in the turbulent seventeenth century (Fig. 9.7). One (7½c) was Michiel de Ruyter himself (1607–76) whose exploits included serving under Maarten Tromp at the victory off Plymouth during the First Anglo-Dutch War in 1652–54, raid-ing the English colonies in North America and shipping off Barbados during the Second Anglo-Dutch War (1665–67), winning the Four Days Battle in 1666, narrowly losing the St James' Day Battle soon afterwards, and winning the bat tles of Solebay, Schoonovold and Texel in the Third Anglo-Dutch War (1672–73).

Fig. 9.7

Eventually he was fatally wounded off Sicily fighting the French. Another (17½c) featured Wilhelm van Gent, who served ably under de Ruyter and was killed at Solebay in 1672. A third (10c) pictured Johan Evertson (1600–66), who achieved lasting fame for the victory of his three ships in 1636 against the four led by the renowned French privateering captain Jacques Colaert based in Dunkirk. Piet Hein (1577–1629) (15c) fought the Spanish across the Caribbean during the Dutch wars of independence in the 1620s, and died in battle with privateers off Ostend. Witte Corneliszoon de With (1599–1658) (20c) fought the Spanish under Piet Hein, and later commanded the fleet against England at the indecisive Battle of Kentish Knock.

Another hero was Maarten Tromp (1598–1653) (12½c) who commanded the Dutch fleet in its victories of Dungeness, Portland, Gabbard and Scheveningen, during which he was killed by a sharpshooter. His son, Cornelis Tromp (1629–91) also merited a stamp (30c) as a distinguished subordinate of Michiel de Ruyter in the battles of the Third Anglo-Dutch War. Tjerk Hiddes de Vries (1622–66) (25c) became a hero for his personal courage in freeing his ship from several surrounding burning vessels during the Dutch defeat at the Battle of Lowestoft in 1665 and taking over a squadron of ships when its commander, Cornelis Evertsen the Elder, was killed during the Four Days Battle in 1666. Evertson (1610–66) had a stamp in his own right (22½c), as a determined opponent of French privateers off the Dutch coast and a highly promising subordinate admiral in the First and Second Anglo-Dutch wars. And his son, Cornelis the Younger (1642–1706) (40c), also became a famous admiral and commanded the Dutch fleet that captured the English North American city of New York in 1672. Until relinquished under the peace treaty of 1674 it was renamed New Orange.

At various dates during 1943 stamps appeared featuring symbols from German mythology – a seahorse, swans, birds, trees, prancing horses and a mounted warrior (See Fig. 9.8 in colour section). They are hard to interpret as ancient mythology was replete with heroic and magical events, and these became subject to retelling, even recreating, by nineteenth-century nationalists and Romantics. The Nazis eagerly followed suit in order to be seen as the courageous inheritors of all the powers forging the nation's destiny. Essentially, the Nazis delighted in selecting stories of heroes challenged almost beyond endurance as they sought to claim, control and civilise their homeland, and bring themselves and their people through numerous trials and tribulations to understand their own virtues and live at one with the natural forces around them. This was exactly what the Nazis, with hindsight rather than foresight, claimed they were doing for the German people. The swans perhaps recalled the hero Lohengrin whom they pulled across the water to rescue the damsel, or ancient stories of the beautiful children turned into swans by an evil stepmother. The trees may have recalled the sacred groves in pagan Prussia where deities and spirits guide, warn and challenge their adherents, or Yggdrasil, the 'world tree', often represented as a mighty ash with serpentine roots that links heaven and earth. The birds recalled the winged messengers from the gods, and birds were also the omens or harbingers of good or bad news and events. The horses may be Achilles' Balius and Xanthos, or those pulling Poseidon's chariot, or any number of equally powerful and fearsome mythological steeds, and the seahorse may be Kelpie, the Celtic water horse feared and admired in equal proportion.

In March 1944 another set of Child and Winter Welfare stamps was issued picturing mothers and young children in various poses (Fig. 9.9). The fund was certainly needed, but at that stage of the war every obstacle got in the way of humanitarian aid. Many Dutch families were desperate for help. Food supplies were already low by March but in the short term the D-Day landings were to make things worse not better. The south of the country was liberated but the failure of the largely airborne Operation Market Garden to capture the bridge across the Rhine at Arnhem brought hopes of a rapid advance to a sudden halt. Northern and western Netherlands along with the port of Antwerp remained in German hands, and

Fig. 9.9

after a Dutch railway strike in September 1944 the Germans blocked all food supplies to the western towns. The bitter fighting across parts of the country and an unusually early and harsh winter made the situation worse; even when the embargo was partially lifted in November barges could not use the frozen canals. By April 1945 there was no gas or electricity and rations had shrunk to 400g of bread and 1kg of potatoes a week. Cheese and meat disappeared completely. More than 20,000 people starved to death.

Despite the speed of the German occupation, in May 1940 some 1,460 officers and men escaped to Great Britain through Dunkirk, and eventually a force of more than 2,700 Dutchmen from across the world donned British khaki uniforms with Dutch arm badges in the Detachment Koninklijke Nederlands Troepen en Groot Brittania. In July 1941 Queen Wilhelmina conferred on it the title The Princess Irene Brigade. After coastal defence duties in Essex, the brigade followed the D-Day landings and saw active service in France, Belgium and then home territory in the Netherlands.

On 15 June 1944, soon after the D-Day landings, the Dutch government-in-exile was permitted a set of stamps for use on Netherlands warships in the Allied fleet. Several featured a profile of Queen Wilhelmina, while others pictured an advancing infantryman, the liner *Nieuw Amsterdam*, a pilot in the cockpit of a fighter and the light cruiser *de Ruyter* (See Fig. 9.10 in colour section). Other values were added when the whole set went on sale in Great Britain in December 1945, although none were on sale in the Netherlands until April 1946, when the political situation had calmed down and the constitutional monarchy firmly re-established.

After helping the Allies in the hopeless task of stemming the Japanese advance, the *de Ruyter* was sunk in a surprise attack by Japanese cruisers in the Battle of the Java Sea on 28 February 1942. The liner *Nieuw Amsterdam* was in the USA when the Netherlands surrendered, and after requisition and refitting by the British government it sailed some 530,000 miles as an Allied troop transport. Dutch pilots formed Squadrons 320, 321 and 322 in the RAF, and others undertook special training as commandos in Burma, and as Special Operations Executive personnel sent behind enemy lines.

It was largely Canadian and Polish troops who liberated the Netherlands, although western areas had to wait until German forces surrendered there on 5 May 1945. On 15 July 1945 a stamp picturing a lion slaying a dragon formally commemorated the liberation (See Fig. 9.11 in colour section). The country had suffered badly. It had the highest percentage death rate of all Nazi-occupied countries in Western Europe – 205,000 men and women, representing 2.36 per cent of the population. Alongside the joyous celebrations, there was a rush to deal with collaborators. Some were lynched, some made to clear minefields, and some imprisoned – although mistakes were made in the haste for justice and a number of guilty verdicts were subsequently quashed. And all holders of German passports were deported.

Illustrations

Fig. 9.1 5*c* Portrait from the Queen Wilhelmina definitive set (1 April 1940).

Fig. 9.2 7½*c* and 80*c* overprinted pre-war 'flying dove' definitive stamps (1 October 1940) and 50*c* from the new 'flying dove' values issued in 1941.

Fig. 9.3 1½*c* + 1½*c* Vincent van Gogh and 3*c*+3*c* Petrus Camper from the Cultural and Social Relief set (11 May 1940).

Fig. 9.4 2½*c* + 2½*c* Jan Ingenhousz and 4*c*+3*c* Aagje Deken from the Cultural and Social Relief set (29 May 1941).

Fig. 9.5 2½*c* Child with dandelion (2 December 1940) and 4*c* Titus Rembrandt (1 December 1941) from Child Welfare sets.

Fig. 9.6 Postally used cover with Dutch Legion stamps (1 November 1942).

Fig. 9.7 10*c* Johan Evertson, 20*c* Witte de With and 22½*c* Cornelis Evertsen the Elder from the Dutch Naval Heroes set (1943–1944).

Fig. 9.8 1*c* Seahorse, 2*c* Swans and 3*c* Tree with Serpentine Roots from the Old Germanic Symbols set (1943).

Fig. 9.9 5*c*+5*c* Mother and Children and 7½*c* +7½*c* Mother and Wheatsheaf from the Child Welfare and Winter Help set (6 March 1944).

Fig. 9.10 Souvenir cover over printed with Government-in-Exile stamps (15 June 1944).

Fig. 9.11 Liberation stamp with Rotterdam postmark (15 July 1945).

10

LUXEMBOURG

The small pear-shaped Grand Duchy of Luxembourg nestles between Belgium to its west, France to its south and Germany to its north. For much of the nineteenth century both France and rapidly expanding Prussia had hoped to annex it, but eventually the Treaty of London in 1867 established a free and neutral Luxembourg that remained in personal union with the King of the Netherlands. However, when King William III died in 1890, his daughter and heir Wilhelmina was barred from succeeding to the Grand Duchy, which passed to Adolphe, Duke of Nassau.

Adolphe's granddaughter, the Grand Duchess Marie-Adelaide, did not flee when the Germans occupied the country in 1914 because it lay in the path of their great curving advance towards Paris. In the face of great suspicions by her countrymen and strong allegations by France regarding her allegedly close relations with the Germans, including the kaiser, she abdicated in 1919. Her successor, her sister Charlotte, did not repeat the mistake in 1940.

As international tensions rose in the 1930s, Luxembourg welcomed Hitler's reassurance in March 1939 that the country's sovereignty would not be breached. A few more soldiers were recruited and rather flimsy barricades built along the border with Germany, but after September 1939 no blackout was ordered and the trains still ran regularly into Germany and France. On 9 May when German troop movements were observed some efforts were made to block the roads from Germany, but on the following day German forces brushed aside the barricades and the token resistance, and by nightfall the country had fallen. The battles continued in Belgium and the Netherlands but fundamentally Luxembourg merely represented a passageway for German armies circumnavigating the French Maginot Line fortresses and advancing on Paris – and, unlike 1914, this time they were successful.

Charlotte and her government fled, the grand duchess settling in London where she symbolised the suffering and unity of her people, and could broadcast to those Luxembourgers who could listen to her in secret. Her son, Jean, joined the British Army. However, the Nazis perceived Luxembourg very differently from the kaiser in 1914. In 1940 its citizens were deemed ethnically German and the Grand Duchy as German territory. After a short period under military control, in late July Luxembourg was incorporated into the German Gau of Trier-Koblenz (later Moselleland) under the German Gauleiter Gustav Simon. He led the vigorous campaign known as

Heim ins Reich (Home in the Reich) to persuade the population by constant assertion, stringent new regulations and finally terror that they were German. The use
of the French language, French clothing, such as berets, and French ways of life
were banned, and all institutions, including the Parliament, that marked the Grand
Duchy as an independent country were suppressed. German laws were introduced,
including those confiscating Jewish property and rendering Jews virtually unem-
ployable. Synagogues were destroyed, and many Jews fled but they were unwelcome
in France. Those remaining were transported to camps, and in June 1943 Simon
declared Luxembourg to be Jew free, although a few survived in hiding. Huge pressure was placed upon Luxembourgers in professions and businesses to join Nazi
organisations, and any reported criticisms of the occupiers could lead to the loss
of employment and even deportation. From 1941 youths were ordered into the
Reichsarbeitsdienst, the uniformed and highly regimented Reich Labour Service,
which by then was transporting provisions to troops, repairing roads and bridges,
and constructing airstrips, as well as undergoing constant Nazi indoctrination.

The stamps reflected the great changes. Pictorial and definitive Luxembourg
stamps remained in use for a short period after the invasion, but from 1 October
1940 they were banned and replaced by the definitive stamps of Germany picturing
President Hindenburg with the overprint '*Luxemburg*' carefully placed just below
the portrait and just above '*Deutsches Reich*' (See Fig. 10.1 in colour section). On
5 December 1940, however, a number of pre-war Luxembourg stamps were reissued with the cents and franc values obliterated, and overprinted with new German
values. The local scenes on the pictorial stamps and the definitive portrait of
Charlotte were left virtually untouched, and the name 'Luxembourg' remained (See
Fig. 10.2 in colour section). Perhaps a shortage of overprinted Hindenburg stamps
necessitated this hurried issue or, less likely, it represented a slight shift in German
attitudes towards harnessing local support. They were soon joined – on 12 January
1941 – by the German set of Winter Relief Fund stamps overprinted '*Luxemburg*'
just above '*Deutsches Reich*' (Fig. 10.3). The Relief Fund surcharge was still appli-
cable so just possibly Luxembourg was officially eligible for some of its proceeds.
A year later, from 1 January 1942, Luxembourgers were obliged to use German
stamps without any overprints.

Fig. 10.3

Many young men joined the French and Belgian resistance movements, but resistance within Luxembourg was largely limited to morale boosting underground pamphlets, anti-German graffiti, and hiding Jews and youths escaping enlistment in the Labour Service. In 1942 the draconian drafting into the Labour Service and conscription into the German Army incited a savagely suppressed general strike, and also encouraged many young men to risk the penalties and try to flee the country. It was the moment that Gustav Simon realised the Germanisation policy stood little chance of real success, and he intensified the arrest and deportation of unsympathetic families. However, many other men – through conviction or pressure or mere opportunism – actively supported the Nazi regime and the eradication of the old Grand Duchy. At the end of the war 2,000 collaborators were found guilty of treason. Most were imprisoned, but nine were executed.

Luxembourg was liberated without a battle in September 1944, and that November the first values in a new series of definitive stamps featuring the Grand Duchess were issued (Fig. 10.4). However, like Belgium, liberation was not the end of Luxembourg's war, as the northern part saw much bitter fighting, numerous civilian deaths and extensive material destruction when the German Seventh Army advanced and then retreated during the Ardennes campaign in December 1944 and January 1945. On 1 March, over two months before the final German surrender, Luxembourg issued a dramatically designed set of four stamps expressing its gratitude to France, Great Britain, the Soviet Union and the United States (See Fig. 10.5 in colour section). The dates on the stamps

Fig. 10.4

– 10.V.1940 and 10.IX.1944 – ignore the painful second liberation of the northern region, which suggests the issue had been printed before the surprise attack, then held back, and then a decision taken to issue them without amendment.

Illustrations

Fig. 10.1 Celebratory cover from the city of Luxembourg posted to Berlin with the set of German overprinted stamps (1 October 1940).

Fig. 10.2 Cover with Luxembourg stamps reissued on 5 December 1940 overprinted with German values.

Fig. 10.3 6pf+4pf Posen City Theatre, 8pf+4pf Heidelberg Castle and 12pf+6pf Porta Niger, Trier, stamps from the overprinted German Winter Relief Fund stamps issued in Luxembourg (12 January 1941).

Fig. 10.4 Examples of the new Grand Duchess Charlotte stamps (6 November 1944).

Fig. 10.5 Cover with the set of celebratory stamps, plus special postmark (1 March 1945).

11

BELGIUM

In 1939 Belgium was barely 100 years old as a sovereign nation, and within that time had endured ethnic tensions between the Dutch-speaking Flemings in the north and the French-speaking Walloons in the south, deep political and social unrest during the surge of industrialisation in the nineteenth century, and the sudden invasion and harsh occupation by the Germans in the First World War.

For centuries before the 1830s, when Belgium fought to separate itself from the Netherlands, the land comprising the 'Low Countries' of modern Belgium, the Netherlands and Luxembourg had been constantly fought over by its mightier neighbours, notably France and Austria. At various times it had splintered into small dependent duchies and counties or been absorbed into large empires. In 1839, though, in a key clause of the Treaty of London Great Britain was so keen to avoid any major power occupying the ports just across the Channel that it made a guarantee of Belgian neutrality in future European conflicts. The German onslaught in 1914 invoked that guarantee.

As political tensions mounted in the later 1930s the Belgian government, with the full support of King Leopold III, announced that it would remain neutral in the event of renewed war across Europe. Belgium released itself from several military treaties it had signed in the aftermath of the First World War, and concentrated upon defensive works along its eastern borders. It was all in vain. On 10 May the Germans invaded again, and eighteen days later Leopold surrendered the army and the country. Although the Belgian monarchy retained significant powers, Leopold's surrender was deemed unconstitutional by his ministers, who wished him to flee abroad and rally resistance, as had Queen Wilhelmina of the Netherlands. By staying a prisoner of the Germans and seeking peaceful accommodation with them, many came to see Leopold as a not-too-unwilling puppet of the Nazis, especially as his pre-war anti-Semitic views were well known, and he conspicuously failed to denounce the German deportation of thousands of Belgian workers. Most of his ministers managed to reach London, where they established a government-in-exile almost as hostile to Leopold as to the Nazis. The Allies, though, found it politically convenient to portray Leopold as patiently suffering for his country's sake.

For most of the war Belgium formed part of a German military administration along with neighbouring Nord-Pas-de-Calais in France, although a north-western region including Eupen, Malmedy and St Vith that Germany had lost in 1918 was reincorporated into the Reich. General Alexander von Falkenhausen exercised final control but the Belgian civil service continued to run most domestic affairs under the authority of the German civil administrator, Eggert Reeder. Living standards declined steadily, the press was strictly controlled, rationing was quickly introduced when food imports dramatically ceased, the black market soared and, despite Belgian protests at the thousands of civilian casualties, the Allies steadily increased the ferocity of bombing raids on railway centres and industrial complexes. When Belgian industrialists sought to avoid making goods for the Nazi war effort rather than just the Belgian market the Germans retaliated by deporting workers and industrial machinery to German factories. The Germans' initial policy of conciliation towards the Belgians soon turned into attempts to woo the support of the Flemings at the expense of the Walloons, and then degenerated into a more ruthless exploitation of the country's economy and systematic harnessing of the numerous collaborators, especially in Flanders, to infiltrate the resistance movement and reinforce the German Army.

Even so, there was no sustained attempt to eradicate Belgian culture, and Flemish culture was largely protected. Indeed, one Red Cross Fund set reclaimed the celebrated painter Anthony van Dyke (1599–1641) for Belgium by featuring his self-portrait and scenes from works undertaken when he lived in Antwerp (See Fig. 11.1 in colour section). Not surprisingly, there was no hint of his time in England, his knighthood or his portraits of Charles I and the Stuart aristocracy. The stamps pictured the miraculous survival of St Sebastian, Jesus healing the paralytic man, the Madonna showing Jesus, and Daedalus warning Icarus not to fly too near the sun with his waxed wings. A sixth stamp featured Jacob Jordsen's *The Good Samaritan.* Although ostensibly merely a charity issue, the selected paintings could be interpreted as silent comments on overweening Nazi ambitions, Belgian suffering and the survival of hope and goodness.

Definitive stamps with Leopold's portrait continued in use throughout the war, and the colourful Winter Relief Fund issue in December 1940 and January 1941 pictured the arms of Mons, Ghent, Arlon, Bruges, Namur, Hasselt, Antwerp and Liège – the principal cities of Belgium's Walloon and Flemish provinces (See Fig. 11.2 in colour section). And until August 1942 Belgium's special railway stamps kept the national arms with the Belgian lion rampant . When further

Fig. 11.3

Chapelle Musicale de la Reine Elisabeth

Muziekkapel van de Koningin Elisabeth

N⁰ 081680

Fig. 11.4

railway stamps were required early in 1942, pre-war definitive stamps showing the king or the national arms were merely overprinted, but not obliterated, with new values and the railway's winged wheel emblem (Fig. 11.3). Other reminders of Belgian royalty and, indeed, past challenges to Germany, were also forthcoming. Queen Elisabeth, King Leopold's mother, was a very active patron of the arts, and a fund raising miniature sheet inscribed 'Queen Elisabeth's Music Hall' in French and Dutch, with a surcharged stamp picturing the completed hall and adorned with the royal lyre and monogram, was issued in December 1941

(Fig. 11.4). Elisabeth was the widow of King Albert of the Belgians who achieved world renown for his defiance of the Germans at the start of the First World War, and for his stalwart leadership of the army during the four years it protected the free northern sector of the country. And it was here, at the front, that Elisabeth made her own mark working tirelessly as a nurse.

In July 1941 a dramatically illustrated set of surcharged stamps raised money for the reconstruction of Orval Abbey in the southern Walloon province of Luxembourg adjacent to the grand duchy of the same name. As the Roman Catholic ecclesiastical hierarchy possessed a relatively high degree of freedom, and certainly great influence, the Germans had no wish to alienate it unnecessarily, and the high-profile building work continued throughout the war, although some supplies suffered delays. The eye-catching illustrations show the monks singing, at prayer, examining plans, painting a mural and carving a statue. That October a particularly large miniature sheet (165x183mm) joined the set (Fig. 11.5). Two years later, in October 1943, an unusual set sought further funds for the abbey. There were six stamps – five pictured different letters from the name 'Orval' and a long sixth stamp repeated them all to show the full name (Fig. 11.6).

Fig. 11.5

The abbey had had a chequered history. Possibly built on the site of an earlier chapel, a Benedictine monastery was started in 1070 but abandoned about forty years later. The buildings were completed by a group of Canons Regular in 1124 and soon afterwards they merged with a group of Cistercian monks who had arrived there. In 1252 fire destroyed the monastery and it took a century to rebuild it. In 1637 it was burnt down by French troops during the Thirty Years War, was rebuilt and then destroyed again by French troops in 1793. The Harenne family

Fig. 11.6

came into possession of the site and in 1926 it was given back to the Cistercians. For the next twenty-two years the monks worked to rebuild the monastery. Its coat of arms shows a gold ring rising out of the water, harking back to the legend of a widowed noblewoman who lost her wedding ring in a spring at Orval only to see a trout bringing it back to the surface for her. She is said to have given Orval its name by exclaiming, 'Truly this place is a Val d'Or' (a Vale of Gold).

St Martin of Tours, a particularly popular saint in Belgium, was commemorated in lengthy sets of stamps in 1941, 1942 and 1943 in support of the Winter Relief Fund (See Fig. 11.7 in colour section). However, Martin had a reputation wider than Belgium. Born in AD 316 in Pannonia in modern-day Hungary, Martin grew up in northern Italy, where his father was stationed in the Imperial Guard. He is said to have become a Christian while still a child. He followed his father into the army, but just before a battle with the Gauls near modern-day Worms he refused as a Christian to shed blood and left the army, although only after a spell in prison on a charge of cowardice. Stories abound of his travels, conversions, miracles, confrontation with the Devil and zealous challenges to heretics. In 361 he joined with Hilary of Poitiers in establishing Ligugé Monastery, the oldest in Europe. In 371 he was popularly acclaimed as Bishop of Tours, where he ordered the destruction of pagan temples and vigorously combated heresy, but always sought the emperor's mercy for condemned heretics. All the Belgian stamps are based upon statues in numerous Belgian churches showing the moment when Martin as a young Roman soldier divided his cloak with a scantily clad beggar he encountered at the gates of Amiens. That night he dreamed that Jesus was wearing the half-cloak he had given away. This, it is claimed, confirmed his Christian faith. Throughout the Middle Ages Tours became a centre of pilgrimage, especially for those from the Low Countries and northern Germany. Successive French kings, and indeed their rivals, used his image and name to rally support in war, and in the nineteenth century ultra-right-wing clerical and military groups refined and promoted his embodiment of mental and physical courage, utter devotion to Christian virtues, and harmonious relations with secular rulers. He became the soldier's saint. His time in the imperial army was highlighted, but not his sudden refusal to spill blood.

After their surrender in 1940, 225,000 Belgian soldiers were imprisoned in Germany. The vast majority were Flemish, and most of these were repatriated the following year, partly to mollify the Flemings and partly because the Belgian and Germany economies needed them. Nevertheless, despite constant pleas, about 70,000 remained as prisoners of war, and three sets of stamps were issued to raise relief funds for them in October 1942, May 1943 and May 1944.

The first two sets pictured soldiers reading, writing or playing the accordion and dreaming of their home and families (Fig. 11.8). The third set, however, comprised an eclectic collection of famous historical figures selected from across

Fig 11.9

the Belgian provinces, all of whom had international achievements to their names (See Fig. 11.9 in colour section). Overall the set seemed to symbolise both the uniqueness and commonalty of the nation's heritage, and perhaps the belief that it had the strength to survive its present ordeal. The first stamp pictured Jan van Eyck (c.1390–1441), a renowned Flemish painter employed first by John of Bavaria, Count of Holland, and then by Duke Philip the Good of Burgundy, which then incorporated much of modern Belgium and the Netherlands. The second pictured Godefroid de Bouillon (c.1060–1100) who became lord of Bouillon – in the Walloon region in the province of Luxembourg – within the medieval duchy of Lower Lorraine. He mortgaged or sold his lands to the Bishop of Liège to raise funds to support, and share the leadership of, the 1095 crusade. After immense difficulties Godefroid led the successful attack on Jerusalem, and became its first crusader-ruler. The third pictured Jacob van Maerlant (c.1235–c.1300) who was born in Bruges and became one of the greatest Flemish poets. His works glorified the virtues of great knights, refined the concept of chivalry and stirred up support for further crusades against the 'infidels'. The fourth portrayed Jean Joses de Dinant, a famous fourteenth-century coppersmith who helped extend the prestige of the Walloon city of Dinant. The fifth showed Jacob van Artevelde (c.1287–1345), a wealthy textile merchant who created an alliance of neutrality between Ghent, Bruges, Ypres and other Flemish towns to ensure the war between England and France would not threaten their prosperity. After several years of uneasy peace he was murdered by an enraged mob suspecting he sought to make the son of King Edward III of England count of Flanders. The sixth pictured the Brussels-born Charles-Joseph de Ligne (1735–1814), whose distinguished military career culminated in the rank of field marshal, friendship with the Holy Roman Emperor Joseph II and Catherine II of Russia, and sympathy, but not overt involvement, with the Belgian revolutionary movement. The seventh portrayed André Gretry (1741–1813), a composer of operas popular across western Europe whose statue stood in his birthplace of Liège. The eighth pictured Jan Moerentorf (1543–1610), who married the daughter of his famous employer, the Antwerp printer Christophe Plantin, and inherited the firm in 1589. The firm's reputation soared and the Moerentorf Bible remained the official Roman Catholic edition for centuries. The final stamp featured the Flemish scholar and priest Jan de Ruysbroeck (1294–1381), who was born near Brussels and attracted many followers because of his popular writings and their challenges to contemporary heresies.

   Christophe Plantin (1514–89) was one of nine sixteenth- and early-seventeenth-century Flemish and Walloon intellectuals to appear on a set of surcharged anti-tuberculosis stamps in May 1942 (Fig. 11.10). All of the diverse figures struggled to pursue their work at a time when major political and religious divisions were erupting into wars and persecution – and when scientists could easily be accused of heresy, as were Christophe Plantin himself and the mapmaker Geradus Mercator (1512–94), who featured in the set.

Fig. 11.10

Fig. 11.11

Both were strongly suspected of harbouring disturbingly liberal Protestant sympathies within their largely authoritarian Roman Catholic communities. The others included the mapmaker Abraham Ortelius (1527–98), the anatomist Andreas Versalius (1514–64), the botanist Rembert Dodoens (1517–85), the mathematician and engineer Simon Stevin (1548–1620), the philosopher Justus Lipsius (1547–1606), the chemist Johann Baptista van Helmont (1579–1644) and the Jesuit hagiographer Jean Bolland (1596–1665).

In June 1944 a set dedicated to the Anti-Tuberculosis Fund followed the same diplomatic pattern of targeting a range of provinces, but this time by featuring scenes from local legends. As legends usually do, they tell of triumphs against the odds – a morale boosting idea in wartime (Fig. 11.11). One example was the story from Namur of the great horse Bayard capable of carrying the four sons of Aymon and incurring the jealousy of Charlemagne, who orders it thrown into a river with a rock tied around its neck. It crushes the rock with its hooves and gallops to freedom. Another was the legend of Geneviève of Brabant who was falsely accused of infidelity by an officer of her husband's court. Sentenced to death by her husband she was spared by the executioner and fled to a cave with her son where they were nourished by a roe deer. Her distraught husband found out she was innocent, and some years later he was chasing the very same deer when it led him to her hiding place.

A complex set issued in August 1941 sought to raise funds for the relief of families of prisoners of war, and somewhat painfully bearing in mind the German occupation it comprised ten portraits of past rulers of the Low Countries when Belgium was merely one component of vast French, Spanish and Austrian kingdoms and empires (See Fig. 11.12 in colour section). First was Philip the Good (1396–1467) who became Duke of Burgundy in 1419 and succeeded in incorporating Namur, Hainault, Brabant and Luxembourg into his Low Countries domain. He was responsible for the capture of Joan of Arc in 1430. He was succeeded by Charles the Bold (1433–77). Not content with ruling Burgundy, Flanders, Artois, Luxembourg, Holland, Zeeland, Friesland and Brabant, Charles tried to add Alsace and Lorraine but was killed at the Battle of Nancy. A third stamp features Joanna of Castile (1479–1555), the heiress uniting Castile and

Aragon in Spain, who married Philip the Handsome who ruled Burgundy (still embracing much of the Low Countries) on behalf of his father, the Holy Roman Emperor Maximilian I, and his mother, Margaret, Duchess of Burgundy. A fourth features Maximilian's daughter, Margaret of Austria (1480–1530), who became regent of the Spanish Netherlands (the name accorded the Low Countries under the Spanish Hapsburgs) in 1507 on behalf of her young nephew, the future Emperor Charles V – Joanna's son. Charles V (1500–58) merited his own stamp as the warrior who grew up in the Spanish Netherlands and went on to wage wars against France, seize northern Italy, halt the advancing Turks outside Vienna and coerce the Pope into refusing to annul Henry VIII's marriage to his aunt Catherine of Aragon. Margaret of Parma (1522–86) was Charles's talented illegitimate daughter who married the Duke of Parma and went on to become a popular and conciliatory Spanish governor of the Netherlands even though the northern provinces wrenched themselves free to become the United Provinces in 1581. Two stamps feature Archduke Albert (1559–1621) and his wife Isabella (1566–1633), who became joint sovereigns of the remaining Spanish Netherlands in 1598. They brought thirty years of peace and prosperity. The final two rulers were Empress Maria Theresa of Austria (1717–80), whose lands included much of modern Belgium, although not modern Netherlands, but extended to modern Germany, Austria, the Czech Republic and Slovakia, and her brother-in-law Prince Charles of Lorraine (1712–80), whom she made joint governor of the Austrian Low Countries with his wife.

Resistance to the German occupation was slow to start but grew widespread, especially when Belgian Jews were rounded up, civilian workers were deported, and ultimate German victory seemed increasingly remote. Underground newspapers ranging from royalist to communist in sympathy flourished, intelligence-gathering groups kept the Allies informed of German troop movements and coastal fortifications, and the well-organised 'Comet' escape route led some 700 shot-down aircrew to safety in Spain. Large-scale industrial strikes occurred, although they were heavily punished, extensive sabotage severely disrupted the railway system, especially after the D-Day landings in June 1944, and, unlike many occupied countries, the assassinations of German officers and noted collaborationists became increasingly common, despite the inevitable reprisals. However, the Germans used informers very effectively. Numerous resistance groups were betrayed, and many thousands of resistance members were arrested and executed.

Collaborators were also numbered in thousands. The pre-war fascist parties in both Flanders and Wallonia sought accommodation with the Nazis, but were treated more as nuisances than useful allies. Nevertheless many Belgians who feared and opposed communism were persuaded to work for the Germans in various civil, intelligence and military capacities after Hitler broke with Stalin in 1941. About 15,000 Belgians served in either the Flemish or Walloon Waffen-SS brigades. Both forces issued propaganda and fund-raising stamps (See Fig. 11.13

in colour section). They had no postal validity, and if affixed to envelopes or parcels they needed to be accompanied by official postage stamps. A 'Flemish Legion' with a semblance of provincial independence was formed just after the German invasion of the Soviet Union, but in 1943 it was reformed as the 27th SS Langemarck Division and dispatched to the Eastern Front where it fought well but incurred heavy casualties. There were also Flemish para-military forces such as the Algemeene-SS Vlaanderen that operated alongside German forces in protecting installations and suborning internal dissent, and sent volunteers to support hard-pressed German and Langemarck forces in the Soviet Union.

In Wallonia it took the pre-war Catholic and fascist 'Rex' organisation some time to win German favour, but its rabid anti-communist and anti-Semitic ideologies eventually triumphed and its members became powerful allies of the Nazis and natural targets for assassination by resistance groups. Leon Degrelle, the Rexist leader, finally secured German support for the creation of a 'Walloon Legion' primarily for combat in the Soviet Union but also as the hope for greater Wallonian autonomy within the Nazi Empire. His faith in these causes was great enough for him to enlist as a private, and by 1943 the increasingly desperate Germans recognised the legion's commitment and turned it into the 28th SS

Fig. 11.14

Wallonien Division with Degrelle as an obersturmführer, or senior lieutenant. In the desperately bitter fighting in the Ukraine and then around the River Narva in Estonia, Degrelle was frequently wounded, decorated and promoted, reaching the rank of standartenführer, or full colonel, in April 1945. After the war he fled to sanctuary in Spain, and was condemned to death in absentia in Belgium.

The Allies liberated most of Belgium in early September 1944. The speed with which it happened precluded any power vacuum, and the return of the government-in-exile was facilitated by the absence of King Leopold in prison in Germany and then Austria. In November the first Liberation set was issued featuring the Belgian rampant lion superimposed on a 'V'. A little later several pre-war Arms stamps were reissued with a large red 'V', but only in December were a few pre-war King Leopold stamps issued with a small 'V' and shadowy crown at his side (Fig. 11.14). Leopold was liberated in May 1945 but unease over his conduct led to a regency under his brother, Prince Charles, and the king's exile in Switzerland until 1950. Still controversial, his brief return led to strikes and rioting, and his belated decision – forced by the government – to abdicate in favour of his son, Baudouin.

However, in December 1944 Belgium's war was not over. On 16 December three well-hidden German armies burst through the Ardennes forests and hills to surprise the weak American forces holding a line approximately along the Belgian and Luxembourg border with Germany. Hitler's aim was to drive across Belgium to Antwerp and split the Allied armies. Initially successful, the Germans rapidly advanced 30–40 miles along a 60-mile front but, despite American chaos, the difficult terrain and appalling winter conditions fatally impeded their progress. By 21 December American forces in the important junction town of Bastogne were surrounded, but when called upon to surrender Brigadier General McAuliffe made the celebrated reply: 'Nuts'. The determined resistance seriously delayed the Germans already hard-pressed timetable. Bastogne was relieved on 26 December, and during a freezing January the Germans were reduced to a fighting withdrawal under major Allied counter-attacks and the loss of most armoured vehicles. Bastogne became both the symbol of American valour and Belgian gratitude. A pair of stamps issued in June 1946 commemorated the achievement and raised funds for a memorial (See Fig. 11.15 in colour section).

Illustrations

Fig. 11.1 1.75f+8.25f Sir Anthony van Dyck self-portrait, 60c+3.40f Christ healing the paralytic (detail) and 1f+5f Madonna and child from the Red Cross Relief Fund set (16 April 1944).

Fig. 11.2 Winter Relief set reissued as a miniature sheet (May1941).

Fig. 11.3 2.50f King Leopold definitive stamp issued in wartime, and the overprinted 2.25f King Leopold and 35c Arms stamps used as additional wartime railway stamps.

Fig. 11.4 Queen Elisabeth's Concert Hall Fund miniature sheet (1 December 1941).

Fig. 11.5 5f+10f stamp from the Restoration of Orval Abbey set (4 July 1941).

Fig. 11.6 5f+30f stamp from Restoration of Orval Abbey set (9 October 1943).

Fig. 11.7 St Martin of Tours Winter Relief Fund sets (5f+5f from 3 November 1941, 10f+20f from 12 November 1942, and 10f+30f from15 November 1943).

Fig. 11.8 Prisoners of War Relief Fund stamps (5f+45f + label from 1 October 1942, and 1f+30f from May 1943).

Fig. 11.9 The set of nine Prisoners of War Relief Fund stamps (31 May 1944).

Fig. 11.10 1.75f+50c Gerardus Mercator and 10f+30f Christophe Plantin from the Anti-Tuberculosis Fund set (15 May 1942).

Fig. 11.11 10c+5c Bayard the horse and 1.75f+5.25f Geneviève of Brabant from the Anti-Tuberculosis Fund set (25 June 1944).

Fig. 11.12 The set of nine Soldiers' Families' Relief Fund stamps (25 August 1941).

Fig. 11.13 Set of four Algemeene-SS Vlaanderen (General-SS Flanders) fund raising and propaganda labels (1941).

Fig. 11.14 3.50f Lion rampant and 'V' stamp from the first Liberation set (10 November 1944), 20c Arms stamps with overprinted 'V' from the second set (13 November 1944) and 2f King Leopold portrait stamp with a 'V' over the crown from the third set (18 December 1944).

Fig. 11.15 Illustrated Belgian–American Association cover with the pair of surcharged Bastogne Memorial stamps (15 June 1946).

12

FRANCE, AND THE CHANNEL ISLANDS

On 10 May 1940 German armies invaded Belgium and the Netherlands, but it was the conquest of neighbouring France that was uppermost in the minds of Hitler and his generals. A few days later a German army burst out of the Ardennes forest, tore a 50-mile gap in the supposedly impregnable French border defences, and carried out a huge sickle movement to reach the Channel coast and cut off the Allied armies in the north. It took just nine days.

After fighting off belated French and British counter-attacks, the German armies marched into Paris, and then continued west, south and east. Some French units fought fiercely, but to no avail. They were strategically and politically leaderless. On 16 June Marshal Pétain, an 84-year-old hero of the First World War, and recently appointed Minister of War, negotiated peace with the Germans – or rather accepted the terms dictated by Hitler. Paul Reynard, the prime minister, resigned rather than accept them, and President Lebrun feebly conceded authority to Pétain, thereby giving any government the Germans negotiated with Pétain a cloak of legitimacy (see map on p. 250).

The French Republic ceased to exist, and the country was splintered into several parts. The long-contested eastern regions of Alsace and Lorraine, which had been held by Germany between its stunning victory over France in 1870 and its defeat in 1918, returned to Germany for incorporation in the Reich. Several *départements* in the far south-east were given to Mussolini. The *départements* of Pas-de-Calais and Nord adjoining Belgium fell under direct military control, and later on so did an important coastal strip 10 or more miles deep running hundreds of miles from the Somme to the Spanish border. The rest of the country was divided into two. The remainder of northern France and a south-western strip running down to the Spanish border were placed under German administration. Finally, Hitler allowed central France and the remains of the south to become a shrunken puppet 'French State' governed by Marshal Pétain from the dismal spa town of Vichy. French humiliation was complete, and post-war France never reconciled its swift defeat and Vichy's active collaboration with the Nazis to its subsequent claims to be a nation that had opposed the horrors Hitler wrought upon Europe.

But that was not how Marshal Pétain and his adherents saw things. They had witnessed the post-war mood of pessimism after 1918 and the lack of confidence and courage that afflicted France after its bitter struggle and huge loss of life. Other factors seeming to signal a national decline caused continual worry, notably rural depopulation and the low birth rate. As a result, the inter-war governments tried to promote the regeneration of the countryside, the virtues of family life and the maintenance of regional cultures. There was an accompanying fear that modern women were seeking lives of selfish hedonism, and there was constant criticism of the heady influence of American popular culture. Other fears were the rise of socialism, and the rampant spread of communist ideology throughout Europe.

In the 1920s and 1930s national and local elections swung violently between right- and left-wing parties, with coalitions quickly formed and quickly broken as financial crises, personality conflicts and opposing views on nationalising industries, supporting the Roman Catholic Church and introducing constitutional reform stretched political groupings and coalitions to breaking point. To Pétain and his followers France seemed impotent in the face of social degeneracy, political paralysis and economic stagnation, and the disturbing threat posed to national security by Hitler and the Nazis. Conversely in the 1930s many influential people in France saw rising German nationalism, authoritarian government, radical economic reforms and apparent clear political thinking as things France itself desperately needed. There was a sense across France that no one seemed able to contain, let alone solve, the morass of debilitating issues. This was compounded during the economic depression by the influx of German Jews that heightened xenophobia and rekindled the nineteenth-century paranoia regarding Jewish warmongers endlessly profiteering and plotting chaos across Europe. On top of all this, the horrors of the First World War contributed to a strong pacifist movement in France.

As Pétain assumed authority in Vichy, families and communities across France were dislocated by thousands of refugees fleeing from the German advance. Perhaps not surprisingly the news of the armistice was greeted with widespread relief, and Pétain's personal popularity soared with his repeated expressions of concern for the plight of the homeless. Equally popular, at least in the short term, were his twin arguments that the armistice had prevented further destruction and now should be regarded as the springboard for national regeneration. A 'National Revolution' based upon love of one's nation, region and family and a heightened regard for working-class culture, education, morality and religion was launched. Collaboration with Germany was explained by the need to secure the necessary period of peace to achieve regeneration, and Jews, communists and resistance fighters were repeatedly condemned, and rigorously hunted down, as enemies of this vital process. Bloody battles occurred between Vichy and British naval and military forces when Churchill decided not to risk French warships and Middle East colonies such as Syria falling into enemy hands. Vichy police had no hesitation in seizing Allied airmen on the run.

Pétain possessed the impressive mystique of a national war hero, as indeed he had been in the First World War, and he looked very much like a trusted elderly father figure. He took care to cultivate this omnipresent image amidst the murky intrigues for positions of power among his key supporters. Pictures and statuettes of Pétain were everywhere, and although France had not issued stamps portraying national leaders since Emperor Napoleon III in the 1860s, the Vichy regime quickly appreciated the propaganda opportunities afforded by these vital everyday items. Stamp exhibitions became common, and commemorative envelopes, souvenir postmarks and patriotic cachets were avidly promoted. Vichy stamps were sold in parts of France under direct German military or civilian control, although surviving envelopes show that stamps of the former French Republic already purchased by families were permitted alongside the new issues. In Alsace and Lorraine German stamps overprinted with the relevant province's name were used for several months until it became obligatory to use German stamps without any additional nomenclature (See Fig. 12.1 in colour section). Italian stamps were mandatory in the south-eastern *départements* granted to Mussolini.

Pétain remained the imposing face of the less-than-imposing Vichy regime. In January 1941 a set featured striking head and shoulder portraits of him looking sage and reassuring in his marshal's uniform (See Fig. 12.2 in colour). His gaze was fixed on the purchaser of the stamps. In 1941 and into 1942 a set of nineteen definitive stamps was issued with Pétain's head in three different civilian or military profiles (Fig. 12.3). High-value 5*f* and 50*f* stamps were added in June and July 1942, picturing Pétain as head of state, again looking directly across his shoulder at the purchaser (Fig. 12.4).

In 1943 two further sets, both sold in se-tenant strips, effectively summarised the ideology of the regime. In February the well-tried military and civilian Pétain portraits were reissued with complementary pairs in bright blue and bright red positioned each side of a white central label picturing a marshal's baton on a tricolour double-bladed axe (Fig. 12.5). Not only was the much-honoured revolutionary French tricolour clearly associated with the Vichy regime but the vision, self-belief and commitment of the nation under Napoleon Bonaparte were called out of the shadows. The stamps contained a hefty surcharge in support of the National Relief Fund. In June another surcharged se-tenant strip appeared. This time portraits of Pétain at each end supported three central stamps with

Fig. 12.3   *Fig. 12.4*

Monsieur B U´ F F E T
10. Rue De LABORDE.
P A R I S. (8ème).

Fig. 12.5

striking pictures labelled '*Travail*', '*Familie*' and '*Patrie*' ('Work', 'Family' and 'Homeland') – the three key values promoted so vigorously by the regime (See Fig. 12.6 in colour section). Honest healthy toil enabled the nation to prosper, disciplined family life stabilised society, and devotion to the country regenerated its pride. In efforts to achieve this moral high ground the regime intensified the laws against abortion, made divorce more difficult, allowed illegitimate children to be legitimised if their parents married, marked Mother's Day with great celebrations, and promoted domestic science, handicraft, physical exercise and moral education in schools. Finally in April 1944 a massive stamp celebrating Pétain's 88th birthday was issued alongside one with a rural scene inscribed 'The Marshal sets up the Peasant Corporation' and another showing factories, saying 'The Marshal gives France the Workers' Charter' (See Fig. 12.7 in colour section). They referred to the establishment of a hierarchy of workers' syndicates from local to national level which aimed at ensuring workers received decent living and working conditions. A few local syndicates worked well, but most of them failed through a general lack of interest and indeed any significant trust in the regime's ideas at this late stage in the war.

The Germans consistently refused to release French prisoners of war, but the Vichy regime sought to cast their sufferings as the nation's necessary redemption for its former moral failings. Prisoners' wives and families were lauded as dutiful penitents, although they risked criminal prosecution if they resorted to adultery or prostitution to alleviate their poverty, as did women whose husbands had chosen or been forced to work in Germany. Surcharged special stamps supported various relief funds, and most promoted the image of the virtuous family. In November 1940 one portrayed a nurse highly reminiscent of the Virgin Mary caring for a bandaged soldier and his wife and child (Fig. 12.8). In January 1941 a pair of stamps portrayed prisoners of war as healthy and far from anguished as they looked patiently at distant hills or read letters from home (Fig. 12.9). That March a pair showed the allegorical figure of Charity aiding a pauper, and more pragmatically food being distributed from the back of a cart (Fig. 12.10). In September 1943 two stamps pictured a prisoner's family bravely striving to make a living on their own (Fig. 12.11). The implication was that Vichy citizens were strong and determined, and Vichy aid and support were ever present. In other words the state was at one with its people.

Fig. 12.8

Stamps avidly promoted rural life and regional loyalties. An early set in December 1940 portrayed agricultural life at its most satisfying, with healthy peasants sowing, harvesting, gathering grapes and herding cattle (See Fig. 12.12 in colour section). In 1941, and again in 1942 and 1943, sets of stamps portraying a range of city and provincial coats of arms both within and beyond Vichy territory strove to strengthen people's identification with their historic locality (See Fig. 12.13 in colour section). In 1943 a set combined several Vichy virtues in portraits of healthy, happy, young country women in the traditional costumes of Picardy, Bretagne, Île-de-France, Bourgogne, Auvergne and Provence (See Fig. 12.14 in colour section).

Fig. 12.11

Fig. 12.9

Fig. 12.10

Many writers and artists left France rather than endure the Vichy regime, but some stayed despite the restrictions on their freedom of expression. In November 1940 a set of stamps raised funds for unemployed intellectuals, a sign of both the dislocation of the war and Vichy's attempt to establish itself as the source of continuity in cultural affairs. The regime chose to remember a carefully selected number of figures. In February 1941 a stamp commemorated Frederic Mistral (1830–1914), a poet famous for preserving the Occitan language in his native Provence. In May 1942 the Romantic composer Emmanuel Chabrier (1841–94) was celebrated. No doubt his partiality for Wagner and frequent visits to Germany helped ensure his favour with Vichy ministers and the Nazis. Soon afterwards a stamp publicised Jules Massenet (1842–1912), a prolific composer of French popular songs as well as operas. In 1944 Charles Gounod (1818–93), the composer of the popular opera *Faust*, appeared on a stamp. His works included the *Marche Pontificale*, which became the anthem of the Vatican City, and also a mass in memory of Joan of Arc, both pieces likely to attract the Vichy regime seeking rapprochement with the Roman Catholic Church as part of its policy of national regeneration (Fig. 12.15).

Other historical figures were honoured if their ideas and achievements served Vichy purposes. In March 1942 the renowned sailor and explorer Jean-François de Galaup, Comte de La Perouse (1741–*c*.1788) was commemorated. After a celebrated role in combating the British in North America in two major wars, his memory was ensured when he disappeared off north-west Australia during what had been a successful voyage combining scientific exploration, the search for new trading links and the identification of possible French naval bases. Later that year a medieval scourge of the villages and towns along the southern coastline of England, the sailor Jean de Vienne (1341–96), appeared in a suitably confident pose on a stamp. And soon afterwards the tercentenary of the birth of the Comte de Tourville (1642–1701) provided another opportunity to portray a French admiral who had defeated English fleets – at the Battle of Beachy Head in 1690 and again off Portugal in 1693 (Fig. 12.16). The regime also allied itself to pioneering scientists by marking the bicentenary of the birth of the chemist Antoine Lavoisier (1743–94), the centenary of the birth of Édouard Branly (1844–1940), the pioneer of wireless telegraphy, and the 150th anniversary of the invention of semaphore signalling by Claude Chappe (1763–1805). Two had

Fig. 12.15

Fig. 12.16

Fig. 12.17   Fig. 12.19

tragic deaths: Lavoisier was executed during the French Revolution and Chappe committed suicide when accused of plagiarism (Fig. 12.17).

The sixteenth and seventeenth centuries, culminating in the reign of Louis XIV (1643–1715) – the celebrated 'Sun King' – proved particularly attractive to Vichy. In 1943 a National Relief Fund set pictured the illustrious military commander Pierre Terrail, commonly known as the Seigneur de Bayard (1473–1524), who was considered the epitome of medieval chivalry, together with Ambroise Paré (1509–90), the renowned surgeon whose books on the treatment of war wounds achieved international fame, François Clouet (1510–72) the court artist, Michel de Montaigne (1533–92) whose famous *Essays* were a witty but scarifying analysis of human behaviour, King Henry IV (reigned 1589–1610), who achieved great popularity for the peace and prosperity he brought to a country wracked by civil war, and the faithful soldier and administrator the Duc de Sully (1560–1641), who assisted Henry in quelling insurrection and encouraging economic growth through the building of roads, bridges and canals, draining of marshes, promotion of animal husbandry and reduction of tolls (See Fig. 12.18 in colour section). To the Vichy regime, stumbling along under the glare of its Nazi overlords, such giants of the past were role models whose skills and achievements could be replicated – once it had regenerated the nation and purged its moral turpitude and chronic self-doubt. Vichy also chose to mark the founding of the famous Beaune Hospital by Nicholas Rolin, the powerful medieval Chancellor of the Duchy of Burgundy, and his wife (Fig. 12.19). The regime, the stamp implied, had become the true legacy of French charitable enterprises in its concern for the poor.

A second National Relief Fund set in 1944 concentrated upon the reign of Louis XIV, whose magnificent court dazzled all Europe and, indeed, its own citizens. It portrayed Jean-Baptiste Poquelin, better known as Molière (1622–73), the celebrated playwright, and Jules Hardouin-Mansart (1646–1708), the chief architect of Versailles, Blaise Pascal (1623–62), the scientist and mathematician, Jean-Baptiste Colbert (1619–83), the king's unpopular but vigorous finance minister, and finally Louis XIV himself (See Fig. 12.20 in colour section). Vichy ignored the corruption and savage infighting surrounding the 'Sun King', much like that surrounding Pétain himself, and concentrated upon the undoubted pride, vision and achievements of that celebrated period. In reality Adolf Hitler had replaced Louis as the state's dominant force, and Pétain's government consistently based its domestic policies upon the notion that France somehow deserved its defeat by its political and moral paralysis after the First World War, but would be resurrected as a strong and confident nation by allegiance to, and imitation of, its strong and confident conqueror.

The surcharged Legion Tricolore stamps issued in 1942, even though they featured a determined French soldier against a background of advancing Napoleonic troops, represented the ultimate collaboration in encouraging Frenchmen to enlist in the German Army (Fig. 12.21). The Vichy regime had high hopes of this legion. It assumed that the French units would enjoy a marked degree of French control, and would lead the Germans to see France as an ally to be trusted with ever-increasing autonomy. Such aspirations were hopelessly misguided as the Germans never perceived the defeated French as much more than subservient sources of cheap labour, plentiful agricultural produce and vital industrial materials – and perhaps extra troops to attach to their hard-pressed armies on the Russian front. A few months after its formation the Légion Tricolore was absorbed into the Légion des Volontaires Français that had already fought outside Moscow and against partisans in Belorussia. In late 1941 members of the Légion des Volontaires had used a special stamp pointedly featuring a bomber heading towards the Soviet Union on their airmail letters, and it was later reissued overprinted with the even clearer inscriptions 'Front de L'Est' and 'Ostfront' (See Fig. 12.22 in colour section). In 1943 and 1944 the legionaries took part in several bitter battles as the German army retreated across the Soviet Union. In April 1942 another dramatic issue pictured legionaries in battle, with one stamp showing legionaries saluting Napoleonic soldiers advancing in their equally ill-fated invasion of Russia (See Fig. 12.23 in colour section). With the survivors of another French force, the Französische SS Freiwilligen Sturmbrigade, the legion became part of the newly created Waffen Grenadier Brigade der SS Charlemagne whose 7,300 troops were sent to fight Soviet forces in Poland in September 1944. The brigade was badly mauled, and in April 1945 the few hundred survivors were sent to defend Berlin where all but a few dozen died.

Fig. 12.21

Increasing food shortages, the relentless conscription of men as labourers in German factories, and the failure to secure the repatriation of prisoners of war weakened the reputation and authority of the Vichy regime, and as Allied forces landed in North Africa, and then in Sicily and south-western France, Germany took charge of the whole of France. From late 1943 until early 1945 Vichy stamps retreated alongside the Axis forces. They were replaced by stamps issued by the French Committee of National Liberation displaying the Cross of Lorraine along-side the restored inscription 'RF' – 'République Française' – and portraying the Gallic cockerel, the Arc de Triomphe or the allegorical head of 'Marianne', the traditional symbol of revolutionary France. Numerous commemorative covers spread across the nation as towns and *départements* were liberated by the Allies. Many Vichy stamps appeared hurriedly overprinted 'RF' and the name of a liberated city (See Fig. 12.24a & 12.24b in colour section).

Pétain and his ministers fled to Germany, and later were arrested and prosecuted by de Gaulle's initial post-war administration. Pétain himself was sentenced to death, but de Gaulle commuted this to life imprisonment. Generally perceived as deluded at best and traitorous at worst, the Vichy regime's stamps reveal its desperate attempts to pursue a policy of social and political reform, albeit under Germany's watchful eyes, after two decades of what Pétain and his adherents believed to be shamefully weak and enervating republican governments.

Fig. 12.25

A Note on the Channel Islands

When the Germans reached the north-west coast of France, detachments went on to occupy the Channel Islands on 1 July 1940. The Germans allowed the use of British stamps to continue, but when supplies ran low in Guernsey and could not be replaced from the mainland, some 2*d* definitive and 1840–1940 Centenary commemorative stamps were cut diagonally in half with each half having an accepted postal value of 1*d* – the most commonly used value (Fig. 12.25).

Commencing in 1940 Guernsey and Jersey saw the introduction of a new simple design featuring the Channel Islands' arms – a shield bearing three lions *guardant passant*. The coat of arms had been brought to England by Duke William of Normandy in 1066 and the stamps were seen as marking the islands' return to formal links with the Continent rather than confirming their ancient link with Great Britain. It was rumoured that the tiny letter 'A' that appears in each corner of the beaded margin of the Jersey version had been inserted deliberately by the local designer, Major N.V.L. Rybot, and stood for '*Ad Avernum Atroix Adolphe*' ('To Hell With You, Atrocious Adolf') (Fig. 12.26). In 1944 a set of six single-colour views of Jersey was issued. They were drawn by a local artist, Edmund Blampied, who managed to include scrolls to the left and right of the 3*d* value tablet that were widely believed to stand for 'GR' – Georgius Rex (Fig. 12.27). They were small morale boosters at a time of steadily increasing shortages, draconian regulations, the deportation of members of the resistance, and the harsh treatment of Russian slave labourers building fortifications and the famous underground hospital.

Fig. 12.26

Fig. 12.27

Illustrations

Fig. 12.1 Souvenir cover with the set of overprinted German definitive stamps for Alsace (15 August 1940).

Fig. 12.2 Souvenir cover with the first set of stamps featuring Marshal Pétain (1 and 25 January 1941).

Fig. 12.3 40*c*, 80*c* and 3*f* portraits in the 1941–42 Pétain definitive series.

Fig. 12.4 5*f* and 50*f* Pétain stamps (June–July 1942).

Fig. 12.5 Souvenir cover with the Pétain se-tenant set + central label (8 February 1943).

Fig. 12.6 Se-tenant strip with portraits of Pétain and representations of *Travail, Familie* and *Patrie* (7 June 1943).

Fig. 12.7 Pétain's 88th birthday set (24 April 1944).

Fig. 12.8 War Victims' Fund stamp (12 November 1940).

Fig. 12.9 Prisoners of War Fund set (1 January 1941).

Fig. 12.10 Winter Relief Fund set (4 March 1941).

Fig. 12.11 Prisoners' Families' Relief Fund set (27 September 1943).

Fig. 12.12 1.50*f*+2*f* Gathering Grapes and 2.50*f*+2*f* Grazing Cattle from the National Relief Fund set (2 December 1940).

Fig. 12.13 Philatelic cover with the first set of city coats of arms (15 December 1941).

Fig. 12.14 60*c*+1.30*f* 'Picardy', 1.20*f*+2*f* 'Bretagne' and 1.50*f*+4*f* 'Île-de-France' from the National Relief Fund set of provincial costumes (27 December 1943).

Fig. 12.15 1*f* Frédéric Mistral (20 February 1941), 2*f*+3*f* Emmanuel Chabrier (18 May 1942), 4*f* Jules Massenet (22 June 1942) and 1.50*f*+3.50*f* Charles Gounod (27 March 1944).

Fig. 12.16 2.50*f*+7.50*f* Jean-François de Galaup, Comte de la Perouse (23 March 1942), 1.50*f*+8.50*f* Jean de Vienne (16 June 1942) and 4*f*+6*f* Anne Hilarion de Costentin, Comte de Tourville (21 February 1944).

Fig. 12.17 Stamps commemorating Antoine Lavoisier (5 July 1943), 4*f* Édouard Branly (21 February 1944) and 4*f* Claude Chappe (14 August 1944).

Fig. 12.18 The six Valois–Orléans period figures from the National Relief Fund (25 October 1943).

Fig. 12.19 The 500th anniversary of Beaune Hospital stamp (21 July 1943).

Fig. 12.20 The six figures from the reign of Louis XIV from the National Relief Fund set (31 July 1944).

Fig. 12.21 The *Légion Tricolore* stamp (12 October 1942).

Fig. 12.22 Cover with overprinted '*Légion des Volontaires Français*' airmail stamp + Feldpost and Paris cancellation dated 22 January 1942 when the legion was serving near Moscow.

Fig. 12.23 Block of 1942 Légion des Volontaires Français stamps and Field Post Examiner's Office postmark dated 4 August 1944 when Axis forces were in full retreat.

Fig. 12.24 30*c* Gallic Cock, 4.50*f* Marianne and 4*f* Arc de Triomphe Post Liberation 'Republique Française' issues (late 1943 onwards). Two covers with Vichy stamps locally overprinted R.F. from Loches and Bordeaux.

Fig. 12.25 Souvenir cover with Guernsey bisected GB 2*d* 1840–1940 Centenary stamp (27 December 1940).

Fig. 12.26 Jersey Arms ½*d* stamp (29 January 1942) and 1*d* stamp (1 April 1941).

Fig. 12.27 Jersey 3*d* pictorial (Gathering Seaweed) stamp (29 June 1943).

13

ITALY

Before the First World War Italy had been an ally, although somewhat half-heartedly, of Germany and Austria, but against a background of political and social unrest its government decided to stay neutral in the autumn of 1914. For several decades the nation's main ambition had been to gain sovereignty over Austrian territory, especially the regions curving around the north and north-east shores of the Adriatic Sea: Trieste, Istria, Fiume, Zara and the Dalmatian coastline. In 1915 Great Britain and France enticed Italy to join the Allies with promises of these regions once the war was won. Despite huge losses, successive Italian campaigns across the mountainous terrain of Friuli-Venezia Giulia bordering Austria–Hungary failed to dislodge enemy forces until 1918 when social unrest began to paralyse the Hapsburg government and broke the morale of its armies. Although Italy was among the victors, the American President Woodrow Wilson insisted that the Allies' commitment to the self-determination of small nations took precedence over any earlier promises made to Italy and it was denied the extensive Adriatic provinces it had so long sought. Dalmatia became part of the new but unstable Kingdom of the Serbs, Croats and Slovenes (later Yugoslavia) instead, and in doing so kindled a festering sense of deep injustice in Italian nationalists that explains much about the country's attitudes and actions in the next war.

In 1918, Italy had annexed Trieste and the Istrian Peninsula to its south, and proceeded to persecute the Slovenes and Croats living there as an intense campaign enforcing the Italian language, customs and education was launched. Many fled to the neighbouring Kingdom of the Serbs, Croats and Slovenes, while many Dalmatian Italians fled to Trieste. To the south, Fiume (modern Rijeka in Slovenia) and its hinterland became a viciously contested area between the Slavs and Italians. The Allies had planned for it to become a small free state acting as a buffer between the hostile countries, but in September 1919 a hotchpotch force led by a renowned Italian nationalist and poet, Gabriele D'Annunzio, seized Fiume and occupied it for fifteenth months until November 1920 when Italy and the Kingdom of the Serbs, Croats and Slovenes agreed it should become independent. Stamps highlighted the changes. In 1918 Italy used some old Hungarian stamps overprinted Fiume, and then a specially designed Fiume set was issued with allegorical figures of 'Italy' and 'Revolution', and

Italian flags being raised. In September 1919 D'Annunzio's popular invasion merited a long set with his portrait. The 1920 agreement was fragile, and various nationalist factions tried to dominate Fiume until in 1924 another bilateral treaty granted Fiume and most of its hinterland to Italy with the eastern coastal enclave of Susak going to the Kingdom of the Serbs, Croats and Slovenes. April 1921 saw stamps overprinted '*Costituente Fiumana*' ('Fiume Constitution'), late

1921 saw the overprints change to '*Governo Provvisorio*' ('Provisional Government'), and in January 1924 to '*Regno D'Italia*' ('Kingdom of Italy') (Fig. 13.1). In due course ordinary Italian stamps were introduced. Again, though, nothing was really settled, as events fifteen years or so later would prove.

By 1924 Benito Mussolini was the ruler of Italy although Victor Emmanuel III remained king. Originally a far left social revolutionary, yet with strong nationalist views,

Fig. 13.1

after 1918 Mussolini increasingly moved to the right to entice the support of Roman Catholics and monarchists as well as strident nationalists. In 1922 a bitter general strike provided him with the opportunity to seize power within the framework of the national constitution. Demanding political power from the fractured government, his relatively small Fascist Party marched towards Rome, all the time loudly proclaiming its aim of restoring law and order. The king and his advisers faced a dilemma. With the current government in tatters, his choice lay between the right-wing Fascists or the left-wing socialists. He chose Mussolini whom he believed would preserve the monarchy, unite warring factions, restore order and promote Italy as a world power.

Mussolini became prime minister, although he was generally known and addressed as '*Il Duce*' ('The Leader'). Within a few years his coalition of parliamentary supporters ensured the Fascists became the ruling party, and in 1928 they became the only party allowed by law. Other Acts ensured regional autonomy was eliminated, and that Mussolini was accountable only to the king – a fatal weakness when his popularity waned in 1943. Nevertheless in the 1920s and 1930s a fervent personality cult surrounded him, and huge rallies provided the opportunity for his emotional oratory to reach thousands of listeners first hand, and then millions through leaflets and newsreels. The '*fasces*' emblem was to be seen everywhere – the bundle of sticks tied around an axe that was the symbol of the authority of ancient Rome's civil magistrates. And, in common with many episodes in ancient Roman history, fascist violence cowed or removed numerous political opponents. In 1935 Italy was officially declared a totalitarian state. As Hitler struggled to achieve power in the later 1920s he envied Mussolini's success, and copied many aspects of the Fascist Party's imagery, propaganda and cult of personality.

In a popular move Mussolini established good relations with the Vatican that ended half a century of tensions between the Roman Catholic Church and Italy's various governments. In 1929 the Lateran Treaty defined and recognised the Vatican City as a sovereign state, and Roman Catholicism was made the sole religion in Italy. Religious education re-entered schools, and marriages in church once again received state recognition. In return Italian bishops swore allegiance to the state, and although the Vatican made no agreement to support the Fascist government it did endorse Mussolini's aid to General Franco's anti-communist campaign in Spain and the Italian invasion of Abyssinia. And, significantly, the Vatican also promised to act neutrally in Italy's international affairs, unless both sides sought its mediation.

Many Fascist social reforms proved both popular and effective. The school leaving age was raised from 12 to 14 and attendance rigorously enforced. Illiteracy fell, but lessons and textbooks had to portray Italy as the greatest force for European civilisation from Roman times, through the Renaissance, into the nineteenth-century fight for unification, and finally the policies of Il Duce himself. Young people's physical fitness became important, and so did the triumph of national sportsmen, notably footballers, whose success as role models was as important as the international honours they brought home. In 1933 a set of stamps marked the International University Games in Turin, and in 1934 another commemorated Italy hosting the Football World Cup Championship – which Italy duly won (Fig. 13.2). In 1937 the state's care, and its political indoctrination, of children was marked by a Child Welfare set promoting the provision of fully equipped summer camps (Fig. 13.3). By then all towns in Italy possessed a *Dopolavoro*, a workers' club with facilities such as sports fields, libraries, theatres and cinemas for adult recreational and cultural activities. This immensely popular state-sponsored movement inspired Hitler to create the even more centralised and party political *Kraft durch Freude* (strength through joy) programme.

Great attention was given to the legacy of famous Italian scientists, musicians and writers, and in 1926 the Royal Academy of Italy was established to promote these various fields and mark great achievements. Numerous stamps recalled

Fig. 13.3

Fig. 13.2

Fig. 13.6

Italy's great cultural figures, such as the nationalist novelist Alessandro Manzoni in 1923, the Roman poet Virgil in 1930, the scientists Antonio Pacinotti and Luigi Galvani in 1934, the composer Vincenzo Bellini in 1935, the Roman writer Horace in 1936, the scientist Guglielmo Marconi in 1937, the Roman historian Livy in 1941 and, in 1942, the composer Gioachino Rossini and scientist, mathematician and philosopher Galileo. Sets in 1932 and 1937 were devoted to a rich mix of historic inventors, composers, writers, philosophers and poets – including the polymath Leonardo da Vinci and the poet Dante Alighieri (See Fig. 13.4 in colour section). Interspersed with these were sets highlighting the continuity of Italy's greatness into the Fascist era. In 1932 the tenth anniversary of the Fascist march on Rome was celebrated, and in 1934 a set marked the tenth anniversary of the annexation of Fiume (See Fig. 13.5 in colour section). Numerous airmail stamps highlighted Italy's modern aeronautical achievements, including the new transatlantic flights to North and South America (Fig. 13.6).

Fascist propaganda portrayed Mussolini himself as a universal or Renaissance man, supremely talented as a sportsman, horse rider, soldier and aviator. He became a god-like figure of heroic stature and tireless energy in promoting Italian greatness, and the violent treatment of opponents was minimised as the justified elimination of traitors and all those who stood in the way of national unity. Stories were promoted that Il Duce's life and character were akin to those of famous saints. He had suffered on behalf of others, it was asserted, much like St Francis of Assisi, and just as St Sebastian had been martyred by being pierced by arrows so shrapnel had pierced Mussolini in the First World War. Even Pope Pius XI said he was a man of Providence, and the Fascists built on this saintly image whenever Il Duce targeted the communists. Not surprisingly a series of sets commemorating the vision, suffering and miraculous achievements of saints – St Francis in 1926, St Benedict and his monastery at Monte Cassino in 1929, and St Anthony of Padua in 1931 – ensured Catholic opinion was gratified while Fascist propaganda sanctified Mussolini's own image by association. The holy years of 1924 and 1933 were also duly acknowledged with sets primarily featuring the Vatican (Fig. 13.7).

Under the Fascists Italy's manufacturing and agricultural output improved, but the government lulled the nation into a false sense of national self-sufficiency and military preparedness when Mussolini sought to establish a second

Fig. 13.7

Fig. 13.8

Roman Empire. In 1929 a lengthy set of new definitive stamps appeared that reflected both the Fascist hold on the state and Mussolini's dreams of recreating the greatness of Italy at the time Octavius Caesar transformed himself into Emperor Augustus. The set, significantly referred to as the 'Imperial' series mixed the Fascist arms, portraits of King Victor Emmanuel III, and an allegory of Italia, with a Classical statue of Romulus, Remus and the wolf, and busts of Julius Caesar and Augustus. Each one had *fasces* images in its lower left and right hand side (Fig. 13.8). The anniversary of the founding of Rome, 21 April, became a Fascist holiday, state-supported archaeological excavations abounded, and ancient monuments were accorded pride of place in numerous localities. In Rome hundreds of buildings were destroyed in order to create the wide Classical Via dell'Impero that passed key imperial sites and led to the Colosseum.

The brutal, prolonged but ultimately successful invasion of Libya in the late 1920s and the brutal but speedier conquest of Abyssinia in 1936 helped fulfil Mussolini's dream, but at the expense of his international isolation, except for Nazi Germany. Nevertheless 1936 saw the new Italian Empire officially proclaimed. Despite the horrors and mismanagement of the Italian occupation, Mussolini preached the need for Italians to breed more children to ensure the new colonies were filled with white settlers to civilise and develop them. Colonial stamp issues reflected mainstream Italian ones – images of mail and passenger aircraft, King Victor Emmanuel III in military uniform, historic Italian heroes – with the addition of numerous scenes of peaceful native life (Fig. 13.9a & 13.9b).

In 1937 and 1938 Mussolini's prestige was at its height. In September 1937 the 2,000th anniversary of the birth of the Emperor Augustus was celebrated with a major exhibition and a set of stamps strongly linking his achievements

Fig. 13.9a

Fig. 13.9b

with those of Mussolini. Individual stamps featured military trophies, the conquest of Ethiopia, the building a new fleet of warships, the election of Augustus to the senior post of consul, and friezes highlighting the prosperity of the state. Diplomatically, one stamp featured a census with a reference to Jesus Christ; less fortuitously one showed a statue of Julius Caesar, murdered because of his overweening ambition (See Fig. 13.10 in colour section). Soon afterwards, in October 1938 a set marked the second anniversary of the proclamation of the new Italian Empire, and tracked its alleged evolution from Augustus, through great Italians such as Dante, Columbus, da Vinci, the nationalist warrior Garibaldi and King Victor Emmanuel II to the First World War's Unknown Warrior, the Fascist March on Rome, the union with Ethiopia, and the current monarch, King Victor Emmanuel III (Fig. 13.11). Mussolini himself was portrayed endlessly everywhere, except on Italy's stamps where the king took priority, although everyone, including the king, knew who was the de facto ruler.

Ironically, however, in January and April 1941, just as Italy's feeble military performances defending North Africa and attacking Greece had rendered Mussolini a chronic liability in Hitler's eyes, a two-part set appeared featuring Il Duce face to

Fig. 13.11

Fig. 13.12

Fig. 13.14

face with the Führer (Fig. 13.12). They had met in January 1941 at the Berghof, Hitler's Bavarian retreat, but it was a humiliating encounter for Mussolini as Hitler had had to order German troops to redeem his defeats in Africa and the Balkans. The stamps, of course, portrayed a far more equal relationship. Eighteen months later, in August 1942, as Italian forces suffered privations and defeats on the Eastern Front and partisan attacks in the Balkans, and the Italian Navy was steadily losing control of the Mediterranean, a War Propaganda set was thought necessary to stiffen Italian resolve. Three stamps (25c, 30c and 50c) featuring the king appeared, each with four different labels. The first featured the navy with the inscription '*La Disciplina E'Arma Di Vittoria*' ('Discipline is the Weapon of Victory'), the second the army with '*Armie Cuori Devono Essere Tesi Verso Lameta*' ('Arms and Heart have to be Directed Towards the Goal'), the third the air force with '*Tutto E Tutti Per La Vittoria*' ('Everything all for the Victory'), and the fourth for the militia with '*La Vittoria Sara Del Tripartito*' ('The Victory will be of the Tripartite Agreement'). No perforations were placed between the stamp and label to ensure as many propaganda labels as possible were stuck on mail.

A little under a year later, on 10 July 1943, Allied forces landed in Sicily and began their long campaign to conquer Italy. As they occupied the island and then successfully landed on the mainland, deliberately nondescript stamps inscribed 'Allied Military Postage' increasingly appeared in common use (Fig. 13.14). The Allied threat prompted the Grand Fascist Council of Italy, completely disillusioned with Mussolini's series of military catastrophes, to vote a motion of no confidence in him on 24 July 1943. The next day the king exercised his authority to dismiss and arrest his prime minister, and the new government under Marshal Badoglio began secret talks with the Allies. The Germans, though, swiftly transferred crack forces to Italy to counter both the Allies and the predicted switch of allegiance by Italy. When, on 8 September, Badoglio finally announced the surrender the Germans disarmed Italian units, massacred many of them, seized their equipment and occupied the whole of northern and central Italy down to the south of Rome.

Later that September, numerous disenchanted citizens of Naples rose in a haphazard but successful revolt against the German forces struggling to organise resistance to the advancing Allies who had heavily bombed the city in preceding months. Between 27 and 30 September fighting raged around Naples until the Germans withdrew the day before Allied tanks arrived. That December the 20c, 25c and 50c values from the Imperial series overprinted '*Governo Militare Alleato*' ('Allied Military Government') were introduced in and around the damaged and still chaotic city (See Fig. 13.15 in colour section).

The Allies permitted the king to establish a pro-Allied government in Brindisi, and then Salerno, and in due course various printings of the 'Imperial' series stamps appeared but without the *fasces* symbols on their lower left- and right-hand sides (Fig. 13.16). Discredited by his long association with Mussolini, on 5 June 1944 King Victor Emmanuel handed over his powers to Crown Prince Umberto, and abdicated on 9 May 1946. By then a new definitive series full of symbols of freedom, families, enlightenment, peace and growth was in use (Fig. 13.17). And shortly afterwards a referendum decided in favour of a clean sweep. A republic was declared, and King Umberto left Italy forever on 18 June 1946. In confirmation, in October a set of large stamps contrasted starkly with Mussolini's obsession with the Roman Empire by featuring the medieval republics of Amalfi, Lucca, Sienna, Florence, Pisa, Genoa and Venice. In an apt analogy the final stamp featured 'The Oath of Pontida' in 1167 whereby the cities of Lombardy united to defeat the Emperor Frederick Barbarossa (Fig. 13.18).

Fig. 13.16

Fig. 13.17

Fig. 13.18

The Vatican

Pope Pius XII held office from 2 March 1939 until his death on 9 October 1958. Prior to his election he had been Papal Nuncio to Germany between 1917 and 1929, and then Cardinal Secretary of State. He had worked to improve state and Church relations when Germany sunk into political and social chaos at the end of the First World War and to mitigate the harshness of the Versailles peace terms. As Secretary of State he spoke against the excesses of the Nazi Party, but in July 1933 he signed a controversial Concordat with Germany under which the Roman Catholic Church could conduct services, make church appointments and run charities, schools, hospitals and youth groups without interference, in return for not involving itself in the country's internal politics, notably by ceasing to guide and support the strongly Catholic Centre Party and Catholic Labour Unions. Not surprisingly over the next decade he issued numerous private and public condemnations of Germany's failure to abide by the Concordat in its persecution of clergy and religious institutions.

Vatican stamps marked two significant decisions taken by Pius immediately after his election. Both revealed his fears regarding the impending international crisis. The first was to order the most triumphalist coronation for a century, thereby elevating the position of the Pope and sending out the strongest possible signal that Rome reached out to every country (Fig. 13.19). The second was the adoption of a personal coat of arms featuring a dove and an olive branch above a stormy sea (Fig. 13.20).

Pius strove in vain to ease international tensions in 1939, and although he followed the public path of political neutrality throughout the war he sought, through sermons, broadcasts and diplomacy, to mitigate the suffering of its countless civilian victims with repeated condemnations of totalitarianism wherever it might be found. He did not, though, name any state or group of victims, and Vatican stamps mirrored both his concern and also its unspecified targets. In September 1942 a set was issued picturing a cluster of vaguely outlined families looking upon the

Fig. 13.19

Fig. 13.20

Fig. 13.21

face of God, and inscribed '*Flagrante Bello Misereor Super Turbam*' which can be loosely translated in this context as 'Take pity during the flagrant uproar of war'. They had the date '1942', and were reissued in January 1944 with the date '1943'. They were reissued again with higher values in September 1945, although dated rather oddly '1944' (Fig. 13.21).

These obvious efforts have not saved Pius from later accusations of culpable weakness in the face of Nazi terror, especially towards the Jews. His failure to mention Nazism by name publicly, even when Poland and its Catholics were ferociously persecuted, was particularly criticised, as was his failure to condemn the forced conversions of Muslim Serbs to Catholicism in Croatia. His defenders argue that outright alienation of Nazi Germany and its allies would have wrecked all chances of influencing their actions, or of supporting the Roman Catholic Church in those countries by more surreptitious, less well-known but possibly more effective means. Pius was extremely well informed about European affairs, and through Papal diplomatic channels he did make his opposition to anti-Semitic legislation and persecution known to the Nazis, and to Admiral Horthy in Hungary, Monsignor Tiso in Slovakia and King Boris and later Regent Kyril in Bulgaria.

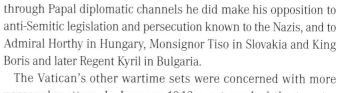

Fig. 13.22

The Vatican's other wartime sets were concerned with more personal matters. In January 1943 a set marked the twenty-fifth anniversary of the Pope's elevation to the episcopate (Fig. 13.22) and in November 1944 a set commemorated the fourth centenary, in the previous year, of the *Pontificia Insigne Accademia di Belle Arti e Letteratura dei Virtuosi al Pantheon* (the Pontifical Academy of Fine Arts and Literature of the Virtuosos of the Pantheon). Through this splendidly named institution the Vatican had honoured a succession of notable architects, artists, sculptors and academics whose work was deemed to promote the Catholic faith. The set chose to feature particularly celebrated members, including the great artist Raphael (1483–1520), who worked for Popes Julius II and Leo X, the architect Antonio da Sangallo (1484–1546), who designed and built several Roman churches and the Vatican's Cappela Paolina, the Baroque artist Carlo Maratti (1625–1713), who painted *Constantine Ordering the Destruction of Pagan Idols* for the Baptistry of the Lateran, and Antonio Canova (1757–1822), the sculptor who was celebrated for his Classical nudes such as *The Three Graces*, *Pysche* and *Theseus Vanquishing the Minotaur* as well as the elaborate tombs of several popes (Fig. 13.23).

Fig. 13.23

Mussolini and the Italian Social Republic

In a skilfully mounted operation, on 12 September 1943 German special forces freed Mussolini from captivity high in the Apennine Mountains, and soon afterwards Hitler made him titular leader of a new Fascist state – the Italian Social Republic – in German-occupied Italy. Mussolini recognised his complete humiliation, but from his headquarters at Salo on Lake Garda he dutifully condemned King Victor Emmanuel as the traitor and praised the Führer as a true friend of Italy. Hitler merely saw the Fascists who gathered around Mussolini as convenient instruments of civil government and repressors of the growing numbers of partisans while the German Army faced the encroaching Allies.

Mussolini could do little except complain when Hitler allowed Croatia to annex parts of the Dalmatian coast that had been ceded to Italy in 1924, or when he allowed Mussolini *de jure* power over two sizable areas of Italy between Germany and the Adriatic Sea while de facto authority rested entirely with the German occupying forces. The northern area including Trento, Bolzano and Belluno became the Operationszone Alpenvorland attached to the civil Gau Tirol-Vorarlberg, and Fiume and Trieste along with Udine, Gorizia and Pola became the Operationszone Adriatisches-Küstenland attached to the Gau Karnten. Across these territories the dual but basically one-sided arrangement meant that both Italian and German stamps could be used, as many souvenir covers testify (Fig. 13.24). The same arrangement placed the Dodecanese Islands under German military control. Here some Italian forces remained loyal to Mussolini and his Nazi protectors, while others were disarmed and cold-bloodedly shot by the Germans.

Mussolini made some attempt to arouse broad support for the new state, but by and large both the trades unions and the major industrialists remained unimpressed by his claims to create a freer economy and a more equitable society. Indeed, but for German money the state would have been bankrupt. Nevertheless, a hard core of Fascist soldiers allowed Mussolini to create a surprisingly effective military force that disrupted partisan advances for a time, and even fought alongside the Germans defending the heavily fortified Gothic Line across the northern end of the Apennine Mountains against major assaults by the Allies, who now included other Italian units. The stubborn rearguard action lasted until mid-April 1945, when finally the Germans were broken. They surrendered on 29 April.

Fig. 13.24

The fall of the Fascist regime in Italy in 1943 meant the disbandment of the Milizia Volontaria per la Sicurezza Nazionale (the National Security Volunteer Militia) or MVSN, who were the legalised successors of the Blackshirts, the violent paramilitary organisation that had helped Mussolini's rise to power, and indeed helped keep him there. However, on 8 December 1943 the Social Republic formally established the Guardia Nazionale Repubblicana (National Republican Guard) or GNR, not surprising composed mainly of former members of the militia and police. In August 1944 the GNR was absorbed into the Social Republic's army, but not before its members had stamped their mark on their new state's postal services. In December 1943, in an attempt to consolidate the rickety new regime and their place in it, senior officers, and notably General Renato Ricci, the commander, arranged for stocks of the current Italian 'Imperial' series definitive stamps in Brescia to be overprinted 'GNR'. They appeared in ordinary use in and around Brescia before the postal authorities realised, but when they did the stamps were withdrawn. However, a combination of circumstances led to their reappearance in February 1944. It seems that Mussolini had given approval for the initial overprinting, although in the general confusion the Minister of Communications did not know this. There was also a fear of philatelic speculation in the very unusual issue. In the event the overprint did not mean very much but nevertheless hurried arrangements were made to print more overprinted stamps at Verona and put them on sale (See Fig. 13.25 in colour section).

Initially the Social Republic had continued to use unaltered stamps from the 'Imperial' series with their largely Fascist imagery. The half-dozen values picturing King Victor Emmanuel could easily be dispensed with out of the lengthy set of twenty-two, but nevertheless in January 1944 five of the six reappeared with the king's face overprinted in red or black with the fasces or '*Repubblica Sociale Italiana*' or both. The high value 50*l* was not used (See Fig. 13.26 in colour section).

The same fasces and inscription overprint was used on the king's face on the express letter stamps from January 1944, and that April Italian parcel post stamps with attached receipt labels appeared with the *fasces* untouched but the royal eagle overprinted '*Rep. Soc. Italiana*' and the Kingdom of Italy arms on the receipt obliterated by another fasces. The arms on Italian postage-due stamps received the same anti-monarchy treatment (Fig. 13.27).

Fig. 13.27

In February 1944 the 1942 War Propaganda stamps picturing the king with labels extolling the Italian army, navy, air force and militia reappeared, sometimes with the *fasces* overprint blotting out the king but not the label, and sometimes with them blotting out both. The twin overprint stamps are comparatively rare, and probably an error. As the Social Republic possessed a modestly strong army and militia, as well as a small but aggressive air force and navy, it is reasonable to assume the overprint was intended for the king but not the labels (See Fig. 13.28 in colour section). Everything suggests Mussolini vigorously portrayed the Social Republic as a lineal descendent of the larger Italy he used to control so thoroughly. However, while encamped at Salo he certainly needed to encourage his forces as his many enemies closed in from every side.

Commencing on 5 June 1944 the first stamp designs specifically from the Social Republic appeared. They strove to link Italian culture, and indeed Italian identity, firmly to the Fascist Republic, and not the monarchy, through featuring several significant religious sites that had been heavily damaged by Allied bombing in recent months (See Fig. 13.29 in colour section). The war was certainly bringing death and destruction to the Italian mainland, and increasingly to many areas within the Republic's tenuous authority. The fifteenth-century church and convent of Saint Mary of Grace in Milan (1.25*l* and 3*l*) were adorned with ancient frescoes. On 15 August 1943 the convent was heavily damaged in a joint British and American air raid. Far to the south in central Italy Saint Ciriaco's Cathedral in Ancona (5c) had a history going back to a pagan temple, and much of its fabric was over 900 years old. During an Allied raid a transept and many stored treasures in the crypt beneath it were destroyed. The delicately structured fifteenth-century palace in Bologna known as the Loggia dei Mercanti (20c) was another victim of bombing. In Rome, a raid in late 1943 severely damaged the beautifully frescoed Basilica of Saint Lawrence Outside the Walls (25c). The Emperor Constantine had built the original oratory on a site where it was believed St Lawrence was martyred in 258. The final building was the hilltop Abbey of Monte Cassino (10c and 1*l*), the site where St Benedict of Nursia had founded the first monastery of the Benedictine Order in or around 530. The Germans made the abbey a strongpoint on their defensive Gustav Line blocking the road to Rome. On 15 February 1944 American air raids virtually destroyed the abbey under the mistaken impression that German troops had occupied it – which they did as soon as the complex was reduced to easily defended ruins. The ensuing battle lasted until 17 May, when the Germans finally withdrew. Two other stamps in the set – a Classical Roman allegory of Fascism (50c) and a drummer boy calling people to arms (30c and 75c) completed the attempt to occupy the high moral ground and arouse more fervent anti-Allied feeling. An accompanying express letter stamp pictured Palermo Cathedral in Sicily, reminding everyone of the huge damage wreaked by the Allies on the ancient port in July 1943 and the theft of the cathedral's renowned bells.

Fig. 13.30

In December1944, as Allied forces and Italian partisans relentlessly eroded Mussolini's territory, the Social Republic issued its last set of stamps. They sought to associate the intensely nationalistic state, with its fast fading hopes of restoring Fascism in Italy, with two intensely nationalistic early-nineteenth-century revolutionaries, Attilio and Emilio Bandiera who, in fact, dreamed of freeing Italy from authoritarian rule (Fig. 13.30). Venetian by birth, the brothers had served in the Austro-Hungarian Navy but became active members of a secret society dedicated to the liberation and unification of Italy from Austro-Hungarian rule in the north and Bourbon rule in the south. Their attempts at inciting revolution were many but always ill-organised and ill-fated. An attempt to seize an Austro-Hungarian warship was betrayed, and they fled to Corfu. From here they were misled into thinking southern Italy and Sicily were ripe for rebellion against its Bourbon rulers, and landed on the Calabrian coast along the 'toe' of Italy to meet and hopefully lead the insurgents. Betrayed again, they and their few devoted followers were executed on 23 July 1844, but their dreams and death turned them into martyrs and inspired another and more successful generation of revolutionaries.

On 28 April 1945 Mussolini and several of his ministers met the same fate, although the legacy of martyrdom eluded them. Communist partisans caught and shot them near Lake Como while attempting to flee to Switzerland.

Illustrations

Fig. 13.1 Fiume stamps overprinted '*Regno D'Italia*' and '*24-IV-1921 Costituente Fiumana 1922*'.

Fig. 13.2 25*c* Tackle from Football World Cup (24 May 1934) set.

Fig. 13.3 25*c* Child clutching ears of corn and 75*c* della Robbia's 'Bambino' from Child Welfare/Summer Camps set (28 June 1937).

Fig. 13.4 1*l*+25*c* Caprera 'Here we make Italy or die' from the 50th Anniversary of Garibaldi's Death set (April–June 1932), 50*c* Portrait from the Tercentenary of Galileo's Death set (28 September 1942), 25*c* Statue of Rossini from 150th Anniversary of his Birth set (23 November 1942).

Fig. 13.5 50*c* Equestrian statue of Mussolini from the Tenth Anniversary of the Fascist March on Rome set (27 October 1932), 25*c* Flying boat over Fiume harbour, and 3*l*+2*l* Roman wall around Fiume from the Tenth Anniversary of the Annexation of Fiume (March–July 1934) set.

Fig. 13.6 25*c* Wings, 2*l* Arrows, and 10*l* Pegasus from the 1930–33 Airmail set.

Fig. 13.7 20*c* St Anthony's installation as a Franciscan monk from the 700th Anniversary of his Death set (9 March 1931), 50*c* Angel and 2.55*l*+2.50*l* Cross of Doves from the Holy Year set (23 October 1933).

Fig. 13.8 1.75*l* Emperor Augustus, 10*l* 'Italia' and 50*l* King Victor Emmanuel III from the 'Imperial' definitive series (21 April 1929 onwards).

Fig. 13.9 10c King Victor Emmanuel in Ethiopia from Annexation of Ethiopia set (May–December 1936). Cover with various Italian colony of Libya stamps.

Fig. 13.10 15c Military Trophies, 1.25l Roman warships, and 2.50l+2l *Fasces* and the Capitol from the 2000th Anniversary of the Birth of Augustus set (23 September 1937).

Fig. 13.11 10c Founding of Rome, 1.25l Tomb of the Unknown Warrior, and 2.75l Wedding ring on a map of Ethiopia from the Second Anniversary of the Proclamation of the Italian Empire (28 October 1938).

Fig. 13.12 75c Hitler and Mussolini stamp from the Italian–German Friendship set (January and April 1941).

Fig. 13.14 2c Allied Military Government postage stamp from the USA set for use in Sicily and Italy after the Allied invasion (1943).

Fig. 13.15 Allied propaganda cover with 50c Italian definitive stamp overprinted *'Governo Militare Alleato'* for use in Naples (10 December 1943).

Fig. 13.16 20c, 30c and 60c Imperial Series definitive stamps reprinted without *fasces* in the margins (1944–45).

Fig. 13.17 25c 'Enlightenment', 50c 'Freedom' and 6l 'New Growth' from the Peace and Reconstruction set (1 October 1945 onwards).

Fig. 13.18 2l Lucca, 4l Florence and 20l 'Oath of Pontida' from the Republic set (31 October 1946).

Fig. 13.19 First day cover with Pope Pius XII's Coronation set and Vatican City postmark (2 June 1939).

Fig. 13.20 5c Arms of Pope Pius XII (12 May 1940).

Fig. 13.21 1942, 1943 and 1944 stamps from the Relief Fund sets (1 September 1942, 31 January 1944 and 1 September 1945).

Fig. 13.22 25c stamp from the Episcopal Silver Jubilee set (16 January 1943).

Fig. 13.23 1.25l Carlo Maratti from the Fourth Centenary of the Pontifical Academy set (21 November 1944).

Fig. 13.24 Souvenir cover with Italian and German stamps posted in Operationszone Adriatisches-Küstenland.

Fig. 13.25 Souvenir cover with 'Imperial' series stamps overprinted 'G.N.R.' (December 1943–February 1944). The thin lettering and late Florence postmark suggest Verona as the source.

Fig. 13.26 Souvenir postcard with the five overprinted King Victor Emmanuel III stamps (plus two other Imperial series values) postmarked Bolgheri in Livorno (Leghorn) province (22 January 1944).

Fig. 13.27 Overprinted 1.25l Express Letter, 1l Parcel Post and 30c Postage Due stamps.

Fig. 13.28 Souvenir cover with the four overprinted 30c War Propaganda stamps (February 1944).

Fig. 13.29 Souvenir cover with the Italian Social Republic set (1944–45).

Fig. 13.30 1l from the Centenary of the Death of the Bandiera Brothers set (6 December 1944).

14

ALBANIA

In 1501, when the Turks finally seized the last Venetian outpost on the Dalmatian coast, their conquest of Albania was complete. For the next four centuries local rule was left in the hands of tribal chiefs, who paid varying degrees of allegiance to their Turkish overlords. Many Albanians became Muslims, not least because careers and sometimes lives often hinged on it. There were some uprisings in the early nineteenth century, but Albanians generally had mixed views on severing complete links with the Ottoman Empire as many feared the expansionist policies of Serbia, Greece and Bulgaria and even greater repression. Indeed it was the Albanian uprisings in 1910–12 that led to Serbian and Greek incursions. The Albanians hurriedly declared independence, leaving an international conference to settle the borders. Many, however, were disgruntled when numerous Albanians were left in western Serbia and many Greeks incorporated into southern Albania. In the First World War the country descended into chaos, with Italy, Greece, Bulgaria and Austria–Hungary all occupying bits of the country, and the rest falling under rival local warlords. In 1920 the Allies decided to partition Albania between Yugoslavia, Italy and Greece, but a combination of belated Albanian unity and American commitment to ethnic self-determination ensured its survival.

Surrounded by predators, the impoverished country endured years of short-lived governments until Ahmed Bey Zogu, a tribal leader and prime minister, who had fled to Yugoslavia after one of the numerous eruptions of violence, returned at the head of a Yugoslav-supported invasion force in late 1924. Zogu became, first, president, and then king, and used his increasingly autocratic powers to crush civil liberties and all opponents. He gained international support and huge loans from Mussolini's Italy, but the price was steadily increasing Italian influence and control over the Albanian economy and army.

On 7 April 1939 Mussolini seized the opportunity provided by the growing European crisis in Czechoslovakia and Poland to invade Albania and replace Zog by King Victor Emmanuel of Italy. It was part of the Italian dictator's desire to recreate a second Roman Empire, and the new Italian regional governors were ordered to introduce the Italian language in schools and secure swathes of land for Italian settlers. In addition control of the Albanian coast helped bolster Italian national pride after Italy's paltry territorial rewards after the First World War and ejection from Albanian soil in 1920. Mussolini believed, too, that it showed Hitler his Italian ally remained a major military force.

A sequence of Albanian stamps reflected the rise and fall of both King Zog and Mussolini. In April 1938 stamps featured Zog and his new bride, the half-Hungarian, half-American Countess Geraldine, in August 1938 another set commemorated the tenth anniversary of Zog's accession, and on 12 April 1939, a week after Zog's wife had presented him with an heir, the complete Albanian definitive and airmail series suddenly appeared overprinted '*Mbledhja Kushtetuése 12-IV-1939 XVII*' which translates somewhat innocuously as 'Constitutional Meeting 12 April 1939' (Fig. 14.1). The overprints, however, publicised a dramatic turn of events – the Albanian Parliament's formal deposition of Zog and the nation's acceptance of a personal union with Italy through their joint king, Victor Emmanuel III. As many of the stamps featured Zog and views of his birthplace, the overprinted issue reinforced the end of this increasingly unpopular dictator. Many Albanians had profited from the long-established links with Italy and welcomed them, and the set was intended to be a notification of a nationally agreed change of dynasty rather than any celebration of Albania's defeat and humiliation. Significantly the postage-due stamps featuring the arms of Albania were not overprinted and, although in due course the crown of Italy replaced the Albanian helmet of Skanderberg, and supporting *fasces* were added, the central Albanian spread eagle was kept intact. Later in 1939 a new definitive set started to appear that carefully mixed images of Victor Emmanuel with pictures of men and women in tribal costumes. The powerful Tosk and Gheb clans were traditional rivals, and care was taken to treat them equally on the stamps. Not surprisingly, notable sites from Albania's Imperial Roman past were included. These included Botrint (Roman Buthrotum), where amidst great publicity for

Fig. 14.1

Fig. 14.2

Fig. 14.3

the past decade Italian archaeologists had been excavating some of the public buildings, temples and amphitheatre in this lavishly equipped army veterans' *colonium* (Fig. 14.2).

In March 1940 a new airmail series featured aeroplanes flying over peaceful Albanian landscapes peopled with waving peasants in regional costumes. One contained a map with the main routes to Italy, and another featured a benign Victor Emmanuel by a harbour looking up at the passing Italian aeroplane (Fig. 14.3). At this stage there was little resistance to the Italian occupation, not least because the day-to-day administration was in Albanian hands, and the Albanian Communist Party was very small and supported the Soviet Union's pact with Nazi Germany. The greatest threats came from nationalist groups, although few sought the return of King Zog.

Everything changed in the autumn. In October Albania became the staging post for Mussolini's invasion of Greece in pursuit of his dream of rivalling Hitler's conquests and restoring Rome's dominance of the eastern Mediterrancan. To many people's surprise not only did the Greeks halt the invasion but they pushed the Italians back into southern Albania and then proceeded to occupy it until April 1941 when Hitler rescued his humiliated ally, and crushed Yugoslavia and Greece before turning on the Soviet Union in the summer. Italy suddenly found itself gifted with large areas of Greece and Yugoslavia to control as well as an enlarged Albania. However, the new situation pleased many Albanians as the largely Albanian-speaking area of Kosovo and slices of land to its north and south had been added to the country. In April 1942 a set of seven identical stamps boldly featuring King Victor Emmanuel celebrated the third year of Italian rule (Fig. 14.4). Exactly a year later a surcharged set picturing a peasant girl rocking a cradle supported the Anti-Tuberculosis Fund (Fig. 14.5). TB was rampant across the impoverished and war-wracked Balkan countries, and many of them issued similar sets at this time.

Fig. 14.4

Fig. 14.5

When Mussolini's government collapsed, German forces hurried to occupy Albania before guerrilla units could occupy the major centres, especially Tirana, the capital. Initially the Germans were successful, forcing the guerrillas back into the mountains and gaining significant support from anti-communist nationalists who avidly sought the retention of Kosovo. Initially, too, the Germans shrewdly allowed Albanians to continue running the country, and the first German set of stamps was markedly low key, being merely the Italian definitive set overprinted with the date '*14 Shtator 1943*' ('14 September 1943') that marked the end of the Italian connection (See Fig. 14.6 in colour section). Under the Albanians there was little persecution of the Jews, and, except in the old Yugoslav province of Kosovo, the Italians and even the Germans remained remarkably restrained in their anti-Semitism.

A couple of stamps were given new values, but no new stamps appeared until September 1944 when a surcharged set with a harrowing picture of a ragged woman clutching a child against a background of a burning hut was issued to support a War Refugees' Relief Fund (Fig. 14.7). The set was far too late to provide effective aid from the German-sponsored government controlling increasingly constricted parts of the country, and the violent civil war had undoubtedly wrought widespread destruction and misery. Communist units had soared in numbers throughout 1944, and a major partisan force, the National Liberation Army, had belatedly joined them in an anti-Nazi alliance and agreed that Enver Hoxha, the communist leader, should take overall command.

By the end of November 1944 most German forces had withdrawn, and a communist provisional government was formed. On 4 January 1945 the Italian definitive set suffered another overprint when it was reissued with the inscription '*Qeverija Demokratike E Shqiperise 22-X-1944*' ('Democratic Government of Albania 22-X-1944') and Albanian values (See Fig. 14.8 in colour section). During the war the major Allies had had few thoughts about the post-war future of Albania, and by and large Hoxha was left to liquidate Axis collaborators, political opponents and dissident clan chiefs (most communist leaders were Tosks and therefore hated the Ghebs) and to stave off Yugoslav domination while at the same time enjoying Tito's recognition and protection. In this process, however, Kosovo had to be given up to Yugoslavia.

On 1 July 1946 a set of overprinted stamps issued announced the establishment of the Albanian People's Republic (Fig. 14.9).

Fig. 14.7

Fig. 14.9

Illustrations

Fig. 14.1 1*q* from Royal Wedding set (25 April 1938), 1*f* from the Tenth Anniversary of Accession set (30 August 1938) and 15*q* from the Constitutional Meeting overprinted set (12 April 1939).

Fig. 14.2 1*q* Gheb man, 50*q* Tosh woman and 5*f* Amphitheatre at Berat from the Italian definitive set (1939–40).

Fig. 14.3 Souvenir cover with the Airmail set (20 March 1940).

Fig. 14.4 25*q* from the third anniversary of Italian Rule set (April 1942).

Fig. 14.5 Souvenir cover with the Anti-TB Fund set (1 April 1943).

Fig. 14.6 2*q* Tosh man, 65*q* King Emmanuel III and 2*f* Vesiri Bridge from the German overprinted Italian definitive set (1943).

Fig. 14.7 1*f*+50*q* from the War Refugees' Relief Fund set (22 September 1944).

Fig. 14.8 Souvenir cover with Italian stamps overprinted 'Democratic Government of Albania 22-X-1944' (4 January 1945).

Fig. 14.9 20*q* Independent Albanian stamp overprinted 'People's Republic of Albania' (1 July 1946).

Fig. 1.2a

Fig. 1.2b

Fig. 1.3

Fig. 2.2

Fig. 2.5

Fig. 2.6

Fig. 2.10

Fig. 2.11 + 2.12

Fig. 2.13b

Herrn

Rektor Schumacher

Mülheim / Ruhr

Holunderstrasse 5

Fig. 2.13a

Fig. 2.19

Fig. 2.23

Fig. 2.24

Fig. 2.25

Fig. 2.26

Fig. 2.27

Fig. 2.31

Fig. 2.32

Fig. 2.34c

Fig. 2.3

Fig. 2.35

g. 2.36

Fig. 2.37

Fig. 2.40

Fig. 2.46

Fig. 2.43   Fig. 2.44

Fig. 2.48

Fig. 2.49

g. 2.51

Fig. 2.53

Fig. 2.56

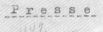

Presse

942

Mr.Joh.H.Huyts

Hoofdredacteur "Nieuwe Rotter-
damsche Crt."

Postbus 824

ROTTERDAM

(Holland - Hollanti)

SJOERD BROERSMA

Journalist

Snellmansgatan 17 A. 9

HELSINKI

FINLAND

Fig. 3.3

Fig. 3.4

Fig. 3.6a

Fig. 3.6b

Fig. 4.4

Fig. 4.6/5.1

Fig. 4.8

Fig. 4.10

Fig. 4.13

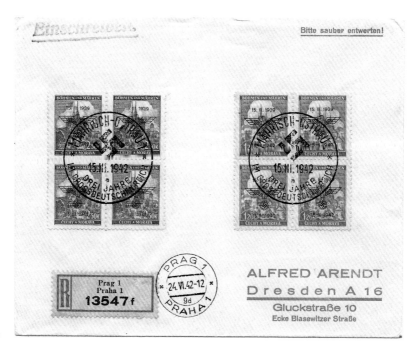

Fig. 4.16a

Fig. 4.16b

Fig. 4.18

Fig. 4.22a

Fig. 4.22b

Fig. 4.25a

ig. 4.25b

Fig. 5.4

Fig. 5.9

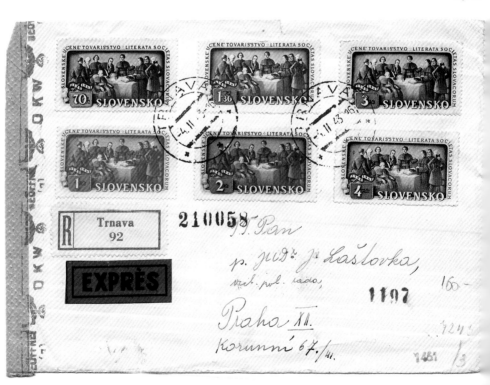

Fig. 5.1

Fig. 5.16

Fig. 5.19

Fig. 6.2

Fig. 6.5

Fig. 6.7

Fig. 6.11

Fig. 6.12

P. Hesse
Erfurt, Winterfeldtstr. 10.
(15)

Einschreiben

ig. 6.13

DAVID FIELD LTD.,
7, VIGO STREET,
LONDON, W.1,
ENGLAND.

g. 6.14a

Fig. 6.14b

Fig. 6.18

Fig. 6.20

Fig. 6.20b

Fig. 6.22

ODENSE FILATELISTKLUBS

25-Aars Jubilæums-Udstilling

7.-8. SEPTEMBER 1940

RØDE KORS KUVERT

Fig. 7.2

Fig. 8.5

Fig. 8.6

Fig. 8.7

Mr. E. Mangor,
C/o B.P.A.,
3 Berners Street,
London, W.1.

Fig. 8.16

Fig. 8.19

Fig. 8.20

Fig. 9.2

Fig. 9.5

AANTEEKENEN.

R GOUDA
Graaf Florisweg
Gd.Gf. № 279

Den Heer J. C. Piek,
Noordplein 45b,
R O T T E R D A M .

5285

Fig. 9.6

Fig. 9.8

Mrs. E. Keene,
36, Poplar Road,
Merton Park,
S.W.19.

g. 9.10

Fig. 9.11

Fig. 10.1

Fig. 10.2

Fig. 10.5

Fig. 11.1

Fig. 11.2

Fig. 11.7

Fig. 11.9

Fig. 11.12

Fig. 11.13

Fig. 11.15

Fig. 12.1

Fig. 12.2

Fig. 12.6

Fig. 12.1

Fig. 12.7

Fig. 12.13

Fig. 12.14

g. 12.18

Fig. 12.20

Fig. 12.22

Fig. 12.23

Fig. 12.24a

Fig. 12.24b

Fig. 13.4

Fig. 13.10

Fig. 13.5

Fig. 13.15

Fig. 13.25

Fig. 13.26

Fig. 13.28

Fig. 13.29

Fig. 14.6

Fig. 14.8

Fig. 15.9

Fig. 15.10c

Fig. 15.10b

Fig. 15.12

Fig. 15.11

ig. 15.13

Fig. 15.15

Fig. 15.21

Fig. 15.30

Fig. 15.31

Fig. 15.34

Fig. 15.35a

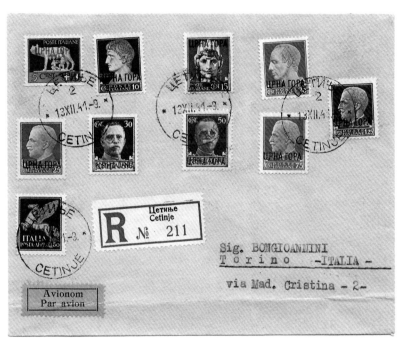

Fig. 15.35b

Fig. 15.39

Fig. 15.38

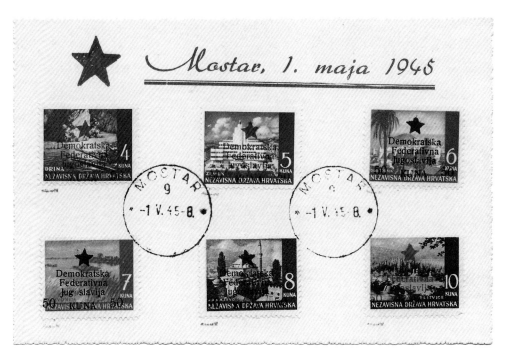

Fig. 15.43

Fig. 15.46

Fig. 15.48a

Fig. 15.48b

Fig. 16.2

CARTOLINA POSTALE

ISOLE JONIE

Fig. 16.3b

Fig. 16.3a

Fig. 16.7

Fig. 17.12

Fig. 17.13

Fig. 17.14

Fig. 17.16

Бессмертна слава Сталинграда!

Fig. 17.19a   *Fig. 17.19b*

27/I- 1944 года

Город Ленинград полностью освобожден
от вражеской блокады.

1 3 2 3 1 9 3 9

URBS VILNIUS

METROPOLIS LITHUANIAE RECUPERATA

KAINA 2 LITAI

Fig. 18.3

Fig. 18.5

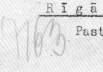

Ierakstit.

God. kungam

A. Muravioff

RIGA
LATVIJA
0155

Rīgā

Pasta kastite 567.

g. 18.8

Fig. 18.12

Fig. 19.2

Fig. 19.13

Fig. 19.17

Fig. 19.19

Fig. 19.18

Fig. 19.22

Fig. 19.23

Fig. 20.3a

Fig. 20.3b

Fig. 20.5

Fig. 20.6

Fig. 20.

Fig. 20.8

Fig. 20.15

Fig. 20.18

Fig. 20.19

Fig. 21.1

Fig. 21.7

Fig. 21.13

Fig. 21.1

15

YUGOSLAVIA

Disintegration of Yugoslavia

As the power of the Ottoman Empire waned across the Balkans during the nineteenth century the Austro–Hungarian Empire had replaced it by annexing territory (such as Croatia), establishing increasingly dependent protectorates (such as Bosnia) or becoming an overbearing neighbour (such as to Serbia). The various ethnic groups prized the autonomy they had achieved, or were struggling to achieve, but with varying degrees of enthusiasm they recognised that coordinated action aimed at creating a larger state was more likely to keep mightier predators at bay as they freed themselves from Ottoman overlordship.

By 1918 Austria-Hungary was in complete disarray militarily and politically after four years of war, and on 1 December the National Council of Serbs, Croats and Slovenes, although riven with ethnic disagreements and power struggles, declared a new Kingdom of the Serbs, Croats and Slovenes. The situation remained highly unstable, and Italy looked enviously at parts of Slovenia and several Dalmatian islands. Serbia was the most powerful component part, especially after it had absorbed Montenegro in November 1918 and its monarch became King Peter I of the new state. (See map on p. 251)

King Peter (1918–21) and notably his successor Alexander I (1921–34) kept the country intact despite the ambitions of Serbians to dominate it and the jealousy spreading among other ethnic groups, especially the Croats. In June 1928 a Serb deputy shot and killed three Croat deputies in the National Assembly, and soon afterwards Alexander suspended the constitution, banned political parties and assumed executive power. The country was renamed Yugoslavia, and henceforth Alexander sought to minimise separatist tendencies and maximise broader nationalist ones through a highly centralised personal government. Many politicians were imprisoned, internal borders were redrawn and new regional names invented, but by the time Alexander was assassinated in Marseilles in 1934 internal tensions, especially in Croatia, were reaching bursting point. In addition, Italy and Germany were opposed to the king's efforts as they cast envious eyes on parcels of Yugoslav land, and the Soviet Union decided the kingdom was fertile ground for communist agitation.

Fig. 15.1   Fig. 15.2

Alexander was succeeded by his 11-year-old son, Peter II, and temporary authority was vested in his cousin, Prince Paul, as regent (Fig. 15.1). Paul eventually bowed to the relentless internal and external pressures, and in 1939 agreed that Croatia could become an autonomous region within the kingdom as a first step towards greater federalisation. A provocative set of stamps celebrated Croat history (Fig. 15.2). Two years later, on 25 March 1941, he signed the Tripartite Treaty in Vienna, although privately he hoped to keep Yugoslavia out of the war. Instead he lost popular support, and two days later the pro-Allied and anti-Croat Serb-dominated army mounted a successful *coup d'état.* King Peter II, now 17, was given full powers just a week before an enraged Hitler ordered the invasion of his kingdom, promising to wipe it from the face of the earth.

He kept his promise. On 17 April, just eleven days after the invasion, Yugoslavia surrendered and, taking full advantage of the internal ethnic divisions, Hitler divided the country between Germany and his allies Italy and Hungary. The royal family fled into exile. Greater Germany was expanded to include northern Slovenia, and Italy added much of western Slovenia and the Dalmatian coastline to its empire. Croatia was substantially enlarged with the inclusion of Bosnia–Herzegovina and allowed to become a puppet state, nominally under an Italian prince turned into a king but actually under Ante Pavelic, the leader of the Croatian nationalist Ustase organisation long opposed by Alexander I. The remaining rump of Serbia fell under German military control with domestic affairs being delegated to a vigorous pro-Nazi Serb civil government. Montenegro became a puppet state under Italian jurisdiction, and Hungary was given various parcels of land it had long sought abutting its borders, including eastern Slovenia. The scene was set for over four years of brutal warfare between the occupying forces and various partisan groups, and equally brutal warfare between the deeply divided partisan groups themselves.

In 1939 the Serbs supported the Allies, but the Croats, the Serbs in Macedonia and Montenegro, and the Muslims in Bosnia and Herzegovina favoured Germany and Italy. But the Croats and most Serbs, wherever they lived, continued to hate each other. In May 1941 the Ustase campaign of genocide against Croatia's Serbs and the forced cession of much of Dalmatia to Italy fuelled the first of many outbreaks of fierce resistance to Axis domination. Royalist Serbs in Serbia and other territories adopted the name Chetniks and rallied to Colonel Draza Mihailovic, a prominent officer closely linked to the London-based exiled royal government. Communist forces spread across old Yugoslavia began to rally to their party secretary, Josip Broz Tito, and sought support from the Soviet Union. Initially the Chetniks and communists joined forces in various Serb uprisings against the Germans and Croats. However, they were fundamentally divided. The Chetniks aimed at the restoration of a monarchy dominated by Serbia whereas Tito promoted a far broader vision of a socialist state, and it was this that gradually gained wide support. Soon the communists and Chetniks fought each other as much as they attacked the Germans and Italians. The fighting across the mountains and valleys of the old kingdom grew so confused that sometimes Chetnik forces joined the Germans or Italians against the communists, while at much the same time engaging in battle with Ustase forces armed by the Germans. It was as much a brutal civil war as a sustained uprising against the Axis invaders with all the accompanying burning of villages and massacre of civilians. Indeed, even the Germans sometimes complained about the widespread cruelty of the Ustase and Chetniks and their tendency to create more enemies than they subdued.

   Overall the Chetniks kept hold of Serbia but were decisively defeated by the communists outside it. Although badly mauled, the communists also survived several major Axis offensives against them. Gradually the Allies lost faith in Colonel Mihailovic and the ability of the monarchy to act even-handedly towards its disparate peoples. As Allied support switched to Tito late in the war, the communists, with some Soviet army support, hounded the Germans out of the old kingdom, set about destroying their internal rivals, notably the Chetniks and Ustase, and looked to replacing King Peter II by Tito.

Slovenia

Throughout the nineteenth century a growing sense of cultural and then political nationalism gradually united the Slovene-speaking territories against the ruling Austrian Empire of which they were part. However, the Slovene nationalist movement was strongly resisted in the ethnically mixed areas, notably Trieste where many wanted stronger links with Italy, and in the east where greater unity with the Slavs was sought. During the First World War, several battles ravaged the region. Austria forcibly conscripted thousands of Slovenes, and executed hundreds of hostile activists, while Italy incarcerated ethnic Slovene refugees as wartime enemies. In 1918 Slovenia willingly joined the new Kingdom of the Serbs, Croats and Slovenes, but the western, northern and eastern borderlands remained bitterly contested. A north-eastern province was coveted by Hungary, and Austria sought the return of Lower Styria. And, as we have seen, Italy successfully held onto substantial lands around Trieste and Fiume.

Despite Yugoslavia's political instability many areas of Slovenia prospered between the wars with urban industrialisation, and rural timber processing, taking advantage of the good rail links into central Europe. The thousands of Slovenes left in Italy, however, were persecuted by the fascists, and by 1941 a militant, if still secretive, anti-fascist organisation was increasingly well organised.

On 6 April 1941, the day Yugoslavia was invaded, the Germans occupied and annexed the whole of northern Slovenia including Lower Styria, South Carinthia and parts of Carniola. Hungary was thrown some bits in the north-east, while Italy was awarded the west and south – basically the rest of Carniola that became known as the province of Ljubljana (in Italian Lubiana, in German Laibach).

On 26 April King Peter II definitive and postage-due stamps of Yugoslavia appeared overprinted *'Co. Ci.'* – for the Italian *Commissariato Civile*. Stamps were frequently found with the overprints in many different positions on them, suggesting the rush to mark and publicise the arrival of the new occupiers. On

5 May the overprint on the Yugoslav definitive, postage-due and, a little later, the airmail stamps was extended to read *'R. Commissariato Civile Territori Sloveni occupati Lubiana'* ('Royal Civil Commissariat for the occupied Slovenian territories Lubiana') and this time three or four lines of dots masked the old kingdom's name (Fig. 15.3). Even so, there was no heavy-handed attempt to emphasise Italian overlordship or alienate the population by completely obliterating the king's

Fig. 15.3

features or his kingdom's name. Indeed, compared with the Germans hounding out the Slovenes from their occupied provinces, and the forced 'Italianisation' of Slovenes in Fiume and Trieste, the Italians exercised a light touch in Ljubljana – until partisan resistance started in earnest, and the Italian governor, Mario Roata, responded savagely by transporting thousands of Slovenes to concentration camps.

There were no more overprinted issues in Slovenia as ordinary Italian stamps were subsequently introduced. When the Germans seized control in 1943 after the Italian surrender no new issues occurred until January 1944, when a stream of Italian definitive, postage-due, airmail and express letter stamps appeared with every symbol of Italian Fascism, imperial history and King Victor Emmanuel overprinted with a flamboyant double-headed eagle with outstretched wings surrounded by either a square or circular frame comprising the dual language inscription *'Provinz Laibach'* and *'Pokrajina Ljubljanika'* (Fig. 15.4). In a deliberate act that highlighted the new (or, for Hitler, renewed) German ownership, this version of the spread eagle comprised the heraldic arms of Carniola when it had been part of the Crown lands of the Austrian Hapsburgs. The Nazi contempt for all things Italian was palpable at this critical stage of the war. When the large Italian express letter stamps were used with overprinted surcharges for the Red

Fig. 15.5

Fig. 15.6

Cross and Homeless Relief Funds, the king's head was still overprinted with the eagle and surrounding inscription (Fig. 15.5).

By 1943 the pro- and anti-communist partisans in Slovenia were fighting each other as much as the German occupiers. Many of the anti-communists allied with the Italians and then transferred loyalty to the Germans. The merciless fighting looked a long way from the peaceful Slovenian scenes featured on a lengthy set of stamps issued by the Germans in early 1945 (Fig. 15.6). They were similar in format to the pastoral and historic sets that appeared in Germany and Poland, and these, too, had a specific wartime agenda. Some celebrated the scenic splendours of Slovenia such as the subterranean lakes in Krizna Jama caves, the wine-growing area of Dolenjskem, and the mysteriously disappearing Lake Zirknitz. Others, though, featured equally impressive sites where historic sites had been severely damaged or destroyed through conflict with partisans. One featured the famous railway viaduct at Borovnice. Here, on 28 June 1942, partisans attacked an Italian train taking Slovenes to concentration camps, but took all those they rescued who refused to join them to the nearby Krim caves and shot them. Another pictured the renowned Turjak Castle that was assaulted and partially burned down in September 1943 by partisans attacking the pro-Axis Slovene militia holding it. Others featured Otocec Castle, Zuzemberg Castle, and the great Cistercian monastery and castle at Kostanjevica, all on the River Krka, and all of them burnt down by partisans. The stamps, of course, pictured all the historic sites to best advantage, and all of them – and perhaps particularly the stamps picturing the Gothic glories of Ljubljana, Kocevje, Ribnica and Neustadtl (Novo Mesto) – reinforced

Germany's claim to these historic Hapsburg lands. They did so just at the time that the partisans were on the verge of complete control of Slovenia. Ljubljana was liberated on 9 May 1945, the last battles occurred on 14 and 15 May, and over the next year or so tens of thousands of anti-communist militia and ethnic Italians were slaughtered by the Yugoslav army and partisan units.

Dalmatia

The Adriatic islands and coastal strip off Yugoslavia had long been coveted by Italy. Their annexation was written into the Treaty of London that led Italy to join the Allies in the First World War, but even though Italian forces seized the whole area in November 1918, along with Fiume, the eventual peace treaties forced the abandonment of everything except the naval base of Zara.

In April 1941 the coastline and islands were divided between Italy and Croatia – both allies of Germany but continually at loggerheads over each other's share. Some large northern islands such as Veglia (now Krk) and Arbe (Rab) were absorbed along with Fiume into Italy, while the more southerly areas of Zara, Split and Kotor, another key port, were placed under an Italian governor.

During May 1941 ordinary Italian stamps came into use throughout the Italian possessions along the coast. The initial exception was Fiume where 'Italianisation' took off where it had left off in the 1920s. Here the Italians marked the retaking of the city and its hinterland around the Riva Kupa by heavily overprinting King Peter II stamps of Yugoslavia '*Zona Occupata Fiumano Kupa*' and adding the initials ZOFK across the horizontal margins. At the same time further King Peter stamps were issued overprinted 'O.N.M.I.' ('*Opera Nazionale Maternita e Infanzia*') in aid of a Maternity and Child Welfare Fund, and a fortnight later they were reissued with an additional arch-shaped overprint around the edge saying '*Pro Maternita e Infanzia*', presumably to clarify the meaning of the initials (Fig. 15.7). Yet another overprinted King Peter stamp in May celebrated a minor but widely publicised Italian naval exploit during the First World War (Fig. 15.8). On 10 February 1918 three fast torpedo boats

Fig. 15.7   Fig. 15.8

entered the Austrian anchorage at Buccari (Bakar) near Fiume and fired six torpedoes before escaping unharmed. They failed to do any damage, but the poet and patriot Gabriele D'Annunzio who took part in the attack ensured Italian morale received a significant boost – especially after the recent Austrian victory at Caporetto. The stamps' inscription '*Memento Avdere Semper*' ('Remember always to dare') was D'Annunzio's motto that related to Buccari. Its initials MAS also reflected the initials of the '*Motoscafo Armato Silurante*', the 'Torpedo Armed Motorboats' used in the raid. The sheets of these stamps had the initials MAS – for the boats and the motto – printed between the horizontal rows.

When the Germans took over Dalmatian territory in September 1943 they refused to attach it to the Italian Social Republic and administered it themselves, although some coastal areas and islands, such as Brac, were incorporated into the puppet state of Croatia and had short-lived issues of King Peter II stamps overprinted with Croatian currency and local names. In Zara and its hinterland a host of heavily overprinted Italian stamps was issued, and the Germans made no subsequent efforts to create new designs. The Italian origin of the numerous stamps remained obvious, and no doubt deliberately so as technically speaking Zara remained Italian while under German occupation. Here the Germans used the Italian Imperial definitive, airmail, express letter and postage-due stamps along with the War Propaganda series including the exhortatory labels with their much vaunted images not quite blocked out by either the inscription '*Deutsche Besetzung Zara*' ('German Occupation Zara) or just ZARA between several rows of black bars (See Fig. 15.9 in colour section). In February in the Gulf of Kotor Italian Imperial stamps were issued overprinted '*Deutsche Militärverwaltung Kotor*' ('German Military Administration Kotor') and in September King Peter II stamps appeared overprinted '*Boka Kotorska*' and new German values (Fig. 15.10).

As the Germans and their collaborators retreated in the face of Tito's partisans and the new Yugoslav army the long-drawn-out conflict of ownership of the Dalmatian coast – except in and around Trieste and Fiume – gradually drew to a decisive close.

Croatia

Ante Pavelic's government placed great store upon the propaganda value of stamps, and while some try to give the impression of a peaceful benign state many more reveal the true nature of the regime. Initially the supposedly Independent State of Croatia (*Nezavisna Drzava Hrvatska* or NDH) used readily available supplies of definitive stamps from the Kingdom of Yugoslavia issued in 1939 picturing young King Peter II. Eight low values were issued with the new country's name overprinted in black capitals across the king's head with black vertical bars across 'Yugoslavia.' Soon afterwards a more thorough job was made of obliterating Peter's image and his kingdom's name using the Croatian chequerboard heraldic emblem and thicker writing. Soon after that two stamps appeared with a large black circle containing new values covering the king's heads (See Fig. 15.11 in colour section). The same determination to eradicate any association with the old kingdom led postage due stamps to receive the same attention. King Peter was further overprinted with the chequerboard, the country's name and the date '10.V.1941' to mark the foundation of a specifically Croatian national army (See Fig. 15.12 in colour section).

Just three weeks before the Axis invasion a Croatian philatelic exhibition was held in Zagreb and was marked by two stamps featuring the city's old cathedral and Kamenita Gate. The stamps were reissued just after the invasion but just before the surrender for a similar exhibition in Brod planned for May. Despite the turmoil, it went ahead and the reissued stamps were reissued yet again with '*Nezavisna Drzava Hrvatska*' and a chequerboard emblazoned in gold (See Fig. 15.13 in colour section).

Over a period of a year from the summer of 1941 a lengthy series of new Croatian stamps appeared highlighting historic sites and the beauties of the landscape. Aiming to reinforce nationalist feelings and a comforting sense of restored glory, the scenes ranged across the whole country, carefully including Bosnia and Herzegovina. Alongside the spectacular mountains, gorges, lakes and rivers, there was a view of Varazdin, the ancient Croatian capital, the medieval cathedral in Zagreb, the city of Osijek, which had been repeatedly rebuilt as occupiers came and went, the Dalmatian island of Hvar, where many nineteenth-century Croat nationalists had been born, and the Adriatic castle at Klis and city of Senj, which had defied both the Venetians and the Turks for many years. There was also the mosque in Sarajevo, where ironically in past centuries Muslims, Jews, Roman Catholics and Eastern Orthodox Christians had lived peacefully together. Another stamp featured the hitherto prosperous town of Banja Luka, where Jews and Serbs were already being heavily persecuted and a concentration camp was rising up nearby. In June 1942 a further Croatian philatelic exhibition was held in Banja Luka, and this was promoted through the stamp reissued with 'FI' inscribed in the corner. That April three commonly used values featuring historic scenes across Croatia were reissued in different colours overprinted with the national shield and the dates '1941–1942 10-IV' to celebrate the country's first anniversary (Fig. 15.14).

In Croatia, as elsewhere in war-torn Europe, stamp exhibitions were deemed important. In September 1943 another exhibition was held in the capital Zagreb for which a large stamp featuring St Mary's Church and the Cistercian monastery was issued (See Fig. 15.15 in colour section). The regime may well have chosen the image as part of its belated attempt to placate Croatia's Roman Catholic hierarchy, especially Archbishop Stepinac of Zagreb, whose initial sympathies with Croat separatism had faded as news of Ustasa atrocities spread across the country. Stepanic bravely made several public protests, but nevertheless a few fanatical priests stayed loyal to the Ustasa, and engaged in the forced conversion and baptism of Bosnian Muslims and Eastern Orthodox Serbs.

Fig. 15.14

Fig. 15.16

Fig. 15.17

In December 1941 a surcharged stamp pictured sword-bearing soldiers with shields emblazoned with the Nazi eagle, Italian *fasces* and Croatian chequerboard (Fig. 15.16). Operation Barbarossa, the Axis invasion of the Soviet Union, was at its high point with the Germans just outside Moscow, and the stamp was raising funds for Eastern Front volunteers. Pavelic had already wormed his way into Hitler's favour by creating a regiment of Croats, Bosnian Muslims and White Russians that began fighting alongside Slovak and Norwegian volunteers in Russia in November. Fierce fighting in 1942 around the Samara River, Kharkov and the Don River, and then Stalingrad, meant the regiment required constant reinforcements. For a time, though, it maintained its strength of just over 5,000 officers and men. There were huge casualties at Stalingrad, however, where the regiment shrank to about 700 hungry and exhausted men who eventually surrendered on 31 January 1943 after flying out their wounded colleagues. In July 1943 a set and miniature sheets picturing Croatian soldiers, sailors and airmen raised funds for Croatian Legion units, with each stamp inscribed with a campaign in which legion forces fought – sailors on the Sea of Azov, airmen at Sevastapol, and soldiers at Stalingrad and the Don River (Fig. 15.17). Croat naval minesweepers and gunboats operated in the Black Sea and along the Adriatic coast. Croat fighter pilots had fought the Luftwaffe during the invasion of Yugoslavia, but afterwards they fought alongside German pilots on the Eastern Front before returning home in 1943 to reinforce the campaigns against the largely communist partisans. In March 1942 funds had been raised for the hard-pressed air force by a surcharged set of four stamps and two miniature sheets featuring innocuous model aircraft in flight rather than any alarming pictures of warplanes in mortal combat across the Soviet Union (Fig. 15.18).

Not surprisingly surcharged stamps raised funds for the Croatian Red Cross organisation, and in 1941 and 1942 the sets took the opportunity to heighten a sense of specifically Croat nationhood by featuring people from acceptable ethnic groups in traditional regional costumes (Fig. 15.19). In 1943 a lengthy set combined mother and child pictures with a nurse caring for an injured young man, strongly implying that the mother was a Croat war widow and the man a Croat soldier. In 1942 and 1944 sets for the National Relief Fund used potentially confusing

Fig. 15.18

Fig. 15.19

Fig. 15.20

arrays of images of martyred saints, slain heroes, crippled soldiers, mother and child, triumphal processions and youthful trumpeters (Fig. 15.20). The regime seemed to be attempting to impress several groups all at once – notably, the Roman Catholic Church, ardent Croat patriots and ordinary hard-pressed families. Croatia certainly needed all the relief it could get, not least because the regime itself was a primary cause of widespread desolation and suffering. Other stamps took up the theme of the historic sufferings and betrayal of Croats. In June 1943 an unusual set featured three tragic seventeenth-century patriots who were later hailed as martyrs (See Fig. 15.21 in colour section). Katerina Frankopan, her brother Fran Krsto Frankopan and her future husband Petar Zrinski were aristocratic poets and scholars who sought greater autonomy for Croatia within the Hapsburg Empire only to be constantly rebuffed and increasingly perceived as traitors at a time when the Turkish threat to the Balkans was intensifying. Alienated by the Hapsburgs and their lands ravaged, the family turned to the French, the Venetians and finally the Turks for support but all their hopes were dashed. Finally they secured an audience with the emperor in Vienna but on arrival Petar and Krsto were arrested, tortured and executed, and Katarina forced into a convent.

The current war was equally confused. Nevertheless on home soil the Croatian army, although increasingly riven with desertions to the communist partisans, still managed to put up a credible performance alongside the German army in containing the Soviet, Bulgarian and partisan offensives in 1944 and 1945. In January 1945 a heavily surcharged set promoted the Croatian Legion's SS Division that contained a hotchpotch of troops gathered together from various badly mauled units and stiffened with German officers in a final attempt to stave off defeat (Fig. 15.22). However, as 1944 turned into 1945 more and more

Fig. 15.22

Croats were fighting other Croats, and when the war ended many of the surviving pro-German Croats were executed by Tito's partisans.

One stamp in particular reveals the regime's brutal policies. Colonel Jure Ritter Francetic was a long standing intimate of Ante Pavelic, and became in turn the Ustasa Commissioner in Bosnia-Herzegovina and founder and leader of the 1st Ustasa Militia – the Black Legion – in Bosnia. As commissioner he had imprisoned and massacred thousands of Jews, Serbs and communists, and continued to do so as leader of the militia. He then waged a vicious but successful war against the Chetniks and communist partisans in east Bosnia until finally in December 1942 he was fatally injured when his plane was forced down near Slunj by either sabotage or partisan fire. The stamp honouring him was issued twice in May 1944, once with a high surcharge for a memorial, and then with a lower one as part of a Ustasa Youth Fund set (Fig. 15.23). The paramilitary Croat youth organisation saw Francetic as a role model, and the other stamps in the set backed this up with pictures of legion troops hurling grenades and guarding a gorge on the River Drina.

The Youth Fund stamps had become increasingly militaristic as the war became increasingly desperate. In November 1942 they had harked back to two nationalist figures in Croatia's past. The first was Matija Gubec (*c.*1538–73) who led an ill-fated Croat peasants' revolt against the landed aristocracy and was tortured to death with a red-hot crown and pliers. The second was Dr Ante Starcevic (1823–96) who intensified Croat nationalism through

Fig. 15.23

Fig. 15.24

Fig. 15.25

his opposition to Hapsburg rule, the creation of the Croatian Party of Rights and his hostility towards the Serbs and Jews (Fig. 15.24). The stamps were issued in sheets of sixteen with nine labels forming a central cross. Each label contained the name of an Ustasa soldier killed in the recent anti-Chetnik fighting around Senj. Most of the commemorative postmarks are from Senj and contain the dates '9.V.1937' and '9.V.1942', marking the fifth year of the originally secretive formation of the Ustasa Youth. In April 1943 two more Youth Fund stamps and a decorated miniature sheet pictured a sombre-faced Ante Pavelic in uniform (Fig. 15.25). He featured in a Nazi-style uniform in a late definitive issue, and also in a 1944 set promoting the Nazi-style Labour Front which called upon all young men to receive instruction and training in all manner of physical and military skills (Fig. 15.26). Pavelic tried to ape

Nazi Germany in many spheres of national life, but he failed to impress his
Nazi overlords or to stabilise the region. His end was as shabby as that of the
Führer – skulking under an assumed identity in the Argentine until badly
wounded by an assassin that hastened his death in 1959.

Fig. 15.26

Serbia

Wartime Serbia included the northern part of Kosovo and the Banat as well as Serbia proper. The Banat was a large triangular parcel of land in the north lying between Hungary and Romania that was claimed by both of them but denied each of them by Hitler to avoid accentuating Balkan jealousies. Serbia was placed under direct German military rule, largely because of its valuable mineral deposits and key central European rail and Danube links. A tame Serbian civil regime under the former Yugoslavian general Milan Nedic, known bizarrely as the Government of National Salvation, was bullied into accepting responsibility for keeping the population quiet, restoring services, registering all undesirable elements and removing them from public office. The ethnic Germans in the Banat largely ran their own affairs. Throughout Serbia the Jews were targeted for elimination and in August 1942 the German commander claimed the country was Jew-free.

Hundreds of thousands of Serbs fleeing persecution in Croatia and elsewhere flooded into the country. Nedic's tactic was to reassure people that the war was over for Serbia, and as long as law and order prevailed the country could look forward to a golden future in the Nazis' New Europe. Propaganda portrayed him as the nation's saviour who had sought German support for the restoration and autonomy of the nation. There were similarities with Pétain's Vichy France, but few Serbs were convinced. Increasingly the Chetniks under Draza Mihailovic and scattered communist groups began to take action against the Germans and Nedic's fascist militia and state police. In reprisal, the Germans carried out several mass executions, and while the communists took little heed of the deaths of civilians, in late 1941 the Chetniks decided to enter into a temporary alliance with Nedic and the Germans against the communists. This uneasy period of cooperation did not stop outbreaks of violence between anti-communist forces but it succeeded in weakening the communist partisans' presence in Serbia – but only for a time. Other major communist forces, and Ustasa units from Croatia, soon ignored the artificial borders Hitler had created.

Serbian propaganda permeated all its stamp issues. Initially Serbia used King Peter II definitive stamps that had been printed with a coloured background or '*burelage*', and overprinted '*Serbien*' diagonally. Unlike Croatia, though, the overprint did not try to eradicate the king's portrait and neither was the old kingdom's name obliterated. The same was true of the first set of Serbian airmail stamps that used pre-war Yugoslavian issues (Fig. 15.27). Treading a perilous path of compromise the puppet civil administration was striving to portray Serbia as a coherent, if occupied, state while not forgetting that King Peter had come from the Serbian House of Karadjordjevic, which had supplied independent Serbia with several of its nineteenth- and twentieth-century monarchs. However, in July 1942 the regime reprinted King Peter stamps with a green *burelage* and then overprinted them with an aeroplane and new 'Air' values, and this time the name 'Yugoslavia' was obliterated and replaced (Fig. 15.28).

Fig. 15.27   Fig. 15.28

Fig. 15.29

A catastrophic explosion in the ancient city of Smederevo on the River Danube led to Serbia's first completely new stamps. The huge medieval castle had been used by the Germans to store ammunition and on 5 June 1941 it exploded, destroying much of the castle and the adjoining town. Well over 2,000 people were killed and many more injured. Four surcharged stamps and two miniature sheets picturing a trail of refugees and the castle as it used to be sought to raise funds for the victims (Fig. 15.29).

Just before Christmas 1941 a set of four Prisoners of War Fund stamps was issued featuring the Virgin Mary holding the crucified Christ. Most Serbs were Orthodox Christians, and the complicated format in which these stamps were printed ensured a variety of Christian symbols were revealed in an attempt to attach the murderous regime to the dominant religious group. Each value was printed in sheets of twenty-five stamps (5x5). The five central stamps were in a slightly different shade and without a pink *burelage*, thereby forming a distinct cross bordered by the other twenty darker-hued stamps. The four *burelaged* stamps adjoining the arms of the cross bore large red-edged Cyrillic letters 'C' – those to the right of the cross facing right and those to the left facing left. The heraldic cross with four 'Cs', one in each quarter, was a widely revered ancient image harking back to a twelfth-century Orthodox archbishop who created it as a symbol of Serb unity. The four 'Cs' stood for a popular alliterative slogan that translates into English as 'Only unity saves the Serbs' (See Fig. 15.30 in colour section). The stamps were reissued near Easter 1942 in different colours and a simplified format under the banner of the Red Cross. The intended recipients of the Prisoners of War Fund presumably were Germans and Serbs who had fought on the Eastern Front or just possibly had escaped execution by partisans. The widows and orphans of Serbian soldiers and militia also merited a fund-raising set in September 1942, and this, too, featured the Serbian Cross by the side of the peasant woman and her naked children. In May 1943 a War Invalids' set, also adorned with the Serbian Cross, featured heroic images of a sinew (or is it a crown?) of thorns encircling a cross-like broken sword, a fallen standard bearer, a woman attending a wounded, perhaps dying, soldier on the ground, and an exhausted but fully uniformed soldier with his arm in a sling (See Fig. 15.31 in colour section). Thoughts of noble warriors, Christian martyrs and devoted women are closely bound up in the set.

The Serbian Cross featured on a dramatic set of surcharged stamps issued to keep alive the message of the anti-Masonic exhibition held in Belgrade from 22 October 1941 to 19 January 1942 (Fig. 15.32). One stamp pictured a Serb peasant as the Biblical Samson pushing down Jewish and Masonic pillars, while the other three featured beams of light blinding a hooded Masonic Jew, burning Masonic and Jewish symbols, and guiding a hand to grasp the head of a Jewish snake. Serb fascists had organised the exhibition with Nedic's support and German funds. It portrayed the Jews as secretly plotting world domination with the masons and communists, and sought to encourage and justify their extermination. The 80,000 visitors were given a set of stamps, and hundreds of

Fig. 15.32

thousands of brochures and leaflets were distributed across the state. A similar event was held in Croatia.

Throughout 1942 and 1943 a lengthy set of stamps featured Serbian monasteries, once again trying to reinforce the regime through its Christian links and sympathies (Fig. 15.33). Most of them had been founded by early medieval Serbian kings or aristocrats, and then endured the ravages of earthquakes and invasions with varying degrees of success. One was Studenica Monastery, a fortified monastery founded in 1190 by King Stefan Nemanjic and adorned with brightly coloured frescoes. It was remembered as the political, cultural and spiritual centre of medieval Serbia, and, although badly damaged by the Turks, fire and earthquakes, its reputation led to its reoccupation in the late nineteenth century. Another was Ravanica Monastery. Built in the traditional trefoil style, its founder Prince Lazar was buried there after his death fighting a massive Turkish army at Kosovo in June 1389. He became a Serb martyr and saint. The

Fig. 15.33

stamp was issued in September 1943, and that February the Germans had violated the monastery and arrested and then killed the Archimandrite Makarije. In December 1943 the set was reissued with a surcharge and inscription on behalf of a relief fund for the victims of an Allied air raid on the industrial city of Nish. No doubt the set was an attempt to unify the increasingly fractured state against the Allied incursions, and Nish was specifically selected by the regime as it had been the scene of a particularly bloody struggle in 1809 when a determined Serbian army just failed to take the city from the Turks. Much heavier Allied raids shook the city in 1944 (See Fig. 15.34 in colour section). By the end of the year the communists and Soviet forces had liberated Serbia.

Montenegro

Gradually wrestling himself free from Ottoman rule, in August 1910 Prince Nicholas of Montenegro proclaimed himself king. He supported his neighbour Serbia in the First and Second Balkan Wars of 1912 and 1913 and during the First World War, only for Austria–Hungary to occupy Montenegro from January 1916 until October 1918. A month later he lost his throne when the Serbian king was preferred as the ruler of the evolving Kingdom of the Serbs, Croats and Slovenes.

When the Royal Yugoslav Army surrendered on 17 April 1941 Mussolini wished to establish Montenegro as merely a province within Imperial Italy alongside Albania. However, King Victor Emmanuel's wife, Queen Elena, was a daughter of ex-King Nicholas, and Mussolini was obliged to create a notionally independent kingdom of Montenegro. Legally it remained so throughout the war, but as Nicholas's grandson and then two Romanov princes refused the crown no king was ever appointed. A governorship of collaborators took charge under Italian authority, and the country was increasingly wracked by battles between partisans and the Italian and German occupying forces and their Montenegrin militia, and between the pro-communist and pro-monarchy partisan groups. The warring factions within these two main groups included those seeking an independent Montenegro, union with Serbia, a federalised Yugoslavia and the lasting recognition or, better still, the dominance of either the Eastern Orthodox or Muslim faiths. From time to time various factions sought accommodation with the Italians and Germans in preference to any compromise with their countrymen. It was a particularly chaotic and merciless war.

In June 1941 King Peter II definitive stamps together with Yugoslav airmail and postage-due stamps were issued overprinted 'Montenegro' in both Roman and Cyrillic script together with the date of formal occupation, '*17-IV-41.*' Around the same time Italian stamps from the 'Imperial' definitive series were issued with 'Montenegro' in Cyrillic across the top or bottom – or, as is often the case, anywhere on the stamp (See Fig. 15.35a & 15.35b in colour section). Late in 1942 more King Peter II definitive and airmail stamps appeared with overprints signifying the use of Italian currency and the Roman script inscription '*Governatorato del Montenegro*' (Fig. 15.36). In due course an airmail set appeared that showed planes flying over deceptively peaceful countryside scenes (Fig. 15.37).

In May 1943, however, an unusual set appeared featuring scenes from traditional Montenegrin life together with a corresponding fragment of poetry on the reverse. The key was the image of Prince Bishop Peter II Petrovic-Njegos on the lowest and highest values (See Fig. 15.38 in colour section). Born in 1813 Njegos succeeded his uncle as Serbian Orthodox Prince Bishop of Montenegro at the age of 17. The warring tribal chiefs and blood feuds rendered stable government difficult, but Njegos turned his court into a 'senate', where the most powerful chiefs discussed and agreed policies under his authority, and a special armed force ensured the decisions were carried out. He faced several internal revolts, some backed up by Ottoman forces, but although occasionally defeated his strong relationship with Russia ensured his survival. By the time of his early death from tuberculosis in 1851 he had secured his country's southern border, crushed internal dissent, established schools, eased tensions with the Ottoman Turks,

Fig. 15.36

Fig. 15.37

and continued sound relations with Russia. Njegos was as much a renowned philosopher and poet as he was a ruler, and *The Mountain Wreath*, the subject of the set of stamps, has been hailed as the most influential Serbian poetical work. The poem tells of a probable, but not certain, massacre of Montenegrin Muslim converts, but sets the shocking event in the context of devoted Orthodox nationalists striving against colossal odds to ensure the survival of Montenegro with its rich culture and traditions. The massacre is deeply regretted but, Njegos seems to be saying, the converts should have been conscious of the values they were rejecting and diminishing. The poem has been used to justify persecution of Muslims as much as to heighten Montenegrin and Serbian nationalism. The 1943 stamp illustrations feature folk dances, people leaving church, a tribal wedding procession, an assembly of chiefs, swearing oaths of allegiance, a wounded standard bearer and scenes of Mount Lovcen, a national symbol, where Njegos himself is buried. They are using the national hero and his poem to reinforce the concept of Montenegrin nationalism while portraying the Italians as the liberators of Montenegro from its absorption into Yugoslavia.

When the Germans took over the occupation it is a mark of the significance of this elaborately produced set that it continued in use. With the 'Air' issue, it was overprinted several times, but far from obliterated, with inscriptions announcing the appointment of a '*Nationaler Verwaltungsausschuss 10.XI.1943*' ('National Administrative Committee') and, probably less seriously, raising money for Montenegran refugees ('*Flüchtlingshilfe Montenegro*') and the Red Cross ('*Crveni krst Montenegro*') (See Fig. 15.39 in colour section). In this context it may be significant that King Peter II definitive stamps, not the Montenegro set, were used in the first instance for overprints announcing the German military occupation – '*Deutsche Militaer-Verwaltung Montenegro*'. At this stage of the war the overstretched Germans were desperate enough to portray some sympathy with the population (Fig. 15.40).

Fig. 15.40

Restoration of Yugoslavia

King Peter spent most of his wartime exile in Great Britain, but gradually the British government lost faith in the pro-monarchy Serbian Chetniks and their dubious allegiance to the Allies and recognised Tito's communist partisans as the more popular and effective anti-German forces. As this transition of Allied commitment took place, Peter's hopes of restoration faded fast, especially in the final two years of the war.

On 27 March 1943 a set of four stamps picturing King Peter were issued by the government-in-exile to mark the second anniversary of the overthrow of the

Fig. 15.41

Fig. 15.42

regent, Prince Paul. A surcharge set raised money for the Red Cross, but both sets had limited UK circulation, largely among political sympathisers and stamp collectors (Fig. 15.41). Another set featuring historic Serb, Slovene and Croat patriots – including Prince Bishop Petar II Petrovic-Njegos – was produced for 1 December 1944 to mark the twenty-fifth anniversary of the formation of the Kingdom of Yugoslavia, but not issued.

Far more significant were the stocks of superannuated Serbian, Croatian, Slovenian, Hungarian and German stamps that from late 1944 onwards were overprinted with new currencies and inscriptions that collectively signalled Tito's recreation of Yugoslavia as a democratic federation of states. In December 1944 three Serbian stamps from the Monasteries set were issued overprinted Democratic Republic of Jugoslavia in Cyrillic and surcharged values (Fig. 15.42). Many similar overprinted inscriptions followed in May 1945. In Mostar twenty assorted Croatian stamps were overprinted with the Communist star, '*Demokratska Federativna Jugoslavija*' and new values, and another seventeen Croatian stamps received similar treatment in Split (See Fig. 15.43 in colour section). In Ljubljana the German set of Slovenian views was reissued overprinted '*Jugoslavija Slovenia*' together with the date '9.5 1945' and a star over the triple peak Slovenian badge. In Maribor the same overprints were used on Germany's Hitler head definitive set, and in Murska Sobota on Hungarian national heroes stamps of 1943–44 (Fig. 15.44). At the same time as the old Kingdom of Yugoslavia's disparate parts were symbolically brought

together in their new configuration by these common inscriptions a general Yugoslavian issue pictured Marshal Tito. Indeed, the first stamps in the Tito set were issued as early as February 1945.

Increasingly popular, the communist leader already possessed a firm grip upon the recreated country not only militarily but also politically. Officially, on 7 March 1945, Tito became the last Royal Yugoslav Prime Minister and Minister of Defence with British, American and Soviet Union support, and King Peter as a helpless accomplice. In August a People's Front was formed, comprising all the political parties willing to cooperate with the communists. It organised national elections for 11 November, but with only a single agreed list of candidates. Few demurred, and on 29 November the new Constituent Assembly abolished the monarchy, formally established a Federal People's Republic and confirmed Tito in his posts. A set of stamps featuring male and female workers marked the event, and throughout 1945, 1946 and 1947 a series of definitive stamps harked back to the partisan war with heroic pictures of male and female partisans in action. They included a view of medieval Jajce where on 29 November 1943 the rebuilding of Yugoslavia had begun with Bosnian and Herzegovinan partisan commanders agreeing to join a federal nation (Fig. 15.45).

During the war the partisans in Slovenia had spread their influence into the Istrian Peninsula lying between Fiume and Trieste. Despite savage campaigns by the Germans after the Italian surrender, the partisans managed to control much of the countryside and execute numerous Italian collaborators. As the Germans

Fig. 15.47

withdrew, Tito's Yugoslav Army advanced, and on 1 May 1945 entered Trieste where the executions continued. Almost immediately the Yugoslavs issued the set of Italian Social Republic stamps featuring the drummer and bombed cities overprinted with Trieste, the communist star, the date 1.V.1945, surcharged values and a firm black bar obliterating the Republic's nomenclature (See Fig. 15.46 in colour section). Several Social Republic stamps also appeared overprinted Fiume/Rijeka with the star, a rising sun symbol, the date 3-V-1945 and new values blocking out the Republic's name (Fig. 15.47).

On 20 June, though, the whole of the long contested region between Fiume and Trieste and stretching north past Udine was divided into two zones by agreement between Allied forces occupying Italy and Tito after a tense local stand-off. A line starting just south of Trieste stretched 15 or so miles to the east and then curved gently north-west to near Gorizia and then north along the Isonzo toward the Italian–Austrian border. Zone A to the west was placed under British and American military control, and Zone B to the east remained under Yugoslav occupation. The mainly Italian port of Pola in the far south of Zone B became an unhappy Zone A enclave in Yugoslav territory.

As numerous stamp issues revealed, Tito never gave up claims to permanent annexation of Zone B and indeed much of Zone A. In July 1945 various Italian stamps were overprinted '*Istra*' with higher values for use across the Zone B peninsula. From early August these were gradually replaced by a set of ten specially designed stamps transferring attention from the bitter past to a peaceful and pastoral future. The specially designed set was inscribed '*Istra*' and pictured scenes across Zone B of grapes, a donkey, a shoal of tunny, an olive branch, oxen ploughing, a castle on the coastline, the village birthplace of the anti-fascist patriot Vladimir Gortan, a famous viaduct across the Solkan that survived the war, and a symbolic scene of reconstruction amidst broken buildings (See Fig. 15.48a & 15.48b in colour section). Two years later the Treaty of Paris awarded Fiume (now Rijeka) and Istra to Yugoslavia.

Illustrations

Fig. 15.1 6*d* King Peter II definitive stamp (1939).

Fig. 15.2 1*d*+1*d* King Tomislav of Croatia (910–28) and 2*d*+2*d* Ante and Stjepan Radic brothers (killed in the National Assembly in 1928) stamps from the Zagreb Postal Employees' Fund set (1 March 1940).

Fig. 15.3 1.50d King Peter II stamps overprinted '*Co. Ci*' (26 April 1941) and '*R. Commissariato Civile Territori Sloveni occupati Lubiana*' (5 May 1941).

Fig. 15.4 50c and 1.75l Italian definitive, 25c and 2l Airmail, 1.25l Express Letter and 5c Postage Due stamps overprinted by the Germans with '*Provinz Laibach*' and '*Pokrajina Ljubljanika*' bordering the Carniola spread eagle emblem (January–March 1944).

Fig. 15.5 2.50l Italian express letter stamps with German Red Cross and Homeless Relief Fund overprints and surcharges (18 March 1944).

Fig. 15.6 20c Borovnice Viaduct, 2l Kostanejevica Castle and Monastery, and 10l Otocec Castle from the Landscapes set (1945).

Fig. 15.7 0.50d King Peter II stamp overprinted '*Zona Occupata Fiumano Kupa*' (16 May 1941).

Fig. 15.8 0.50d King Peter II stamps further overprinted 'O.N.M.I' and '*Pro Maternita e Infanzia*' (2 June 1942). 50p King Peter II stamp overprinted '*Memento Avdere Semper Bvccari*' and l1 surcharge (17 May 1941).

Fig. 15.9 Souvenir cover with Italian 'Imperial' definitive, express letter and War Propaganda stamps overprinted 'Zara' in between rows of black bars (4 November 1943).

Fig. 15.10 Cover with Italian 'Imperial' definitive stamps overprinted '*Deutsche Militärverwaltung Kotor*' and new values (9 October 1943). Cover with King Peter II stamps overprinted with bars obliterating the old kingdom's name and currency, and new German values and '*Boka Kotorska*' (16 September 1944).

Fig. 15.11 Souvenir cover with the three initial Croatian overprints on King Peter II stamps (1941). The cover's '*Pomoc*' ('Help') postmark refers to the National Relief Fund campaign in July 1942.

Fig. 15.12 0.25d King Peter II stamp with the Founding of the Croatian Army overprint (10 May 1941).

Fig. 15.13 Yugoslav 1.50d+1.50d Kaminta Gatre, Zagreb and 4d+3d Zagreb Cathedral overprinted '*Nezavisna Drzava Hrvatska*' ('Independent State Of Croatia') and labels marking the Brod Philatelic Exhibition (10 May 1941).

Fig. 15.14 The 75b Varazdin stamp from the Views set (1941–42), the 2k Zagreb Cathedral stamp reissued with the anniversary inscription '1941–1942 10.IV' and chequerboard (10 April 1942) and the 100k Banja Luka stamp reissued for the Philatelic Exhibition there (13 June 1942).

Fig. 15.15 Stamp commemorating the Zagreb Philatelic Exhibition (12 September 1943) and available the same day with the inscription '*Hrvatsko More 8.IX.1943*' celebrating the return of Sibenik after the Italian surrender.

Fig. 15.16 Eastern Front Volunteer Fund stamp (3 December 1941).

Fig. 15.17 Croat Legion Relief Fund miniature sheet (1 July 1943).

Fig. 15.18 Aviation Fund miniature sheet (25 March 1942).

Fig. 15.19 Examples from Red Cross sets: 4k+4k Turopolje regional costume (12 October 1941), and 4k+2k Bosnian regional costume (4 October 1942).

Fig. 15.20 Examples from National Relief Fund sets : 4*k*+2*k* 'Pomoc' Triumphal Arch (5 July 1942) and 7*k*+3.50*k* the martyrdom of St Sebastian (15 February 1944).

Fig. 15.21 Famous Croats set (3) (7 June 1943).

Fig. 15.22 Croatian Storm Division set (Certificated) (9 January 1945).

Fig. 15.23 12.50*k*+287.50*k* Jure Ritter Francetic stamp (22 May 1944).

Fig. 15.24 Illustrated first day cover with the Croat Ustasa Youth Fund set and Senj postmark (22 November 1942).

Fig. 15.25 Pavelic Youth Fund miniature sheet (10 April 1943).

Fig15.26 Labour Front miniature sheet (20 August 1944).

Fig. 15.27 2*d* King Peter II and 40*d* Airmail stamps with diagonal *'Serbien'* overprints (5 June 1941).

Fig. 15.28 Overprinted 20*d* King Peter II stamp from the Airmail set (5 July 1942).

Fig. 15.29 Smederevo Explosion Relief Fund miniature sheet (22 September 1941).

Fig. 15.30 Prisoners of War Fund (5 December 1941). Se-tenant strip from the 1*d*+3*d* sheet with 'C' stamp with facing left, pale stamp forming part of the cross, and 'C' stamp facing right + ordinary sheet stamp.

Fig. 15.31 7*d*+13*d* Mother and Children from the War Orphans' Fund set (13 September 1942). War Invalids' Fund miniature sheet (16 May 1943).

Fig. 15.32 Anti-Masonic Exhibition Set (1 January 1942).

Fig. 15.33 1.50*d* Ravanica from the Monasteries set (3 September 1942).

Fig. 15.34 16*d* Studenica from the Monasteries set reissued overprinted for the Bombing of Nish Relief Fund (11 December 1943).

Fig. 15.35 1.50*d* King Peter II stamp overprinted 'Montenegro' in Roman and Cyriilic script and date '17-IV-41-XIX'. Cover with Italian 'Imperial' series definitive and Airmail stamps overprinted 'Montenegro' in Cyrillic (June 1941).

Fig. 15.36 8*d* King Peter II stamp overprinted *'Governatorato del Montenegro'* and *'Valore Lire'*.

Fig. 15.37 2*l* Budva and 20*l* Mount Durmitor (20*l*) from the Airmail set (1943).

Fig. 15.38 20*l* Prince Bishop Peter II Petrovic-Njegos and 1.25*l* 'Taking the Oath' and fragment of poem from the National Poem set (9 May 1943).

Fig. 15.39 Examples of Italian Montenegro National Poem and Airmail stamps overprinted by German military authorities *'Nationaler Verwaltungsausschuss 10.XI.1943'* (November 1943), *'Flüchtlingshilfe Montengero'* and surcharged (22 May 1944) and *'Crveni krst Montenegro'* and surcharged (August 1944).

Fig. 15.40 4*d* King Peter II stamp overprinted by German military authorities *'Deutsches Militaer-Verwaltung Montenegro'* with black bars and new values in liras.

Fig. 15.41 Souvenir cover with Yugoslav Government-in-Exile Second Anniversary of Royalist Coup set (27 March 1943).

Fig. 15.42 7*d*+3*d* Serbian Monasteries stamp overprinted 'Democratic Republic of Yugoslavia' in Cyrillic and surcharged (December 1944).

Fig. 15.43 First day souvenir card with Croatian stamps overprinted in Mostar with the star and '*Demokratska Federativna Jugoslavija*' and new values (1 May 1945).

Fig. 15.44 10*c* Slovenian stamp overprinted in Ljubljana with the star and triple peak emblem and '*Jugoslavija Slovenia 9*5 1945*' and the similarly overprinted 70*f* Hungarian stamp from Murska Sobota and 42*pf* German Hitler head stamp from Maribor (June 1945).

Fig. 15.45 5*d* Jajce, 4*d* Tito and 16*d* Partisans from the Yugoslav set (1945–47).

Fig. 15.46 Souvenir cover with Italian Social Republic stamps overprinted with red or black bars and stars, 'Trieste', the date '1.V.45' and new values by Tito's Yugoslav government.

Fig. 15.47 Italian Social Republic stamps overprinted by Tito's Yugoslav government '3.V.1945', 'Fiume/Rijeka', a star and rising sun, and new values.

Fig. 15.48 Cover with a mix of Italian Social Republic and Italian Airmail stamps (without fasces) overprinted ISTRA and new values by Tito's Yugoslav government (July 1945). Souvenir cover with the set of ZONE B views (February – March 1946).

16

GREECE

The Classically styled wartime stamp issues of Greece bore little relation to the horrors inflicted upon it during the Axis occupation as resistance groups fought among themselves as well as against the Italians, Germans and Bulgarians.

For centuries Greeks had lived with varying degrees of repression within the vast European lands of the Ottoman Empire, but with the naval and diplomatic help of Great Britain, France and Imperial Russia they had achieved independence by 1829. During the nineteenth and early twentieth centuries Greece sought to enlarge its territory to include more of the Greeks who had lived under Ottoman rule. In due course the Ottomans ceded Thessaly, and Great Britain gave Greece the string of Ionian Islands along its west coast when the pro-British King George I ascended the throne in 1863. During the First Balkan War of 1912–13, Greece, Bulgaria, Serbia and Montenegro defeated the ill-organised Ottoman Turks and at the peace settlement Greece secured Crete, several Aegean islands and southern Macedonia. During the ensuing Second Balkan War against Bulgaria, Greece secured Western Thrace, and, after Bulgaria's further defeat in the First World War, Greece was awarded Eastern Thrace with the exception of a small slice of land surrounding Istanbul. At this time Greece also gained northern Epirus from Albania but lost it again in 1924 when Mussolini successfully lobbied on behalf of Albanian interests.

Not surprisingly, by the 1930s the region was seething with ethnic, religious and political discontent, and much of this partisan fury was let loose throughout the 1940s. A pair of Greek stamps inscribed '*Entente Balkanique*' and featuring the arms of Greece, Turkey, Romania and Yugoslavia inadvertently revealed the seething jealousies. In 1934, and again in February 1940, these four nations agreed to suspend all territorial claims against each other and their neighbours, but significantly Italy, Bulgaria, Hungary, Albania and the Soviet Union, all of whom desired expansion and greater influence in the the region, had refused to sign. Italy and Bulgaria in particular looked jealously upon Greece's recent territorial aggrandisement (Fig. 16.1).

Fig. 16.1

An over confident Mussolini tried to emulate Hitler's military successes, and invaded Greece by way of Albania in October 1940. But the country was defiant and the far smaller Greek Army held the Italians at bay and even triumphantly occupied southern Albania for several months – during which it enforced the use of overprinted Greek stamps (See Fig. 16.2 in colour section). However, on 6 April 1941 Hitler decided to secure the Balkans by delaying his invasion of the Soviet Union and conquering Yugoslavia and Greece first. Erupting first from Bulgaria and then from conquered Yugoslavia, German forces overran Greece in just over a month, sweeping aside Greek, British, Australian and New Zealand troops, and later launching a successful but costly airborne landing on Allied-held Crete.

Greece was pulled apart by the victors. Germany retained authority over key strategic areas including Athens, central Macedonia, eastern Thrace, western Crete and several important Aegean islands. Hitler threw western Thrace, eastern Macedonia and a few islands to Bulgaria, and allowed Italy to control the rest of the country, which was mainly rural in character. Initially the growth of resistance was slow, but by the time of the Italian surrender in 1943 partisan units were better organised, and the most violent and long-lasting guerrilla war outside the Soviet Union was well under way. The Germans, aided by Greek collaborators and Bulgarians, seized the military initiative from the Italians, as well as all the territory granted to them earlier. A particularly grim series of campaigns were launched against both the communist and right-wing guerrillas – who, when they not fighting the occupiers, were hounding and killing each other.

King George II fled to Crete, then Egypt and on to Great Britain, but the king remained a divisive rather than a unifying figurehead. The Communist Party had had widespread, although not overwhelming, support in pre-war Greece, and George had allowed himself to be allied with the right-wing dictatorship of Ioannis Metaxis to secure political stability, and his throne. Nevertheless the monarchy remained recognised by the Western Allies, and the soldiers, airmen, sailors, and warships that escaped after the invasion were formed into Royal Hellenic units under Allied command.

A Greek puppet government was establishment by the three occupying powers but its authority was severely limited because neither the occupiers nor the people as a whole trusted it. The government's use of mainly anti-communist Nazi and fascist collaborators, and the creation of brutal Security Battalions whose main targets were communists and their real and alleged sympathisers, did nothing for its general popularity. By the summer of 1943 most Jews in the Bulgarian and German occupied zones had been deported to concentration camps, and then the Germans concentrated upon the ex-Italian regions and islands. Despite a number of Greek communities bravely hiding Jews, the great majority perished.

Many Greeks died too. The beleaguered government had little control over the rapacious exploitation of agricultural produce and raw materials by all the Axis powers. Up to 300,000 Greeks died of hunger in and around Athens in the winter of 1941–42. And the endless rounds of sabotage, ambushes and assassinations, and ensuing arrests, torture and executions, led to the estimated death of 21,000 Greeks at the hands of the Germans, and 9,000 by the Italians. However, 40,000 Greeks were killed by the Bulgarians, whose crude attempts to 'Bulgarise' the north-east Greek provinces caused outrage and widespread resistance. Everything Greek – language, schools, newspapers and place names – became Bulgarian, and thousands were expelled, deported or executed to make way for Bulgarian settlers. Bulgarian stamps, not Greek, were mandatory. When the Italians occupied the Ionian Islands to the west of the Greek mainland they treated them as new Italian colonies rather than an occupied country, and introduced Italian stamps overprinted '*Isole Jonie*' as part of a policy, albeit less harsh than the Bulgarians in Macedonia, of cultural Italianisation. When the Germans took over they merely added 'Greece 2.10.43' to the overprinted stamp, signalling its return to that country (See Fig. 16.3a & 16.3b in colour section).

Nothing controversial appeared on any stamps issued by the puppet government. There was no hint of any German or Italian connections, or any sign of anti-communist propaganda. Instead there was a modest and, everyone probably realised, hopeless attempt to unify the nation by recalling its ancient gods and historic sites. But at least it solved the problem of what designs to put on the stamps.

To the ancient Greeks winds were gods. Each was associated with a season and the state of the weather, and each was recognised by the direction in which it blew. They were sometimes represented as horses from the stables of the storm god Aeolus but more often as winged men, as portrayed in two sets of wartime stamps. There were four chief winds: Zephyr, the west wind who brought the welcome spring and early summer breezes, is pictured holding a harvest of fruit and flowers; Notus, the south wind who brought the storms of late summer and autumn, holds an amphora of wine or grain; Boreas, the north wind of cold winter, clutches a conch shell symbolising the roar of storms; and Euros, the east wind who could interrupt the others at any time of the year, was often seen holding an upturned vase giving, or wasting, valuable water. There were also four lesser winds: Lips, the south-west wind, can be seen controlling the stern and steering of a ship; Apeliotes, the south-east wind, whose cloak safely holds fruit and ears of corn; Skiron, the north-west wind, who clutches a cauldron heralding winter; and Kaikias, the north-east wind, whose curved shield is full of hailstones. Like all Greek deities, these gods acted on whims, or on thoughts of revenge or reward, and brought happiness and misery to humans in about equal measure (Fig. 16.4).

Between 1942 and 1944 an increasingly lengthy set, whose values finally ranged from 2 to 5,000,000 drachmae, was forced upon the government by rampant inflation largely caused by the forced 'war loan'

Fig. 16.4

to Germany, together with vast payments covering the costs of occupation. The selection of supremely attractive historic sites included the windmills on Mykonos, the fortress at Heraklion on Crete, Meteora Monastery high on the sandstone pillar on the edge of the Plain of Thessaly, the grand villas on the island of Hydra, Mount Athos Monastery, the famous city of Edessa in Macedonia, the island of Corfu, the castle at Burzi on the island of Skiathos, the high-arched stepped bridge across the Aoos River at Konitza in Epirus, and Ekatontapiliani Church at Paros (Fig. 16.5). The serenity of the sites belies the facts that famine decimated the population of Hydra in 1943–44, much of Muslim Konitsa was destroyed towards the end of the war, the Germans deliberately set fire to Edessa in 1944 in retaliation for a soldier shot there, and many lives were lost on Corfu in the German bombardment after the Italian surrender.

Fig. 16.5

Fig. 16.6

In one direct reference to the ravages of war, in June 1944 five stamps from the Views set and five from the Winds set were reissued surcharged 100,000 drachmae in aid of the victims of an Allied air raid on the important port of Piraeus, not far from Athens. The set was much delayed as the RAF attack had occurred on 11 January (Fig. 16.6). Disease,

Fig. 16.8

Fig. 16.9

hunger, homelessness, shattered families and abject poverty were widespread, but no Red Cross Fund sets were forthcoming from the government. Instead there were a number of specific charity issues which were mandatory on mail for a period of time – usually three or four weeks from the date of issue. The Postal Staff Anti-Tuberculosis Fund was targeted a number of times through surcharges and inscriptions overprinted on ordinary stamps, such as the otherwise superannuated 1927 ones picturing the Monastery of Simon Peter and Corinth Canal and reissued in December 1942 and December 1943 respectively (See Fig. 16.7 in colour section). In October 1943 three stamps picturing a child, a mother and child and the Madonna and Jesus were issued for a Child Welfare Fund (Fig. 16.8). In July 1944, when the internal military, political and economic situation was utterly chaotic, another ten stamps from the Winds and Views series were reissued inscribed and overprinted '50,000 + 450,000 drachmae' for postage and a surcharge on behalf on the Children's Convalescent Camp Fund (Fig. 16.9).

The Germans started to withdraw from Greece in late 1944 to avoid being trapped by the Soviet armies advancing westwards across the Balkans to their north. British forces landed and freed Athens on 14 October, but there was no peace until 1949 when the British- and American-backed forces of the returning government-in-exile finally triumphed over the communists. King George himself only returned in September 1946 after a general election and a plebiscite in the middle of the civil war that decided in favour of a parliamentary monarchy system of government. Not surprisingly these decisions incited a violent communist backlash, and not surprisingly the hard-pressed government promoted its cause through a series of dramatic stamp issues. In October 1945 a set inscribed with the word '*OXI*' ('NO') glorified the exact day five years earlier when Greece defied the Italian ultimatum, and on various dates that year a series was issued celebrating the famous moment in the struggle for independence when, in the 1820s, the citizens of the island of Psara blew up their hilltop fort and magazine together with themselves and a large part of the Ottoman invading force (Fig. 16.10). That December a set of black-edged stamps mourned the death of President Roosevelt, in September 1946 the pre-war King George II stamps returned along with the king himself, and then a Victory set featured Greek troops in Albania and in Italy, the Greek memorial at El Alamein, and Greek women transporting supplies in the successful Greek battle of the Pindos Mountains against the Italians (Fig. 16.11).

Fig. 16.10

Fig. 16.11

Illustrations

Fig. 16.1 8*d* Entente Balkanique stamp (27 May 1940).

Fig. 16.2 Souvenir cover postmarked 26 December 1940 with Greek stamps overprinted for use in occupied Albania.

Fig. 16.3 75*c* King Victor Emmanuel III I 'Imperial' series stamp overprinted '*Isole Jonie*' (April 1941) and souvenir cover (certificated) with the six stamps the Germans additionally overprinted 'Greece 2.10.43' (22 October 1943).

Fig. 16.4 5*d* Notus stamp from the Airmail Winds sets (15 August 1942).

Fig. 16.5 75*d* Edessa from the Historic Views sets (15 September 1944).

Fig. 16.6 15*d* Heraklion, Crete from the Views set surcharged and overprinted in aid of victims of the Piraeus air raid (11 June 1944).

Fig. 16.7 1927 25*d* Monastery of Simon Peter and 5*d* Corinth Canal overprinted with 10 drachmae surcharge and Anti-TB Fund inscription reissued on 1 December 1942 and 1 December 1943 respectively.

Fig. 16.8 25*d*+25*d* Child from the Child Welfare Fund set (1 October 1943).

Fig. 16.9 10*d* Apiliotis stamp from the Winds set surcharged and overprinted for the Children's Convalescent Camp Fund (20 July 1944).

Fig. 16.10 20*d* 'OXI' stamp from the Resistance to the Italian Ultimatum set (28 October 1945) and 3*d* stamp from the 'Glory' of Psara set (March–August 1945).

Fig. 16.11 60*d* stamp from the President Roosevelt mourning set (21 December 1945), surcharged 8*d* stamp from the Restoration of King George II set (28 September 1946), and 500*d* Greek infantry in Albania stamp from the Victory set (October 1946–May 1947).

17

THE SOVIET UNION

To the surprise and horror of Josif Stalin, the First Secretary of the Communist Party, at dawn on the 22 June 1941 3 million troops of his erstwhile ally, Nazi Germany, invaded Soviet territory backed up by 3,600 tanks, 7,000 artillery guns and 2,500 aircraft. Since September 1939 a Treaty of Friendship had existed between the two nations, with the recent brutal defeat and partition of Poland agreed between them as well as extensive trade agreements. Admittedly the treaty was one of short-term convenience between the two countries whose leaders loathed the ideologies underpinning each other's regimes and remained deeply suspicious of each other's territorial ambitions. Hitler believed the speedy military defeat of Soviet Russia was essential to his extension and consolidation of power across western and middle Europe, and notably the final defeat of troublesome Great Britain. The campaign – called Operation Barbarossa in honour of a formidable medieval German warrior – was brilliantly successful in its initial three-pronged onslaught.

The Baltic states of Estonia, Latvia and Lithuania, recently annexed and terrorised by the Soviet Union under the agreement with Hitler, were quickly annexed and terrorised by Germany. German forces spread eastwards across the Soviet Union seizing numerous cities and, literally, millions of prisoners in the floundering and encircled armies belatedly trying to mount counter-attacks. Leningrad in the north, Moscow in the centre and the Crimea in the south were the primary targets. By the beginning of July Hitler jubilantly assumed the total defeat of the Soviet Union was imminent, but Stalin was beginning to recover from the personal shock that had caused a total paralysis of his will.

The vastness of the Soviet Union, the ultimate inadequacy of German forces and supply lines, the interference of Hitler in military decisions, the enhanced output of Soviet factories relocated safely behind the Caucasus mountains, and the sheer numbers and powers of endurance of Russian troops all contributed to the eventual demise of Barbarossa in the greatest conflict in military history and certainly the most costly in terms of lives lost. Stalin never envisaged the surrender of the Soviet Union, whatever the cost in terms of destruction and loss of life, and he stiffened the resolve of his generals with the dismissal, imprisonment and even execution of those who lacked the necessary aggression in the face of the continuing German onslaught. Since its inception in 1917, the Bolshevik leadership had fully appreciated the power of continual propaganda promoting the benefits and achievements of the new state, especially in comparison with the former Tsarist regime, and lauding the heroic efforts of devoted communist workers. The regime never let the darker truth of countless deaths through poverty, forced migration and the purges of real and imagined dissidents get in the way of an uplifting story, and it ensured that all aspects of regional cultures and traditions were suppressed in favour of the overarching Communist ideologies.

The desperate wartime struggle altered this long-standing practice. In their ignorance of German racial intolerance, many people in the western Soviet republics, notably the Ukrainians and Cossacks, hailed the invaders as liberators from centralised Communist tyranny. They were soon disabused, but nevertheless thousands of former Soviet citizens preferred military service under German authority to the punitive hardship of German prisoner-of-war camps. However, just as Tsarist Russia had called upon its hard-hit and largely demoralised citizens to rally in opposition to the 1812 invasion by Napoleon Bonaparte by appealing to their latent, and hopefully overriding, loyalty to their motherland, so Stalin adopted a similar approach using all the propaganda resources at his disposal. He, in common with the tsars, recognised that, whatever the people's perceptions of the current regime, there existed a deeper, and older, legacy of stubborn devotion to what was often termed 'Mother Russia' – a mystical, part-religious, part-pagan concept of a land that at its best, whether in the distant past or distant future, provided for and protected its people. In turn, its people, and their leaders, must protect the land. It was a sacred duty that surpassed secular patriotism. In the dark days of 1941 Stalin accepted that religion and regionalism must join Communism in motivating and uniting the disparate peoples of the Soviet Union to face the invaders.

Stamps had always softened the harsh realities of Soviet dictatorship through the cult of the heroic citizen and reverence for Lenin, the creator of the Bolshevik state, but now their images and inscriptions took on radical new dimensions. The first wartime stamp, issued in August 1941, reproduced a Soviet poster of a

Fig. 17.1   Fig. 17.2   Fig. 17.3

mother quietly seeing her uniformed son off to war. There is a stoical parting and the clear message is that patriotism transcends family feeling and both mother and son are calmly doing what the state expects of them (Fig. 17.1). The second stamp, in the desperate times of December 1941, was more wide-ranging in its exhortations, and featured the hammer and sickle flag accompanying a heroic band of citizens. They were all in civilian clothes, and seemed to vary widely in age, but leading them forward were the archetypical young communist male and female workers enthusiastically raising the nation's flag aloft (Fig. 17.2).

Soon, though, the images underwent a drastic change. In January 1942 a pair of stamps targeted a particular ethnic group. They commemorated Mir Ali Shir (1441–1501), the renowned and influential Uzbek poet, musician, composer, painter and sculptor whose fame still shone brightly among the Muslims of the southern Soviet Union (Fig. 17.3). In April 1943 a set marked the life of the famous explorer Vitus Bering (1681–1741) who spent much of his life in the service of Tsar Peter the Great surveying the Russian–Siberian coast and the west coast of America, and seeking the elusive north-east passage between Asia and North America (Fig. 17.4). Not surprisingly, in October 1943 a pair of stamps commemorated the playwright Ivan Turgenev (1818–83), whose works spoke of the stultifying Tsarist regime, the tortured emotions of those seeking self-fulfilment in this depressing atmosphere, the hopes for radical change, and, by contrast, the eternal glories of the forests, rivers and plains of the vast Russian countryside (Fig. 17.5).

Fig. 17.4

Fig. 17.5

The popular Russian fables elaborated upon, or completely invented, by Ivan Krylov (1769–1844) were marked by an issue in November 1944, even though Krylov himself was much praised and rewarded by the Tsars. For the wartime Communist regime, though, he had the virtue of popularising essentially Russian stories delighting in, and sometimes satirising Russian characteristics. His witty and 'knowing' stories, it was said, made Russians everywhere appreciate they were Russian (Fig. 17.6). Far less popular with the Tsarist authorities was Alexander Griboedev (1795–1829) whose major work, the verse comedy *Wit Works Woe* (or *Woe from Wit*) satirising the repressive nature of Imperial Russia's minutely stratified society, was banned from publication in his lifetime. He, too, was celebrated in a pair of stamps in January 1945, with

Fig. 17.6

the aim, it is reasonable to assume, of showing that the Communists were the people's
liberators (Fig. 17.7).

No doubt it was the orchestral pieces
and operas of Nikolai Rimsky-Korsakov
(1844–1908), such as *Scheherazade, The
Snow Maiden, Sadko* and *Tsar Saltan*, which
celebrated treasured Russian traditions
and stories, together with his commitment
to creating an essentially Russian style of
musical composition, that led him, despite
his lengthy service in the Tsar's navy, to
be honoured with a set of stamps in July
1944 (Fig. 17.8). In similar vein, the pre-war
denigration of the stubbornly independent-
minded Cossack culture was reversed in the
stamps issued in November 1944 ostensibly
to mark the centenary of the birth of the
painter Ilya Repin (1844–1930). Alongside
his portrait, they replicated his huge canvas
Reply of the Cossacks to Sultan Mahmoud IV,
painted during the 1880s, which pictured
the Cossacks living near the Dneiper River
in 1676 jauntily compiling their reply, full
of insults and profanities, to the Sultan's
demand that they submit themselves to his
rule (Fig. 17.9).

Contemporary writers could be propaganda tools too, such as Maxim Gorky

Fig. 17.7

Fig. 17.8

Fig. 17.9

Fig. 17.10

(1868–1936) in June 1943. In a life bespattered with controversy, Gorky had publicly opposed the Tsarist regime and suffered arrest as a consequence. He had
befriended Lenin, who later warned him against criticising civil repression. In
1929 Stalin enticed him back to Moscow from self-imposed exile in Capri, and
he received copious gifts and honours for his favourable portrayal of communist
life, even in the gulags. It did not stop him being arrested in the purges of 1935,
with his death soon afterwards creating widespread if only whispered suspicions
about secret service involvement in his passing (Fig. 17.10). Another pair of
stamps in October 1943 celebrated the poet Vladimir Mayakovsky's (1893–1930)
pre-revolution agitation and post-revolution works encouraging Bolshevik troops
to eliminate counter-revolutionary White Russian forces. His *Left March! For the
Red Marines 1918* led him to become the most celebrated contemporary Soviet
poet. In the end, though, he shot himself, disillusioned, perhaps like Gorky,
with the stultifying atmosphere of the new regime – nothing had really changed

Fig. 17.11

(Fig. 17.11). It was their formidable literary output, though, that was remembered, not their dismal deaths.

Interspersed with these issues heightening devotion to regions and cultures, but firmly within the Communist version of the Motherland, there were many others extolling the heroism of rural and industrial workers and also individual soldiers and pilots.

During the war Stalin ordered the restoration of traditional badges of military rank and also phased in a series of awards for distinguished service, most named after famous Russian generals and admirals of the past. These awards were publicised in no less than four sets of stamps. They included the Order of the Great Patriotic War, Order of Suvorov, Order of Kutusov, Order of Ushakov, Order of Nakhimov, Order of Bogdan Chmielnitsky and Order of Alexander Nevsky (See Fig. 17.12 in colour section).

The term 'Great Patriotic War' referred to the 1941 German invasion, but previously the title had referred to the defence of the Motherland against Napoleon's invasion in 1812 and the Germans and Austrians in the First World War. Stalin was reverting to the same carrot and stick approach as his predecessors. Count Alexander Suvorov (1729–1800) was a general distinguished by his speed, aggression and success against the Ottoman Turks, Polish rebels and French revolutionary armies, and also by the devotion he inspired in his men. Field Marshal Mikhail Kutuzov (1745–1813) was, perhaps, the most illustrious Tsarist general, achieving lasting fame for his defence of Russia against Napoleon, inflicting huge casualties in the particularly bloody battle of Borodino and hounding the French during their terrible retreat. Fyodor Ushakov (1744–1817) was a renowned admiral who imposed a series of defeats on Turkish fleets during the Russo-Turkish War of 1787–92, and later successfully assaulted Revolutionary France's Mediterranean bases in Corfu, the Ionian Islands and Naples. Another admiral, Pavel Nakhimov (1802–55) skilfully outmanoeuvred and annihilated the Turkish fleet and fiercely defended Sevastopol against repeated French and British attacks during the Crimean War. Bogdan Chmielnitsky (c.1595–1657) was a controversial figure in Cossack history, but his leadership in wrestling Ukrainian Cossack territory free from Polish and Lithuanian control was undoubtedly the reason for the creation of a medal in his name rather than his treaty with the Russian Tsar that led eventually to the Cossack state's loss of independence. The most celebrated figure was Alexander Nevsky (1220–63), a charismatic ruler of the medieval Russian state of Novgorod, whose stunning defeats of the invading Swedes and north German Teutonic Knights became moments of lasting national pride. His call that 'Whoever will come upon us with a sword, by the sword will perish' became the cry of patriots, and Sergei Eistenstein's 1938 film on his victory over the Teutonic Knights on the frozen Lake of Peipus heightened the popular reverence of his name.

Alongside the issues rallying support through appeals to carefully selected historical events and figures, the heroic achievements of current servicemen of far more humble rank were eulogised in several series of vividly drawn commemorative stamps. In November 1942 a series pictured five Heroes of the Soviet Union, all killed trying to stem the initial German onslaught in 1941 (See Fig. 17.13 in colour section). Lieutenant Viktor Talalikhin was a night fighter pilot who rammed an enemy plane, Captain Nikolai Gastello drove his blazing plane into an enemy fuel depot, Major General Lev Dovator was a daring cavalry commander killed courageously defending Ruza, and Alexander Checkalin and Zoya Kosmodemyanskaya were youthful resistance fighters tortured and hanged by the Germans. Their key propaganda value was their continuing courage and aggression right up to their deaths. Zoya became an icon for many soldiers, and the stamp shows the young girl being led away by her German captors to be hanged after withstanding interrogation, and, some accounts say, torture and rape. Doubts were cast upon some of these stories after the war – notably whether Captain Gastello deliberately aimed his damaged plane at the tanks or it was merely beyond his control, and also whether Checkalin and Kosmodemyanskaya were betrayed by captured colleagues or by local peasants who opposed the partisans' acts of destruction to ensure villages did not fall intact into German hands. During the war, though, they were hailed as Heroes of the Soviet Union at a desperate time in Russian history. Several of these dramatically illustrated stamps were reissued in April 1944.

That July new Heroes of the Soviet Union were celebrated in equally heroic style. One was the young Chechen machine-gunner Khan-pasha Nuradilov, credited with over 900 kills in his all-too-brief service career before his death near Stalingrad in 1942. Two others were Alexander Matrosov, who threw himself onto a German pill-box, blocking its machine gun with his chest to allow his colleagues to advance, and a highly successful and much decorated fighter pilot, Boris Safanov, who was eventually killed defending an Allied convoy around the Kola Peninsula in the far north-west of Russia. Finally there were two celebrated female snipers, Natalya Kovshova and Mariya Polivanova. Their short but notable careers ended when they were wounded and trapped, with their rifle ammunition exhausted, by a party of Germans. Spurning capture and inevitable execution, Natalya released the pin on a grenade and blew up several Germans coming towards them as well as themselves (See Fig. 17.14 in colour plates).

Interspersed with these inspiring issues were others that eulogised the strenuous but devoted labour of ordinary citizens and the heroic actions of anonymous serving soldiers. Unlike most other war-torn countries there were no stamps with relief fund surcharges – personal sacrifices, even death, were expected of civilians as much as soldiers. Historians make much of the ferocious centralisation of the Soviet Union, the ruthless labour schedules expected of its citizens, and the omnipresent threats of savage punishment for the slightest reluctance to obey orders, but at a time of utter crisis and faced with an equally brutal enemy one

Fig. 17.15

Fig. 17.17

Fig. 17.18

way or another the people rallied to the 'Motherland' and were justifiably proud of their sacrifices and achievements. The propaganda was shrewd but not necessarily cynical. A set in 1942–43 pictured food packers, women sewing uniforms, and parcels being distributed to soldiers (Fig. 17.15). Alongside this, a set contained vivid action pictures of anti-tank gunners, guerrillas attacking a train, hidden wireless signallers, machine-gunners about to open fire and the determined defenders of Leningrad, and it did not forget the munitions workers (See Fig. 17.16 in colour section). Another set in 1943 pictured snipers, anti-tank troops, mine throwers and army scouts, and also military nurses (Fig. 17.17). As the fortunes of war turned in the Soviet Union's favour, the battle for Moscow and Leningrad and the liberation of Stalingrad, Sevastopol and Odessa were celebrated, and so was the final liberation of Russian soil in 1945 (See Fig. 17.18, and 17.19a & 17.19b in colour section). And of course, as the postcard in Fig. 17.20 (the translation for which can be found on p. 202) reveals, most ordinary Russian soldiers – as soldiers everywhere – held fast to thoughts of the women they had left behind.

Fig. 17.20

Fig. 17.21

The Soviet regime carefully balanced all the issues drawing upon past and often tsarist glories, sanctioning regional cultures and identities, and eulogising ordinary citizens' virtues with numerous issues heightening the achievements and authority of the Communist leadership. In January 1943 a set of stamps mixed military scenes with images of Lenin to mark the twenty-fifth anniversary of the Russian Revolution, in September 1943 Karl Marx, the author of *The Communist Manifesto*, was remembered, and in October 1943 two sets picturing battle scenes were firmly linked to the twenty-fifth anniversaries of the Red Army and Navy and the Young Communist League (Fig. 17.21). In May 1944, when Soviet armies were approaching the German border, the powerful legacy of the founder of the state was remembered in a set entitled 'Twenty Years Without Lenin'

Fig. 17.22

(Fig. 17.22). The set nevertheless ensured Stalin was portrayed as Lenin's political and ideological heir. As post-war Soviet policies revealed only too clearly, there was no further thought of encouraging regional identities and culture, and the heroics of the tsarist past were quickly forgotten, as indeed were the astounding wartime efforts of ordinary citizens. Everything emanating from the Kremlin signalled that it was Stalin and the Communist regime who had saved the nation.

Illustrations

Fig. 17.1 Mass Mobilisation stamp (August 19412).

Fig. 17.2 National Defence stamp (December 1941).

Fig. 17.3 30k Portrait from the fifth centenary of the birth of Mir Ali Shir (January 1942).

Fig. 17.4 30k Bering sailing round Mount St Ilya from the Bicentenary of the Death of Vitus Bering set (April 1943).

Fig. 17.5 30k Portrait from the 125th Anniversary of the Birth of Ivan Turgenev set (October 1943).

Fig. 17.6 1r Portrait from the centenary of the death Ivan Krylov (November 1944).

Fig. 17.7 60k Portrait from 150th Anniversary of the Birth of Alexander Griboedev set (January 1945).

Fig. 17.8 60k Portrait from the centenary of the birth of Nikolai Rimsky-Korsakov (July 1944).

Fig. 17.9 60k *Reply of the Cossacks to Sultan Mahmoud IV* from the Birth Centenary of Ilya Repin set (November 1944).

Fig. 17.10 60k Portrait from the seventy-fifth anniversary of the birth of Maxim Gorky (June 1943).

Fig. 17.11 30k Portrait from the fiftieth anniversary of the birth of Vladimir Mayakovsky (October 1943).

Fig. 17.12 15k Order of the Great Patriotic War, 20k Order of Alexander Nevsky (May–June 1944) and 2r Order of Bogdan Chmielnitsky (February 1945) from the War Orders and Medals series.

Fig. 17.13 30k Captain Nikolai Gastello, 1k Alexander (Shura) Checkalin, 2k Zoe (Zoya) Kosmodemyanskaya from the War Heroes set (November 1942).

Fig. 17.14 60k purple Alexander Matrosov, 60k emerald Mariya Polivanova and Natalya Kovshova, 60k blue Boris Safonov from the War Heroes set (July 1944).

Fig. 17.15 20k Distributing parcels to soldiers, 30k Food packers, and 45k Women sewing uniforms from the War Episodes series (November 1942–February 1943).

Fig. 17.16 30k slate-blue Guerrillas attacking a train, 60k Defenders of Leningrad and 1r Machine-Gunners from the War Episodes series (November 1942–January 1943).

Fig. 17.17 30*k* blue Scouts, 30*k* brown Mine thrower, and 60*k* Sniper from the War Episodes series (March–May 1943).

Fig. 17.18 30*k* sepia and scarlet Stalingrad, 30*k* slate-green Leningrad and 30*k* emerald Odessa from the Liberation of Russian Cities set (March 1944).

Fig. 17.19 Miniature sheets marking the liberation of Leningrad (4x30*k* dated 27–1–1944) and the relief of Stalingrad (4x3*r* soldier and banner).

Fig. 17.20 The card reads:

23 October 1943.

Be greeted, dear Mussenka. I send you greetings and best wishes. Here nothing has changed. The day before yesterday I sent you also the money for October – 800 *roubles* – and the finance department has sent the certificate. So from November till April you will get the money in a regular way via the military commander's office of Karpinsk [a town behind the Ural mountains, beyond the furthest reach of the German army, but no doubt supplying the Russian army with trained men and goods]. The weather is autumn-like but good. Nearly astonishing [word indistinct]. Write to me saying whether you received my letters! I kiss you intensely and embrace you.

Your Lenja.

Fig. 17.21 15*k* soldiers carrying Lenin's banner from the 25th anniversary of the Russian Revolution (January 1943), 30*k* Portrait from the 125th Anniversary of the Birth of Karl Marx set (September 1943), 60*k* Tank and infantry from the 25th Anniversary of the Red Army and Navy set (October 1943), 30*k* Bayonet fighter and flag from the 25th Anniversary of the Young Communist League set (October 1943–April 1944).

Fig. 17.22 60*k* Lenin as an orator, 1*r* Lenin Mausoleum, and 3*k* Stalin, Lenin and revolutionaries from the Twenty Years Without Lenin set (30 May 1944).

18

THE BALTIC STATES

Hugging the eastern coast of the Baltic Sea, Lithuania, Latvia and Estonia shared long borders with Imperial Russia and then the Soviet Union to the east while also remaining vulnerable to aggression from powerful neighbours to the south and west, such as Poland and Prussia. Historically their borders were fluid, and their independence often perilous.

Lithuania

Lithuania is the southernmost state. It has a complex history that explains much about its wartime ordeals. In the fourteenth century Gerdiminas, the Grand Duke of Lithuania (*c.*1275–1341), expanded the country through shrewdly balanced alliances and wars until it include modern Belarus, Ukraine and parts of Poland and Russia. In 1569 Lithuania and Poland came together as a two-nation commonwealth under a single monarch, but after a period of internal conflict and decline it was gradually broken up and annexed between 1772 and 1795 by Prussia, Austria and Russia. Lithuania became a province of Imperial Russia, but its language, largely Roman Catholic religion, schools and culture survived the periodic and perilous attempts at 'Russianisation'.

During the First World War Germany occupied Lithuania, but it handled the situation carefully to mollify the numerous Baltic Germans and also take advantage of the general anti-Russian feeling. In 1917 a national conference in Vilnius, the capital, declared the country a German Protectorate, but in February 1918 it changed this to an outright Declaration of Independence. However, by the end of December 1918 the Red Army was at the border. As the German occupying forces left, Soviet forces seized Vilnius and laid historic claim to Lithuanian territory. Neighbouring Poland was also fighting Soviet forces, but it too laid claim to parts of Lithuania, and captured Vilnius. In 1920 the Soviet Union recognised an independent Lithuania, but Vilnius remained in Polish hands and Lithuania remained officially at war with Poland for the next nineteen years. And in 1924 Germany became aggrieved when Lithuania seized the old East Prussian city and hinterland of Klaipeda with its Lithuanian-speaking majority.

In 1926, amidst growing political tension, Antanas Smetona (1874–1944) came to power on the back of a coup supported by the army, and two years later he was virtually a dictator, but enjoying wide-ranging support. However, he possessed weak and ill-equipped armed forces and little international support – except ironically from the Soviet Union, which shared his suspicions of Poland and Germany. Pressures mounted in the 1930s. The Nazis bullied Lithuania into returning Klaipeda, and Poland successfully forced favourable trade agreements. And finally in 1939 the Molotov–Ribbentrop Pact assigned Lithuania, along with Latvia, Estonia and eastern Poland to the Soviet Union's 'sphere of influence'.

Soviet forces invaded Poland on 17 September 1939, and seized Vilnius two days later. Stalin returned the historic capital to Lithuania, but only in return for permission to station thousands of troops across the country. In June 1940 Smetana fled when the country was unable to resist renewed Soviet pressure to create a pro-Soviet government. A rigged election in an atmosphere of terror secured a favourable outcome, and in August the Soviet Union accepted Lithuania's application to join it as a Soviet Socialist Republic.

A series of stamps reflect the country's changing fortunes. In January 1939 a set and a miniature sheet celebrated Lithuania's twentieth anniversary of independence with pictures portraying the proclamation of independence and President Smetana (Fig. 18.1). In October the set was reissued with the celebratory overprint '*Vilnius 1939-X-10*' (Fig. 18.2). In May 1940 another set and miniature sheet marked the return of Vilnius with a portrait of the medieval ruler, Gediminas, and scenes of Vilnius and the first capital at Trakai (See Fig. 18.3 in colour section). Between March and July 1940 – during the period of encroaching Soviet occupation – a 'Liberty' set pictured a mix of Lithuanian legends, angels and peaceful modern scenes, but soon afterwards, on 21 August, they were reissued, along with two older definitive stamps, overprinted 'LTSR 1940 VII 21'. The initials stood for '*Lietuvos Tarybu Socialistine Respublika*' or 'Councils of the Socialist Republic of Lithuania') and the date was when the new government 'requested' admission to the USSR (Fig. 18.4).

The peaceful images on the 'Liberty' set were a travesty of what happened in the new Soviet Republic. Between the wars literature, music, art and education had prospered, as had the Catholic Church. Now all political, cultural and

Fig. 18.1   *Fig. 18.2*

Fig. 18.4   *Fig. 18.6*

religious institutions were banned, except the Communist Party and its youth arm. A ruthless programme of rural collectivisation was begun which impoverished farmers and stunted production. Thousands of 'enemies of the people' such as former army officers, political figures and academics were deported to the appalling Soviet labour camps.

Barely a year later, on 22 June 1941, Hitler invaded the Soviet Union. Within a week Germany occupied all Lithuania. Some welcomed the Germans as liberators, but despite all the lingering hopes of autonomy the country became part of the administrative Reichskommissariat Ostland, and all Lithuanian local officials functioned under the direct orders of German officers and civil administrators. Numerous collaborators served in German auxiliary forces and labour battalions, but many others, notably among the minority Russians and the rigorously persecuted Jews, became pro-Soviet partisans.

The rapidity of the initial German advance led to a number of distinctive overprints appearing on the definitive USSR stamps hitherto used across the country. The town of Rokiskis (now Rakischki) in the north-east was one – with the '*Laisvas 1941-VI-27 Rokiskis*' overprint highlighting both the German conquest and its rapid completion. As the capital city, 'Vilnius' was a particularly celebrated overprint circulating largely across the south and east, and '*Nepriklausoma Lietuva* 1941-VI-23' supposedly proclaiming an 'Independent Lithuania' was also commonly used in this early stage of Operation Barbarossa (See Fig. 18.5 in colour section). Indeed, very briefly, the Germans allowed strongly anti-communist Lithuanian provisional governments to operate in various localities until there was time to consolidate Nazi authority. Their hopes of lasting autonomy were soon dashed.

On 4 November 1941, a complete set of 'Deutsches Reich' Hitler definitive stamps overprinted '*Ostland*' was issued for use in all three Baltic States along with part of Belarus and north-east Poland. The Baltic States, and indeed all 'Ostland', were perceived by Hitler as little more than sources of supply of raw materials and mass labour, and as providing reasonably secure ports and bases for military operations in the Soviet Union. The use of overprinted German stamps rammed home, much like the Soviet ones earlier, their political, military and economic subservience, and their denial of any cultural and, therefore, national identify (Fig. 18.6).

Latvia

For centuries Latvia, the middle Baltic State, had little identity as a country. As a result of various wars, in the sixteenth century the region fell under Polish–Lithuanian domination, in the early seventeenth century the Swedes ruled the area, and during the eighteenth century first one half of the region and then the other were annexed by Imperial Russia. During the First World War Latvian battalions fought alongside the Imperial Russian army against Germany, but during the Russian Civil War (1917–22) Latvians could be found fighting on both sides as well as against the Germans occupying part of their country. In November 1918 independence was declared. However, the Soviet Union only relinquished its claims to Latvia in August 1920 after a brief but unpopular Latvian Soviet Republic held power and a Soviet invasion primarily aimed at securing the great port of Riga had been defeated. In the early 1920s a democratically elected government became popular, largely because its distribution of expropriated great estates to peasant farmers was a great political as well as economic success. However, the increasing social and political unrest caused by the world depression in the early 1930s led Karlis Ulmanis, the prime minister, to impose authoritarian rule in May 1934. It was a gamble that paid off as improving living standards gave the regime stability and popularity.

The country became proud of its culture, institutions and prosperity. In November 1938 the twentieth anniversary of independence was marked by a set of seven stamps with peaceful regional scenes and portraits of President Ulmanis flanked by a determined group of patriotic citizens, and General Janis Balodis, the Minister for War, flanked by past and present infantrymen and scenes of battle. The message was clear – peace and prosperity have relied upon, and still rely upon, our national strength and determination (Fig. 18.7).

In May 1939 the fifth anniversary of authoritarian government merited a set of eight carefully chosen stamps. Six of them proudly pictured the Independence Memorial, an eagle and the national flag, Jelgava Castle (restored and extended in 1937 after extensive internal damage in 1918), the Civic Hall at Daugavpils

Fig. 18.7

Fig. 18.9

(near the scene of a major battle against Soviet forces from September 1919 to January 1920), and key buildings and institutions showing the prosperity of Riga, the state capital. The other two showed the president waving at a crowd, and an eagle soaring aloft with the national flag (See Fig. 18.8 in colour section). In October 1939 two stamps complemented these urban scenes with a celebration of the harvest festival and the country's agricultural prosperity – and, thereby, the success of government policy (Fig. 18.9).

Between January and August 1940 a lengthy definitive set was issued picturing the Latvian coat of arms, officially adopted in June 1920 (Fig. 18.10). It combined ancient and modern symbols. The sun symbolised statehood, and the three stars represented the historical regions of Vidzeme, Latgale and Courland-Semigalia. Courland and Semigalia in the west are symbolised by the dragon on the left, which is red on the official arms, and Vidzeme and Latgale in the east by the griffin on the right, which is silver. It was a morale boosting, but short-lived, set at a time of high tension. Some months earlier, in the autumn of 1939, Latvia, along with Estonia and Lithuania, felt it had little option but to sign a mutual assistance treaty with the Soviet Union. On 16 June 1940, with thousands of troops now stationed in the country, the Soviet Union demanded a new pro-Soviet government on the pretext that Latvia was hosting anti-Soviet conspiracies. Knowing that Soviet forces were massed along its borders, and that the Soviet-manned bases within the country were now operational, Ulmanis gave in. A rigged election quickly followed, and on 5 August the new Latvian Socialist Republic was admitted into the Soviet Union. Between October and December 1940 a replacement definitive set of stamps appeared with the new Soviet Republic's coat of arms featuring ears of corn surrounding a sunset over the Baltic Sea together with the red star and hammer and sickle emblems of international communism (Fig. 18.11). The initials PSR stand for *Padomju Sociálistiská Republika* or Soviet Socialist Republic. In Lithuania President Smetana fled the country, but in Latvia President Ulmanis was arrested and died a few years later in, it has been assumed, a Soviet prison.

Fig. 18.10

Fig. 18.11

As in Lithuania, the mass deportations and crushing of national culture and institutions got quickly underway, and as in Lithuania they were suddenly terminated by the swiftness of the German invasion. Riga was seized on 1 July and a couple of weeks later Russian definitive stamps were issued overprinted '*Latvija 1941.1.VII*' to publicise the overwhelming victory (See Fig. 18.12 in colour section). In due course they were replaced by the ubiquitous German definitive stamps overprinted '*Ostland*'. For over three years Latvia became a killing ground for its Jewish and Gypsy populations, and thousands of Jews were deported there from Germany, Austria and Bohemia–Moravia. Many Latvians collaborated with the Germans, and it has been estimated that over 200,000 joined units of the Wehrmacht and Waffen-SS. Others, though, joined resistance groups, notably the pro-independence units and their bitter rivals, the pro-Soviet partisans.

In 1944 heavy fighting took place as Soviet armies advanced westwards. While thousands of Latvian conscripts fought in both German and Soviet armies, tens of thousands Latvian refugees fled to Sweden and Germany to escape both the devastation of war and the renewal of Communist repression. In early October the remnants of the German Army Group North were cut off in what became known as the 'Courland Pocket' when Soviet forces reached the Baltic Sea at Memel. Hitler would not sanction a complete withdrawal by sea, let alone surrender, as he had convinced himself that the new faster and quieter submarines under development could turn the tide of the war from the bases still operational along the Baltic coast. Courland would then become the spring-board for a massive counter-attack. It was, though, the Soviet submarines that decimated German shipping, including those packed with refugees, in the Baltic. Nevertheless, the Courland army held its ground,

Fig. 18.13

fighting off several attacks, until the remaining men – recently estimated at 189,000 Germans and 14,000 Latvians – surrendered to Soviet forces on 12 May 1945. For much of the time a perilous sea and airborne postal service existed, and a special army mail stamp and, as supplies dwindled, three definitive stamps were overprinted 'Kurland' together with commonly used values for use by the encircled troops (Fig. 18.13).

Estonia

Estonia, the northernmost state, also passed into Imperial Russian hands in the early eighteenth century, and grew prosperous as well as peaceful throughout the next two centuries. A distinctive language and literature evolved, and there was little hostility towards Russia, even during the abortive 1905 revolt inside Russia, largely because successive tsars allowed the Baltic Germans to dominate local affairs. In February 1917, after the collapse of Imperial Russia, German forces occupied the country and drove off a Bolshevik attack. Estonian independence was formally proclaimed on 23 February 1918, and the Estonians drove off another Soviet invasion. On 2 February 1920 the Soviet Union renounced all claims to Estonian territory, and under a parliamentary democracy Estonia enjoyed a period of prosperity as land reforms gave peasants secure holdings and external trade expanded. Unusually, in 1925 minority groups, including the Jews, were guaranteed cultural autonomy within the state.

Fig. 18.14

In 1934 Konstantin Pats, the elected head of state, pre-empted the triumph of an anti-communist and pro-presidential political party by a coup establishing himself as an authoritarian president and prime minister. As the country was prosperous, he encountered little popular opposition in crushing his opponents. Pats determined features adorned the country's new definitive stamps issued between 1936 and 1940, and during this period sets and miniature sheets appeared highlighting the Estonian Literary Society, the centenary of the city of Parnu's internationally celebrated mud baths, Beach Hotel and Sanitorium, and the country's postal service (together with the centenary of the first adhesive postage stamp) (Fig. 18.14).

However, Pats' policy of strict neutrality in the tense years of the later 1930s proved as futile as the different machinations of Lithuania and Latvia in thwarting Soviet and German aggression. And ironically it was the action of the Polish submarine *Orzel*, in seeking shelter in the Estonian port of Tallinn and then escaping without internment during the Soviet attack on Poland, that gave Stalin the excuse to accuse Estonia, and the other Baltic States, of being far from neutral. The same remorseless pressure as that exerted on Lithuania and Latvia led first to a forced agreement allowing Soviet troops to create bases within Estonia, and once that was achieved to demands for elections ensuring a new pro-Soviet government alongside free access to Estonian territory for unlimited numbers of troops. In due course on 6 August 1940 the new Estonian Socialist Republic was admitted, at its request, to the Soviet Union.

Pats was arrested alongside tens of thousands of other 'enemies of the state'. The deportations, executions and crushing of national institutions continued until the German onslaught the following summer. There was no stamp issue or overprints marking Estonia's new status within the Soviet Union, but the Germans ensured the Soviet Union's definitive stamps were soon overprinted '*Pernau 8.VII.1941*' (See Fig. 18.15 in colour section). Unusually the German authorities in Tartu printed three stamps adorned with both the swastika and Estonian lions for local and then general use in August 1941. Unusually, too, the Germans issued a set of six stamps with impressive views of major Estonian castles, bridges and cities for a Reconstruction Fund (Fig. 18.16). The stamps were available briefly in both Germany and Estonia, and probably the fund was primarily concerned with rendering the better parts of Estonia suitable

Fig. 18.16

destinations for imported German settlers. As elsewhere in the Baltic States, tens of thousands of Estonians fought in Soviet or German military units on the Eastern Front, and eventually took part in either the defence or liberation of Estonia itself.

The Baltic States had no governments-in-exile, and the Western Allies had greater post-war interests than the fate of these small nations. No serious military consideration could be given to forcing Stalin to reverse their incorporation into the Soviet Union. As a result the 'Russianisation' of Lithuania, Latvia and Estonia picked up where it had left off in 1941.

Illustrations

Fig. 18.1 30*c* President Smetana and 35*c* Proclamation from the Twentieth Anniversary of Lithuania's Independence set (15 January 1939).

Fig. 18.2 35*c* Anniversary stamp overprinted '*Vilnius 1939.X.10*' (28 October 1939).

Fig. 18.3 Recovery of Vilnius miniature sheet (6 May 1940).

Fig. 18.4 10*c* Angel and 30*c* Liberty Bell from the Liberty set (May and July 1940) and reissued overprinted '*LTSR 1940 VII 21*' (21 August 1940).

Fig. 18.5 Cover with Soviet Union definitive stamps overprinted '*Nepriklausoma Lietuva* 1941-VI-23', and Soviet Union stamps overprinted '*Laisvas 1941–VI–27 Rokiskis*', and '*Vilnius*'.

Fig. 18.6 5*pf* German definitive stamp overprinted '*Ostland*' (4 November 1941).

Fig. 18.7 5*s* Landscape and 10*s* General Balodis stamps from the Twentieth Anniversary of Latvian Independence set (17 November 1938).

Fig. 18.8 Souvenir cover with the Fifth Anniversary of Authoritarian Government set (13 May 1939). The postmark, 15 May, is the anniversary date.

Fig. 18.9 The Harvest Festival pair of stamps (8 October 1939).

Fig. 18.10 5*s* stamp from the Latvian National Arms set (January–August 1940).

Fig. 18.11 3*s* from the Latvian Soviet Socialist Republic Arms set (October–December 1940.

Fig. 18.12 Postcard with Soviet Union definitive stamps overprinted '*Latvija 1941.1.VII*' (July 1941).

Fig. 18.13 20*pf* German definitive and armed forces mail stamps overprinted '*Kurland*' and new values.

Fig. 18.14 'Kuuport Parnu' miniature sheet (20 June 1939).

Fig. 18.15 Cover with the set of Soviet Union definitive stamps overprinted '*Pernau 8. VII 1941*' (July 1941).

Fig. 18.16 The 1941 Tartu swastika issue (7 August 1941) and 20*k*+20*k* Stone Bridge, Tartu from the German-sponsored Reconstruction set (29 September 1941).

19

HUNGARY

It is not surprising that wartime Hungary, and its stamp issues, constantly harked back to the nation's historic days of glory long before the dismemberment of the ramshackle dual monarchy of Austria–Hungary after its defeat in the First World War. In 1867, weakened following the Franco-Austrian War and the Austro-Prussian War, rampant nationalism in Hungary had forced the Hapsburg Emperor Franz Joseph to agree to what became known as the Austro-Hungarian Compromise, which split his vast domains into a union of two distinct entities. Though he remained Emperor of Austria, the Hungarians insisted on him being King of Hungary, one of his hereditary titles, and not emperor.

In November 1918 chaos reigned across the collapsing kingdom. It was overrun with various occupying forces, and several ethnically centred provinces struggled for independence. Czechoslovakia was wrestling itself free, and Serbia and Romania ignored the Armistice and continued their offensives against Hungary. Emperor Karl I surrendered his powers as King of Hungary, although he did not abdicate, and a new liberal prime minister rendered the country helpless by ordering the disarmament of the army.

For a brief but bloody period in the summer of 1919 a communist regime led by Bela Kun held power in Hungary but its leaders fled in the face of the multiple pressures – the advancing Romanian army, chronic food shortages and widespread opposition to its hurried plans for industrial and agricultural nationalisation. Significantly, the violent episode created a deep and lasting dislike of the Soviet Union, and also of Jews as so many of the widely hated Hungarian communist leaders were Jewish.

Admiral Miklós Horthy de Nagybánya, the former commander of the Austro-Hungarian Navy, led the right-wing internal Hungarian opposition to the communists. By agreement, the Romanian army finally left the country, although only after pillaging vast swathes of it, and Horthy's forces ruthlessly crushed all left-wing opponents and made the Jews the scapegoats for the pitiful state of the country. By November 1919 Horthy was in firm control, and in March 1920 he became regent for the absent king and was endowed with wide-ranging political and military powers.

The victorious Allies decided to give priority to ethnic claims to independence rather than protect the historic borders of the old Kingdom of Hungary. Late

Fig. 19.1   Fig. 19.3   Fig. 19.4

in 1919 Hungary was obliged to sign the Treaty of Trianon, whereby it lost more than two-thirds of its pre-war lands, most of its timber and iron ore sources, half of its industrial plants and two-thirds of its credit and banking institutions. Ten million Hungarians found themselves living in the newly defined Romania, Czechoslovakia or Yugoslavia. The treaty also banned the active restoration of the monarchy, and Horthy was obliged, not entirely reluctantly, to oppose two attempts by Karl to regain his throne.

Fig. 19.5

Between 1921 and 1931 Horthy's prime minister, Count Istvan Bethlen, pacified extremists on the left and right through concessions, jobs and electoral manipulation. In addition he brought the country out of international isolation by gaining it membership of the League of Nations and signing a treaty of friendship with Mussolini's Italy. His overriding ambition was the revision of the Treaty of Trianon, a policy that brought him enhanced popularity at home and necessitated increasingly friendly contact with influential nations. His successors, especially Gyula Gombos, prime minister in 1932–36, drew close to Hitler's Germany. A trade agreement meant that Germany assisted Hungary to struggle out of depression, but the price was dependency upon Germany for raw materials, and the growing presence of extreme right-wing political and paramilitary organisations. Anti-Jewish legislation and violence intensified.

Horthy retained a deep suspicion of Stalin's attitude towards Hungary, and certainly made it public. Although he chose alliance with Hitler, he managed to maintain some independence to avoid descent into a puppet state. But Hitler wielded great influence, not least by pandering to Hungary's territorial ambitions. After the 1938 Munich Agreement Hitler allowed Hungary to annex nearly a quarter of neighbouring Slovakia, a decision greeted with wild enthusiasm by its ethnic Hungarians and celebrated with the issue of two large Hungarian stamps picturing the nation's patron saint St Stephen and the much venerated St Stephen's Crown of Hungary and overprinted '*Hazateres 1938*' ('The Homecoming 1938') (Fig. 19.1) Equally celebratory were the numerous covers containing mixed Czechoslovakian and Hungarian stamps, and franked with Hungarian special postmarks from annexed Slovakian towns, notably the important city of Komárom that was split in half by the partition nearly twenty years earlier (See Fig. 19.2 in colour section). In January 1939 a new pictorial set was issued inscribed 'Hungary For Hungarians' with carefully selected images of the symbolic statue of the 'despairing' northern provinces, Munkacs Castle in Carpathia at the extreme eastern end of Slovakia, the Cathedral of St Elizabeth of Hungary in Kosice (Kassa in Hungarian) in Slovakia, Admiral Horthy formally entering Komarom, and Hungarian soldiers receiving flowers from girls in national costume (Fig. 19.3).

For a couple of years Hungary was relatively peaceful and seemed to be profiting from its friendship with Hitler. In July 1939 the Girl Guides Rally at Godollo merited a set of four stamps, heavy in their emphasis upon the dove of peace (Fig. 19.4). Perhaps Godollo's name as the place in which King Karl renounced his powers in 1918 was as important as the rally. That October a set and miniature sheet presaged a series of issues highlighting Hungary's strong Protestant community and its historic roots in the nation's struggle for autonomy within the Hapsburg Empire (Fig. 19.5). It pictured notable Bible translators, and also Zsuzsanna Lorantfly (1600–60), a wealthy seventeenth-century aristocrat whose family estates in Royal Hungary – the recently reoccupied part of Slovakia – became an influential centre for Protestant culture in the midst of the predominantly Roman Catholic Hapsburg Empire, and was not far from the border with the still dangerous Ottoman Empire. Another stamp and miniature sheet celebrated Gabriel Bethlan (1580–1629), a warrior prince of Transylvania who became King of Hungary but, threatened with defeat by the Hapsburgs, renounced his throne in return for freedom of worship for Protestants (Fig. 19.6). These issues, of course, said as much about Hungary's national identify as they did about religion, and numerous wartime sets tied famous saints, especially St Elizabeth of Hungary, to the national cause. All Hungary's definitive stamps possessed essentially religious images – of St Stephen, the revered eleventh-century Christian

Fig. 19.6

king, St Stephen's equally revered crown that was still used at coronations, the Madonna, and renowned churches and cathedrals across the country (Fig. 19.7). In January 1940 a set raising funds for Hungary's antiquated air force attempted to heighten patriotism by showing a winged St Elizabeth holding St Stephen's crown aloft and soaring into the sky followed by a squadron of planes (Fig. 19.8). That March stamps marking the twentieth anniversary of Horthy's regency included one with an angel at St Elizabeth's Cathedral in Kassa (Fig. 19.9). Another Aviation Fund stamp in 1941 used the image of the Madonna (Fig. 19.10).

Summer 1940 saw the worst floods in living memory blighting the country to the south and east of Budapest. Endless rain had fallen upon the snow-laden ground and frozen subsoil. A set of stamps and miniature sheet raised money for the relief of victims (Fig. 19.11). Later

Fig. 19.7

Fig. 19.8

Fig. 19.9

Fig. 19.10

Fig. 19.11

Fig. 19.12

Fig. 19.14

in the year, however, it was the jealously coveted province of Transylvania, now in Romania, that dominated stamp issues. In July 1940 a set celebrated the fifth centenary of the birth of Matthias Corvinus (1440–90). Born in Transylvania, he was elected King of Hungary in 1458 and spent the rest of his life fighting back the Turks, dealing with jealous neighbours and extending his kingdom to include Moravia, Silesia, Bulgaria, Dalmatia, southeastern Germany and eastern Austria, and still finding time to promote Renaissance culture and art (Fig. 19.12). Although his kingdom collapsed after his death due to baronial squabbles, peasant revolts and Turkish invasions, in the nineteenth and early twentieth centuries Hungarians revered his Christian leadership and forging of a great kingdom. In September 1940 a stamp laden with imagery – St Stephen's crown flanked by Matthias Corvinus and St Stephen himself – and the inscription *'Kelet Visszatért'* ('The East Returns') marked Hitler's forced transference of North Transylvania from Romania to Hungary (See Fig. 19.13 in colour section). A few weeks later further stamps reinforced Hungary's hatred of Romania by raising money for a Transylvanian Relief Fund, thereby exploiting the charge of chronic maladministration (Fig. 19.14). Their dramatic images show the Madonna cradling a martyr, a mother sacrificing her child to the fatherland, and a modern soldier leading the people to safety as did Prince Csaba, the legendary Hungarian warrior seen riding behind him. Not surprisingly Romania's stamps marking its reoccupation of Transylvania in 1944 were also surcharged for famine relief.

In April 1941 two definitive stamps were issued with the overprint *'Deluisszater'*, triumphantly announcing 'The South Comes Home' (Fig. 19.15). Horthy had granted permission for German troops to cross Hungary during the invasion of Yugoslavia and was rewarded with two parcels of land mainly inhabited by ethnic Hungarians and largely commensurate with the territory taken away by the Treaty of Trianon. It gave Hungary a far longer border along the River Drava. Hungarian troops had taken part in the Yugoslavian campaign, and then joined Germany in its attack on the Soviet Union in June. Initial successes, notably at the Battle of Uman, seemed to presage the destruction of the Bolshevik threat once and for all, but the poorly equipped Hungarian forces ended up at Stalingrad, where the ferocious campaign of attrition and in due course a massive Soviet counter-attack virtually wiped out the Second Hungarian Army in January 1943. The Soviets had deliberately targeted Hitler's weakest allies.

Stamp issues mirrored the ephemeral triumphs and encroaching despair. In September 1941 a dramatic set pictured the achievements of Count Istvan Szechenyi (1791–1860) (Fig. 19.16). From an old Hungarian family, Szechenyi

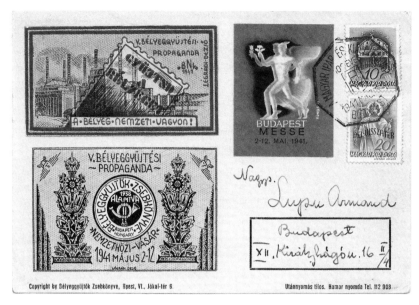

Fig. 19.15

sought to reinvigorate Hungary by instilling a sense of
national purpose and modernisation into what he thought
was a decadent aristocracy. He improved the roads, railways
and navigability of the Danube, founded the Academy of
Science, and built the first suspension bridge in Budapest.
Somewhat a tragic hero, he remained loyal to the Hapsburgs
throughout the 1848 revolution, and committed suicide after
constant attacks for continuing to support Austria's absolute

Fig. 19.16

rule in Hungary. Nevertheless the count's reputation as a devoted Hungarian
survived, and undoubtedly Horthy's wartime regime perceived his devotion to
national unity and regeneration as the key factor in remembering the timely
150th anniversary of his birth.

In March 1942 Admiral Horthy's Aviation Fund prompted another surcharged
set glorifying airmen as the modern cavalry, but in September a Red Cross
set reminded the nation of the hard-pressed nursing services (See Fig. 19.17
in colour section). Soon afterwards the war took the life of the regent's son,
Stephen, who was killed in an air accident while serving as a pilot on the
Eastern Front. A mourning stamp was issued on 15 October, with Stephen's portrait set against a squadron of planes and historic horsemen (See Fig. 19.18 in
colour section). In December three Red Cross Fund stamps and accompanying
miniature sheets pictured Stephen Horthy's widow, mother and nurse tending a
wounded soldier (Fig. 19.19). The tide of war was turning against Hungary and
the destruction of the Second Hungarian Army in January 1943 not far away.

From now on a series of issues recalled past heroes and heroines as Horthy's
regime strove to rally the increasingly dispirited nation. In December 1942 a set

Fig. 19.17   Fig. 19.20

Fig. 19.21

harked back to three celebrated medieval kings of Hungary, all of whom were engaged in constant wars against mighty opponents (Fig. 19.20). Ladislaus I (1077–95) crushed internal anarchy, secured his kingdom against the Holy Roman Emperor, made Christianity the national religion, and died just before going on crusade. Bela IV (1235–70) suffered defeat by the Mongols largely because local magnates were disloyal but returned to triumph over both. Finally Lajos the Great (King of Hungary 1342–82, King of Poland 1370–82) secured the Hungarian throne against the Turks and the Venetians, and then inherited and defended the Polish throne as well. By implication and association Horthy's concept of the authoritarian ruler defending and extending the nation, ensuring internal stability and encouraging religious devotion, education and equitable laws was the linear descendant of these valiant aims and achievements.

At various times in 1943 and 1944 new definitive stamps were issued, many of them portraying national heroes and heroines (Fig. 19.21). There were appropriately warlike portraits of King Ladislaus I, of Prince Arpad, an almost mythical ninth-century hero who led the Magyars out of the east and settled them in Carpathia, of Milos Toldi (c.1320–90), a roving knight who became a folk hero for his exploits alongside hard-pressed Hungarian monarchs, of Janos Hunyadi (c.1387–1456), Regent of Hungary, who stood firm against the Ottoman Turks despite the internal jealousies ravaging the country, and of Pal Kinizsi (1432–94), a general celebrated in folk tales for his personal bravery and victory over the Turks.

Further definitive stamps brought the series steadily up to date. They included Ferenc Rakoczi (1676–1735), who led a major but ultimately unsuccessful war of liberation against the Hapsburgs, enduring desertion by the French at a critical moment, and Miklos Zrinyi (1508–60), who distinguished himself in the defeat of the Turks outside Vienna, and, despite the Hapsburg Emperor turning against him, sacrificed his life defending the city of Szigetvar against Suleiman the Magnificent. The final two were Andras Hadik (1710–90), a Hungarian general who had the unusual distinction of outmanoeuvring Frederick the Great and seizing Berlin in the Seven Years War – presumably a stamp the Nazis would have frowned upon – and Artur Gorgey (1818–1916), the military leader of the ill-fated 1848–49 Hungarian revolt against the Hapsburgs. The stamps resonate with the devotion and courage of the protagonists, most of whom campaigned against internal jealousies as often as they faced external threats. There is a strong streak of fatalism that runs through many of their stories as the nation they were defending was betrayed from within or by its allies, or faced completely overwhelming odds. But, of course, in 1943 and 1944 not everyone could foresee – or wanted to face – the dramatic outcome of the war.

Several women were included in the definitive series. The Madonna was one, and so was St Elizabeth of Hungary (1207–31), the devout daughter of King Andrew II of Hungary, who married Ludwig of Thuringia only to find her piety constantly derided by her husband's family and court. Ludwig was away a great deal on imperial business, and in his absence Elizabeth ruled wisely and generously through times of flood and famine, but she was hounded out of the country when Ludwig died. Undaunted, she adopted the Franciscan rule, but died exhausted, aged just 23. A third stamp featured St Margaret of Hungary (1242–71), the daughter of King Bela I, whose life was dedicated to God in gratitude for the country's delivery from a Tartar invasion. Subsequent stories asserted that seventy-four miracles were linked to her name. Another stamp portrayed Elizabeth Szilagyi, the wife of Janos Hunyadi and mother of King Matthias Corvinus. A powerful noblewoman, she launched a civil war against King Ladislaus V, who had imprisoned Matthias, and after the king's death she ensured her son was elected his successor. The raven she used to send messages to her son in prison became the symbol of the Hungarian Post. Other famous women pictured included Dorothy Kanizsai, who ensured the Hungarian dead were given Christian burial after the disastrous defeat in 1526 by the Turks at Mohacs, Zsuzsanna Lorantfly (mentioned earlier), the creator of the Protestant cultural centre at Sarospatak, and Ilona Zrinyi (1645–1703), the wife of Imre Thokoly, Prince of Hungary, and the widely celebrated defender of Mohacs Castle during its three year siege by Hapsburg forces.

These glamorous figures and their widely known stories might have been inspiring, but reality was becoming a nightmare. Indeed the lengthy set of stamps issued in March 1943 picturing ordinary medieval soldiers to raise funds for modern wounded soldiers more than hinted at the dire situation, as did the Red Cross set in March 1944 with its images of helmeted soldiers, fallen men and lonely women and children (See Fig. 19.22 in colour section). In the same month a dramatic set featuring Louis Kossuth at the height of the 1848–49 Hungarian

Fig. 19.24

Fig. 19.25

Fig. 19.26

revolt was probably more depressing than uplifting in recalling the failure of that world-famous political and military campaign (See Fig. 19.23 in colour section). The sole Christmas issue of the war years came in 1943. With images of the Nativity, its intended appeal to the nation at a time of trial against the Soviet Union and communist sympathisers within Hungary itself was obvious, although it may well have been self-defeating as the forces of atheism were so much in the ascendant (Fig. 19.24).

Most Hungarians had been lukewarm supporters of Hitler's Russian campaigns, and, although Horthy had to endure Hitler's anger at the poor showing of the Hungarians at Stalingrad and promise to intensify his deportation of Jews, the regent was uncomfortably aware that the Allies were likely to win the war and the hated Soviets would arrive first. He sought contact with the Allies regarding a negotiated surrender, and when rebuffed he promised unconditional surrender when the Western Allies set foot in the country. In desperation Horthy even attempted to secure Stalin's promise that Hungary would remain autonomous should it surrender to the Soviet Union.

The Germans, though, anticipated his surrender and in March 1944 they occupied the country. Controversially Horthy remained regent, possibly because he feared a totally German-led administration would treat the country like Poland or even the Ukraine, but when he announced an armistice with the Soviet Union in October soon after its troops advanced into Hungary he was deposed and imprisoned in Germany. Authority passed to dedicated pro-Nazi Hungarians under a German governor, the armistice was ignored by Hungarian and German forces, and a savage battle raged around Budapest as Soviet forces advanced across the country. By April 1945, when German forces finally retreated from western Hungary the Soviet-sponsored premier of Hungary, General Bela Miklos, had agreed to the restoration of its pre-war borders, to huge reparations, to the confiscation of the great landed estates, and to direct Soviet involvement in the nation's recovery. The subjection of Hungary to a superior power had occurred yet again, and the reissuing of the 1943–44 definitive series overprinted 'Felszabadulas 1945 Apr 4' ('Liberation 4 April 1945') had a hollow ring to many, if by no means all, Hungarian citizens (Fig. 19.25). In May 1945 a stamp appeared portraying Endre Bajcsy-Zsiliniszky, a journalist who spoke out against the Jewish persecution, promoted socialist unity among Slav nations, and was hanged in 1944 by the Nazis for his leading role in the resistance movement (Fig. 19.26). It was the first of many picturing communist-inspired patriots and martyrs.

Illustrations

Fig. 19.1 Enlarged 70f St Stephen's Crown definitive overprinted '*Hazateres 1938*' (1 December 1938).

Fig. 19.2 Souvenir cover with mixed Hungarian and Czechoslovakian stamps and Komárom postmark dated 12 November 1938.

Fig. 19.3 20f+10f Admiral Horthy entering Komárom and 40f+20f Girls welcoming soldiers from the 'Hungary for Hungarians' set (16 January 1939).

Fig. 19.4 20f Dove of Peace from the Girl Guides' Rally set (20 July 1939).

Fig. 19.5 40f+20f Zsuzsanna Lorantfly from the National Protestant Day set (2 October 1939).

Fig. 19.6 Prince Gabriel Bethlan miniature sheet issued with the National Protestant Day set.

Fig. 19.7 20f St Stephen from the definitive set (21 June 1939).

Fig. 19.8 20f+20f St Elizabeth from the Admiral Horthy Aviation Fund set (1 January 1940).

Figs 19.9 20f Angel and Kassa (Kosice) Cathedral from the Twentieth Anniversary of the Regency set (1 May 1940).

Fig. 19.10 32f+32f Madonna from the Admiral Horthy Aviation Fund set (24 March 1941).

Fig. 19.11 'Stemming The Flood' miniature sheet (6 May 1940).

Fig. 19.12 20f+10f Equestrian Statue from the 500th Anniversary of the Birth of Matthias Corvinus set (1 July 1940).

Fig. 19.13 Celebratory cover with mixed Hungarian and Romanian stamps, including the Recovery of Northern Transylvania stamp (top right-hand corner) and postmark from the pro-Hungarian Transylvanian city of Marosvasarhely (now Targu Mures in Romania).

Fig. 19.14 32f+50f Mother offering her child to the Fatherland from the Transylvanian Relief Fund set (2 December 1940).

Fig. 19.15 Celebratory cover with Hungarian stamps overprinted 'South Comes Home' (21 April 1941).

Fig. 19.16 16f Szechenyi and Academy of Sciences from the Count Szechenyi set (21 September 1941).

Fig. 19.17 20f+20f Archer and Aircraft from the Admiral Horthy Aviation Fund set (15 March 1942) and 3f+18f Blood Transfusion from the Red Cross Fund set (1 September 1942).

Fig. 19.18 Stephen Horthy mourning stamp (15 October 1942).

Fig. 19.19 6f+1p Stephen Horthy's widow from the Red Cross Fund set (1 December 1942).

Fig. 19.20 8f+8f Ladislaus I, 20f+20f Bela IV and 30f+30f Lajos the Great from the Cultural Fund set (21 December 1942).

Fig. 19.21 *4f* Janos Hunyadi, *6f* Miklos Zrinyi and *30f* St Margaret from the 1943–44 definitive series.

Fig. 19.22 *12f+2f* Mounted Warrior from the Wounded Soldiers' Relief Fund set (March–April 1943) and *50f+50f* Nurse and the Fallen from the Red Cross Fund set (1 March 1944).

Fig. 19.23 *30f* Louis Kossuth exhorting his followers from the Louis Kossuth set (20 May 1944).

Fig. 19.24 *20f* the Nativity from the Christmas issue (1 December 1943).

Fig. 19.25 Madonna and St Stephen's Crown definitives overprinted '*Felszabadulas 1945 Apr 4*' (Liberation 4 April 1945).

Fig. 19.26 Bajcsy Zsilinszky memorial stamp (1 May 1945).

20

ROMANIA

Romania issued a vast number of stamps during its tumultuous political upheavals and military engagements in the late 1930s and throughout the war. All of them were intended to promote particular twists and turns of internal controversies and military fortunes, and they provide a unique record of the convoluted events in this deeply troubled country.

Much of the troubles blighting peace and stability in the Balkans stemmed from the mutual jealousies of neighbouring countries as a result of, first, the decline of the Turkish hold on the Balkans and, later, the territorial settlements after the collapse of the Russian and Austro-Hungarian Empires. As the Ottoman Empire's power waned, especially after the Russo-Turkish War of 1877–78, Romania had grown as a collection of ethnic regions willing to place themselves under the same ruler – Prince Karl of Hohenzollern-Sigmaringen, who became Prince of Romania and, in 1881, King Carol I. The first two provinces, Moldavia and Wallachia, had amalgamated in 1859. In 1878 they were joined by Southern Dobruja, and soon after 1918 by Bessarabia, Bukovina and Transylvania. Romania had reached its maximum extent, and by joining the Allies in the First World War it had achieved its aims of uniting all those regions populated by Romanians.

Romania sought to remain neutral in the Second World War, but both internal and external stresses made it impossible. And the country's instability was exacerbated by the actions of Prince Carol, later King Carol II. His reputation in tatters as a result of his adultery and the breakdown of his marriage, he renounced his right of succession in 1925, and his young son Michael succeeded to the throne in 1927. Then in 1930 Carol renounced his renunciation and usurped Michael's place.

The country entered another turbulent decade. The general economic recession fed discontent with the endless factions involved with parliamentary government, and stimulated the growth of Romania's fascist Iron Guard, an authoritarian organisation initially favoured by Carol. In 1938 he instituted a personal dictatorship, but its popularity swiftly turned to disillusionment as vast swathes of territory were snatched away by neighbours with seemingly little royal protest. In 1939 Great Britain and France guaranteed Romania's independence but a year later France's surrender and the British retreat across the Channel rendered their pledges meaningless. Under the Molotov–Ribbentrop

Pact of August 1939 Germany formally acknowledged the Soviet Union's interest in ex-Russian territory in Romania. As a result, Stalin pressurised Carol into returning Bessarabia and Northern Bukovina. A little later Hitler and Mussolini pressurised him into ceding northern Transylvania back to Hungary, and southern Dobrudja to Bulgaria, in their attempts to pacify these countries and avoid outright war across the region. Germany and Italy preferred to exert their control across a malleable and reasonably peaceful region. In return Hitler, with

Fig. 20.1

his eyes on the vast Ploesti oilfields, promised Carol that Germany would protect the remaining rump of Romania. The result, though, was political chaos within Romania combined with a future irretrievably linked to that of Germany.

In 1938 Carol was suspected of ultimate responsibility for the murder of Corneliu Codreanu, the charismatic leader of the Iron Guard, as an obvious rival for control of the country. However, in September 1940 he was forced to appoint General Ion Antonescu, whose authoritarian inclinations were almost as extreme as Codreanu's, as prime minister, along with Horia Sima, one of the new Iron Guard leaders, as a senior minister. They swiftly dispatched Carol and

Fig. 20.2

his mistress into exile, and his young son Michael nominally became king again. Later that year Romania joined the Axis powers, German troops entered the country, the Iron Guard murderously revenged itself on its political enemies, and the country's already harsh anti-Semitic laws were rigorously enforced.

A series of stamps reflected the tumult. In June 1940 a set marking the tenth anniversary of Carol's accession pictured him as a suitably confident soldier and airman, and an accompanying set celebrated eight sites of key historic significance in the formation of the nation, including Khotyn Castle in Bessarabia, Hurez Monastery in Wallachia, Sucevita Monastery in Bukovina, Alba Iulia Cathedral and a typical fortified church in Transylvania, and the huge post-1918 victory arch in Bucharest (Fig. 20.1). Soon afterwards, though, everything changed. In October a series of definitive stamps pictured the young King Michael in uniform (Fig. 20.2). By then the Iron Guard was at the peak of its influence and in November 1940 two stamps portrayed the murdered Codreanu alongside his movement's fascist emblems. In January 1941 two stamps and a miniature sheet used this brief time of triumph to belatedly mark the deaths of two Iron Guard members, Vasile Marin and Ion Mota, who had been killed several years earlier fighting for General Franco during the Spanish Civil War (See Fig. 20.3a & 20.3b in colour section).

Once again, however, the political wheel turned. For a few months Antonescu worked in uneasy partnership with Horia Sima and the Iron Guard. Together they denounced most of the diplomatic agreements made by King Carol, notably his accord with Yugoslavia, and they strengthened Romania's military links with Germany. But mutual suspicions abounded, primarily centred on who held supreme power. As the Iron Guard violently revenged itself on ex-King Carol's key supporters and publicly attacked Antonescu for failing to consolidate the 'revolution', Antonescu used his growing support amongst senior Nazis in Berlin and Romania to order the Romanian army to crush the Iron Guard and thereby consolidate his virtual dictatorship. Henceforth his destiny was inalienably tied to Hitler's.

In May 1941 a set of five stamps promoting King Carol I's Endowment Fund reminded the nation that this well-respected German-born monarch was also a Romanian patriot who put his nation's wishes before his own personal German sympathies in the First World War (Fig. 20.4). Stamps showed his impressive public library and equally impressive equestrian statue, but one portrayed him alongside King Michael to reinforce the strongly nationalist message and instil loyalty to the country's monarch – and, thereby, his appointed ministers. Later that year Antonescu honoured the commitment to combat communism alongside Hitler, and Romanian troops quickly advanced into the provinces of Bokovina and Bessarabia that had been unwillingly ceded to Stalin the previous year. The Endowment Fund set was quickly reissued, twice, one overprinted '*Cernauti 5 Iulie 1941*' – a major city in Bukovina – and the other '*Chisinau 16 Iulie 1941*' – a key town in Bessarabia (See Fig. 20.5 in colour section). They were popular victories, and 1941 was the high point of Antonescu's career.

Fig. 20.4

Now, though, a fatal but probably inevitable decision was taken to wage a war of aggression beyond the territory awarded to Romania after 1918. It is quite likely that Antonescu sought the reversion of northern Transylvania from Hungary if he proved that Romania was the more enthusiastic ally of Germany. Certainly the overall number of Romanian troops sent to the Eastern Front during the war exceeded the combined total all of Germany's other allies. In August 1941 Romania occupied territory in Soviet Ukraine between the rivers Dniester and Bug, an area the Romanians called Transdniestria. A few weeks later a set of celebratory stamps was issued picturing Prince Michael Voda Patrascu (1558–1601), one of Romania's greatest heroes, who briefly consolidated Walachia, Moldavia and Transylvania under his personal rule in 1600 (See Fig. 20.6 in colour section). Antonescu had done much the same.

If the analogy of Prince Voda's stand against an eastern threat – in his case, the Turks – was lost, a few days later a set of four stamps and a miniature sheet trumpeted Romania's contribution to the Anti-Bolshevik Crusade (See Fig. 20.7 in colour section). One stamp pictured King Michael, in whose name ostensibly these

victories were achieved, the second emphasised the historic links by picturing two
renowned border castles, the third showed a line of modern soldiers steadfastly
advancing, the fourth pictured silhouettes of German and Romanian soldiers
alongside their respective national emblems, and the two stamps of the miniature
sheet pictured German and Romanian soldiers on one and their national badges
on the other under the overall inscription '*Fratia De Arme*'. Five days later the set
and miniature sheet were reissued overprinted '*Odesa 16 Oct 1941*' to celebrate
the hard-won seizure of the Black Sea port between the Dnieper and Bug (See
Fig. 20.8 in colour section). The siege had lasted seventy-three days, cost Romania
90,000 casualties, and was followed by the slaughter of thousands of Jews.

In December 1941 yet another set, a lengthy one of sixteen historic sites,
celebrated the full recovery of Bessarabia and Bukovina (Fig. 20.9). Picturing
ancient and peaceful monasteries, churches and trading centres of essentially
Romanian origin, the stamps presented a vastly different picture of the regions
from the ravages of the recent exploitation of their resources and persecution of
their Jews. In November and December 1942 three sets celebrated the first anniversary of the 'liberation' of Bukovina and Bessarabia, and the incorporation of
Transdniestria (Fig. 20.10). The images on the Bukovina set harped back to coats
of arms, and the Transdniestria set celebrated the seventeenth-century national
chronicler Miron Costin (1633–91), who lived when much of Transdniestria was
accepted as part of Romanian Moldavia. The Bessarabian set, though, contained
three completely different designs, all calculated to cement the nation's current

Fig. 20.9

Fig. 20.10

Fig. 20.11

Fig. 20.12

1943

Fig. 20.13

CONSILIUL DE PATRONAJ

LEI 600

ties with Germany and Italy. King Michael was dragged into two of the stamps, one picturing him apparently taking the lead in studying a map with Marshal Antonescu, and the other showing his portrait along with those of Antonescu, Hitler and Mussolini. The third stamp in the set pictures a line of troops crossing the River Prut when Romania recaptured Bessarabia, and has the head of Antonescu where normally the king would be portrayed.

By then, though, the tide of war was turning against Romania, and indeed against Antonescu himself. Since June 1942 tens of thousands Romanian soldiers had become casualties or prisoners in and around Stalingrad, and by February 1943 the Axis defeat had cost the country 150,000 men. Romania's economic problems soared as its produce and materials poured into Germany, often with payment delayed or ignored, and Allied bombers were now reaching its oilfields. Stamp issues throughout 1943 reflected the increasingly gloomy situation. A sombre and heavily surcharged Red Cross set and miniature sheet pictured a nurse attending a badly wounded soldier (Fig. 20.11). Two sets, each of five stamps picturing cultural figures and martyred patriots from eighteenth- and nineteenth-century Transylvania, raised funds for refugees from the province annexed by Hungary (Fig. 20.12). The overall theme was the long and bitter struggle to be free from Hungarian oppression then – and now. Another heavily surcharged set and accompanying miniature sheet marked the second year of war, but its muted themes showed a soldier protecting a woman and child, a sword breaking chains of oppression, and a sword and castle defending the nation (Fig. 20.13).

Internally, confusion reigned again. Early in 1943 King Michael made a broadcast parting with the Axis, while Antonescu authorised ministers to seek a negotiated peace with the Allies. Opponents of Antonescu, including army officers, diplomats, democrats and the king himself, began to plot his downfall. Nevertheless in September 1943 a stamp celebrating the third anniversary of Michael's reign contained an image of Antonescu as prominent as that of the king himself (Fig. 20.14). Antonescu had managed to survive through a successful military campaign that had stabilised the front to the north and east of Romania.

In November 1943 eight dramatic stamps enthusiastically celebrated past and present victories of the Romanian Army (See Fig. 20.15 in colour section). These included troops helping the Russians defeat Turkey at the Battle of Calafat in 1877, and attacking Austria–Hungary in the First World War. More recent scenes showed Romanian forces advancing on Stalingrad, pounding Odessa, seizing Russian oilfields and besieging Sevastopol. The following year they would be a stark and embarrassing reminder of the country's vast but ill-fated efforts on the Eastern Front. The final stamp of the set pictured King Michael alongside General George Bibescu (1804–73), an early-nineteenth-century elected ruler of Wallachia, who sought good working relations with Imperial Russia, the dominant power in the province, while also trying to implement economic reforms. Ultimately he failed, and after a brief period of power he was exiled – ironically much like Michael himself.

As 1943 turned into 1944 the Soviet advance on Bessarabia and Odessa could not long be delayed. To Antonescu's chagrin, his overtures to the Western Allies collapsed as they insisted on unconditional surrender, and Stalin both courted and dominated the growing Romanian Communist Party. By the summer of 1944 Romanian and German troops were fighting Soviet forces deep inside Bukovina and Moldavia. A 1944 set of stamps, both retrospective and yet aspirational, deliberately portrayed the Bukovinan town of Radeseni at peace and prospering – presumably when under Romanian rule in the 1920s and 1930s – with its ancient church, modern school, busy agricultural institute and families picking apples (Fig. 20.16).

Fig. 20.14

Fig. 20.16

With strong internal support, King Michael arrested Antonescu on 23 August 1944, and suddenly Romanians found their country had unilaterally switched sides. Confusion reigned as for a time Romanian forces did not know whether to support or oppose German and Soviet troops, and Romanians generally remained deeply divided in their loyalties to Hitler and Stalin. Nevertheless by early September Romanian troops were fighting alongside Soviet ones in

pushing the Germans and their Hungarian allies out of Transylvania. In February 1945 a set of eleven stamps celebrated the recapture of northern Transylvania late in 1944, providing a final brief glimmer of national pride (Fig. 20.17). Once again the stamps pictured regional cultural figures – Transylvanian scholars and teachers such as Gheorghe Sincai and Gheorghe Lazar, and nationalistic clergy and bishops such as Ioan Micu Klein and Andrei Saguna – alongside the political revolutionaries such as Vasile Nicols, Ion Oarga and Marcu Giurgiu, who had led the ultimately ill-fated 1784 revolt against Austrian rule. Most of the figures had appeared earlier on the 1943 Transylvanian Refugees' Fund sets.

Fig. 20.17

In 1945 Romanian armies continued to advance alongside Soviet ones into Hungary, Yugoslavia, Austria and Czechoslovakia. There was much heavy fighting, and Romanian casualties fighting the Germans – about 167,000 – were at least as heavy as those incurred fighting for them. As part of their post-war division of European power Prime Minister Winston Churchill had already signalled to Stalin that the Soviet Union could have dominance over post-war Romania.

On 30 April 1945, just as the war was grinding to a halt, a startling set of six stamps of Romanian figures signalled the extent of communist influence. Indeed, as early as 6 March 1945 Petru Groza, Moscow's chosen communist candidate, had become Prime Minister. The link between the six new stamps was the inscription saying all six were martyred during the Nazi terror (See Fig. 20.18 in colour section). However, three of the men were Ion Duca (1879–1933), a pre-war prime minister, Virgil Madgearu (1887–1940), a leading pre-war economist, and Professor Nicolae Iorga (1871–1940), an historian, influential journalist, and also a pre-war prime minister, who were murdered by the Iron Guard for opposing its extremist ideas and actions. The other three were young communists – Ilie Pintilie (1903–40), Bernath Andrei (1908–40) and Filimon Sarbu (1916–40) – who had died after their arrest as saboteurs and agitators. Alongside portraits of the men, each stamp had a picture of a violent attack purporting to be linked to the martyrdom. The trio of elderly influential pre-war figures had nothing to do with the younger communists, but it suited the new regime to portray pre-war and wartime Romania as a brutal hotbed of right-wing fanaticism freed at last by the liberators from the Soviet Union.

Another set in May 1945 was equally obvious in its message. One stamp showed a hand pulling back a curtain to reveal the sun's rays illuminating the Kremlin, while two others pictured Marxist books against a flaming torch and fluttering Romanian and Soviet flags. The fourth stamp portrayed the thirteenth-century Russian hero, Alexandru Nevsky (1220–63) with the early nineteenth-century Romanian hero, Tudor Vladimirescu (1780–1821). The link – somewhat ironic in the circumstances – was that both had fought valiantly to keep Mongol or Turkish hordes from overrunning their countries (See Fig. 20.19 in colour section). Just in case the Soviet Union's dominating influence was not apparent, a hurriedly organised Trades Union Congress was held in war-torn Romania in June 1945 and an accompanying set of stamps pictured Lenin and the communist writers Karl Marx and Friedrich Engels (Fig. 20.20).

Fig. 20.20

Antonescu was executed as a war criminal on 1 June 1946, and King Michael held on to his throne only until 30 December 1947 when the communist-controlled government declared Romania a Soviet-style republic. Bessarabia and Northern Bukovina returned to the Soviet Union.

Illustrations

Fig. 20.1 8*l* Portrait and 16*l*+2*l* Triumphal Arch stamps from the Tenth Anniversary of King Carol II's Accession sets (8 June 1940).

Fig. 20.2 10*l* from the King Michael definitive series (20 October 1940).

Fig. 20.3 20*l*+5*l* from the Corneliu Codreanu set (November 1940) and the Ion Mota and Vasile Marin miniature sheet (13 January 1941).

Fig. 20.4 7*l*+38*l* Foundation Building and Statue from the King Carol I Endowment Fund set (9 May 1941).

Fig. 20.5 7*l*+38*l* Endowment Fund stamp overprinted *'Cernauti 5 Iulie 1941'*.

Fig. 20.6 6*l* Prince Michael Voda Patracsu from the Conquest of Transdniestria set (6 October 1941).

Fig. 20.7 20*l*+20*l* Romanian soldiers from the Anti-Bolshevik Crusade set (11 October 1941).

Fig. 20.8 Anti-Bolshevik Crusade miniature sheet overprinted *'Odesa 16 Oct 1941'*.

Fig. 20.9 1.50*l* Soroca, 3*l* Dragomirna and 39*l* Rughi from the Restoration of Bessarabia and Bukovina set (1 December 1941).

Fig. 20.10 9*l*+41*l* Arms from the First Anniversary of the Liberation of Bukovina set (November 1942) and 18*l*+32*l* King Michael and Marshal Antonescu from the First Anniversary of the Liberation of Bessarabia set and 12*l*+38*l* Miron Costin from the First Anniversary of the Incorporation of Transdniestria set (December 1942).

Fig. 20.11 16*l*+84*l* Nurse and wounded soldier from the Red Cross Fund set
(1 March 1943).

Fig. 20.12 62*l*+138*l* Vasaile Nicola, Ion Oarga and Marcu Giurgiu, executed leaders
of the ill-fated 1784–5 revolt against Austria, from the Transylvanian Refugees'
Fund sets (August and October 1943).

Fig. 20.13 Second Year of War miniature sheet (22 June 1943).

Fig. 20.14 Stamp marking the third anniversary of King Michael's reign
(6 September 1943).

Fig. 20.15 3.50*l*+3.50*l* Stalingrad, 5*l*+5*l* Odessa and 7*l*+7*l* Sevastopol from the
National Artillery Centenary set (10 November 1943).

Fig. 20.16 5*l*+145*l* Stefan Thomsa Church and 32*l*+118*l* School from the Radeseni
set (1944).

Fig. 20.17 11*l* Gheorghe Sincai and 35*l* Avram Iancu and rural scenes from the
Liberation of Northern Transylvania set (February 1945).

Fig. 20.18 20*l*+180*l* Professor Iorga and 36*l*+164*l* Filimon Sarbu from the War
Victim's Relief Fund set (30 April 1945).

Fig. 20.19 80*l*+420*l* Tudor Vladimirescu and Alexandru Nevsky from the First
Romanian Soviet Congress Fund set (20 May 1945).

Fig. 20.20 155*l*+445*l* Lenin from the Bucharest Trades Union Congress set (30 June
1945).

21

BULGARIA

Early twentieth-century Bulgarians, like their jealous neighbours in Romania and Hungary, could look back upon their country's chequered history with considerable pride. In the tenth century and again 200 years later great leaders arose who created extensive Bulgarian empires, and encouraged trade and the arts. However, weakened by warring internal factions, the whole region south of the Danube was conquered by the Ottoman Turks by the early fifteenth century. Christianity was almost, but not entirely, eradicated. The Turks crushed numerous revolts, but in 1878 their waning empire endured a crushing defeat by Russia with Bulgarian help, and Bulgaria achieved the de facto autonomy it had long sought – although it remained a *de jure* tributary of the Ottoman Empire until 1908.

Unfortunately, in the 1870s the western European powers did not want to replace Turkish influence and power with an overlarge Bulgaria, and the 1878 Treaty of Berlin created a modestly sized nation centred around Sofia and Moesia south of the Danube, which angered those Bulgarians within the new state as much as those left outside it. The deep sense of being cheated accounted for much of Bulgaria's aggressive approach to international affairs in the decades to come. The country became heavily militarised, and in 1885 it seized Eastern Rumelia, a large swathe of Ottoman land abutting southern Bulgaria, and decisively defeated the Serbs who opposed the annexation.

In 1912 Bulgaria led Serbia, Greece and Montenegro to victory against the Ottoman Turks, pushing them almost entirely out of Europe. A key outcome was the creation of an independent Albania. However, grievous misunderstandings between Serbia and Bulgaria over each country's contribution to victory and each country's territorial aggrandisement at the expense of Turkey in northern Macedonia quickly led to another war between the two fractious allies. A quarrel with Greece over the division of southern Macedonia led to further bloodshed, and Bulgaria also managed to alienate Romania by not ceding the fortress of Silistra after the Turkish defeat. In the renewed warfare in the summer of 1913 Bulgaria found itself isolated but confident that its borders would be significantly extended beyond those of 1878 and 1885. To its surprise and horror the Serbs, Greeks and Romanians first held off Bulgarian attacks and then advanced into Bulgarian territory, and when the Romanians threatened its capital, Sofia, a completely humiliated Bulgaria sued for peace.

The peace treaties set the regional scene for the First World War and the territorial jealousies of the interwar years and the Second World War. Hitler and Mussolini were to unearth a host of mutual antipathies to play upon as they sought overall Balkan supremacy. In 1913 Bulgaria was stripped of most of its earlier gains. Southern Dobrudja went to Romania, and Macedonia was divided between Serbia and Greece as well as Bulgaria. Italy sought complete control of the Adriatic and became disgruntled at Albania acquiring independence. Victorious Serbia turned its attention to rivalry with Austria–Hungary over Bosnia–Herzegovina. And Bulgaria became a myopic revanchist power, whose disastrous alliance with Germany and Austria–Hungary in the First World War came about largely because all its hostile Balkan neighbours were pro-British, French and Russian. As Bulgaria believed Austria–Hungary and Germany could satisfy its territorial claims, King (or more properly Tsar) Ferdinand joined them in September 1915. After initial success in reoccupying much of the contested regions, the Balkan campaign was reduced to trench warfare and mutual attrition until the demoralised Bulgarian army eventually mutinied under a united Allied attack through Macedonia. Impoverished and saddled with huge reparations, Bulgaria lost its Aegean coastline to Greece, its Macedonian territory to Yugoslavia, and Dobruja to Romania. His country in tatters, Ferdinand abdicated in October 1918 and his son, Boris III, took over the reins.

Boris endured years of political instability, with military, communist and agrarian factions at each other's throats. He narrowly avoided assassination on several occasions. In 1934, though, a quasi-military coup sought to reduce Boris to a puppet king, prompting his successful counter-coup and assumption of personal rule in the following year. The new stability proved popular, and Boris steered a careful course of neutrality as European tensions mounted. However, the lure of recovering lost lands proved irresistible, and Bulgaria's central position in the Balkans rendered it strategically important in the Second World War. In September 1940 Hitler and Mussolini secured the return of Southern Dobrudja from Romania, and in early 1941 Hitler's decision to support the ailing Italians in their conquest of Greece led to a mixture of veiled threats and lures of further territory which caused Boris to join the Axis and allow German troops passageway through the country. As Stalin was still Hitler's ally, and Axis victory seemed assured, the move was popular. Yugoslavia and Greece surrendered in April 1941 and, without having engaged in any of the fighting, Bulgaria received large parts of Macedonia and Thrace (virtually all of today's Macedonia and eastern Serbia).

In September 1940 a set of four stamps celebrated the recovery of Dobrudja between the Danube and the north-east coast (See Fig. 21.1 in colour section). The first pictured a smiling peasant couple in region costume, the second Bulgarian flags advancing over fields of wheat, and the other two maps of Dobrudja itself. All four pictured Boris. Peasant life and rural prosperity were essential ingredients in Bulgarian national life, with both the monarchy and major political parties

Fig. 21.2

Fig. 21.4   Fig. 21.3

keen to secure peasant support. Although some Bulgarian definitive stamps portrayed Boris, several others in the series honoured the shepherd, the bee-keeper and the ploughman (Fig. 21.2). And between 1940 and 1944 an intermittently issued series highlighted a range of key rural occupations (Fig. 21.3).

In October 1941 five stamps celebrated the reoccupation of Macedonia. One showed a smiling young woman in regional costume, three others showed a peaceful Macedonian monastery, a coastal village and a radiant sunset over an island, and the fifth pictured a map and Tsar Boris (Fig. 21.4). The reality of Bulgarian occupation, though, was the opposite of peaceful. Bulgaria imposed its own education system, church and culture, deported thousands of Greek officials, priests and teachers, and replaced numerous Greek farmers with Bulgarian settlers. The harshness of the occupation, and widespread Bulgarian corruption, led to revolts that were savagely crushed.

The days of peaceful expansion faded fast. Bulgarian troops started to fight resistance groups in German-occupied Balkan territory, and, although Boris kept Bulgaria out of Operation Barbarossa, the Soviet Union attacked Bulgarian shipping in the Black Sea and the illegal Bulgarian Communist Party began to plot against the government. The Fatherland Front was established by a coalition of communists, army officers and resistance groups, and grew steadily stronger as the tide of war turned against the Axis. A public outcry successfully halted Nazi demands that Bulgarian Jews were to be deported to Poland, but Boris allowed Jews from the newly occupied lands to be transported, ostensibly as forced labourers. In August 1943 Boris endured an angry haranguing by Hitler for refusing to send troops to the Eastern Front. Still defiant, Boris did, however, notionally declare war on Great Britain and the United States. Soon afterwards,

Fig. 21.5

he died suddenly and many believed German agents had poisoned him. His young son, Simeon succeeded him, although a regency ruled in his name and strove to cope with the ominous thought of defeat at the hands of the Soviet Union. As a prelude Allied aircraft started to bomb Sofia and other rail and industrial centres.

Not surprisingly stamp issues sought to boost welfare funds and stimulate patriotism. In November 1940 a set celebrated famous

Fig. 21.6

historical figures whose lives in various centuries had been devoted, whatever the very real personal and professional perils they faced, to reinvigorating an essentially Bulgarian culture and achieving a greater degree of national autonomy (Fig. 21.5). Among them were Petko Slaveykov (1827–95), who translated the Bible into Bulgarian and sought an autonomous Bulgarian Church, Bishop Sophronicus of Vratsa (1739–1813), who was a leading teacher and writer promoting a national cultural revival in an almost lawless diocese, Martin Drinov (1838–1906), who co-founded the Bulgarian Literary Society, wrote a new constitution, and promoted Sophia as the capital city, and Kolyu Ficheto (1800–81), an architect who promoted and refined a Bulgarian style in the churches, houses and bridges he designed. In December 1940 a pair of stamps marked the 500th anniversary of the invention of printing, and, more significantly, Nikola Karastoyanov's establishment of the first Bulgarian printing press in Samokov in 1828 (Fig. 21.6). All these figures were representative of the period later Bulgarians termed the National Revival as the country passed, often painfully, from an increasingly disgruntled Turkish province through a principality to a fully autonomous kingdom. It was a time of hope, vision, national awakening, striving and triumph—before the devastation and humiliation of the Second Balkan War and the First World War.

A third set, in May 1941, reinforced the uplifting message. It was devoted to the short but romantically heroic life of Hristo Botev (1848–76), who initially was forced into exile in 1867 after a public speech denouncing Turkish oppressors and their privileged Bulgarian collaborators. He became the editor of an inflammatory newspaper, the *Word of the Bulgarian Emigrants*, and published revolutionary poetry creating the image of a peasantry united against tyranny and striving to create a genuinely socialist state. When his friend Vassil Levski, the leader of an insurgency, was hanged in 1873, Botev succeeded him and launched another revolt in 1876. After early successes it was crushed with extreme cruelty and Botev himself was killed when a detachment of rebels was surrounded (See Fig. 21.7 in colour section). Nevertheless the popular image of the poetic rebel combined with the widespread European denunciation of Turkish atrocities stimulated support for Russia's declaration of war against Turkey – and Bulgaria's liberation in 1878.

In July 1941 a set of stamps portrayed the mechanised parcel post service with illustrations of modern weighing machines together with trains, lorries and motorcycles speeding up the system. These images of national efficiency were repeated the following year, in a set proudly picturing the Palace of Justice, the National Bank and a workers' hospital (Fig. 21.8). In 1942, too, the nation's youth was celebrated in a set entitled 'Work and Joy', a title reminiscent of the Hitler Youth and Nazi Germany (Fig. 21.9). Health, culture and comradeship were the key features, with the five stamps picturing outdoor camp life, the national flag being hoisted and young people enjoying folk music and dancing. A grimmer aspect of life intruded in September 1942 with a graphically illustrated War

Fig. 21.8

Fig. 21.9

Invalids set (Fig. 21.10). The six stamps pictured a haggard soldier on crutches, a soldier and his family, first aid being administered on a battlefield, a widow and orphans at a graveside, a cloaked figure looking at the Unknown Soldier's Memorial, and Boris's wife, Queen Giovanna, visiting the wounded in hospital. A label attached to the stamps possessed the dates '29.III.1915' and '27–8.X.1941' indicating the set embraced casualties from the start of Bulgaria's active embroilment in each of the world wars.

Fig. 21.10

A major historical set of ten stamps was issued intermittently during 1942 and 1943. Most, though, were issued in May 1943 when the war was turning against the Axis (See Fig. 21.11 in colour section). Not surprisingly each striking image harked back to a memorable moment of crisis, heroism and glory in Bulgarian history, much like, it strongly implied, the present time and the dire need for similar heroes. One pictured Kubrat, the legendary seventh-century hero who, against all the odds, united the warring Bulgar tribes to create a great nation. Another two, probably linked to Kubrat, showed horsemen about to level their spears in a charge and the carving of a grand equestrian frieze. A scene of the baptism of King Boris I highlighted the successful reign (852–89) of this warlike Christian monarch and his ruthless crushing of all external Serbian and Croatian threats and internal pagan revolts. Another stamp honoured Saint Naum (c.830–910), a scholar and missionary sheltered by Boris I when German bishops opposed his attempts to create a uniquely Slavic liturgy. With Boris's protection, Naum founded a literary school, and also a monastery at Lake Ohrid (which still exists). Two more stamps highlight the reign of Simeon I, a son of Boris I. His lengthy reign – 893 to 927 – was later seen as a golden age when military victories over the Hungarians and Byzantine Emperor were accompanied by the blossoming of Slavonic literature and the new Cyrillic script.

The set then moves through the centuries, but still concentrates upon the hard-won battles for religious and cultural as well as political nationhood and autonomy. One stamp illustrated the trial of Basil, a Bulgar physician who was condemned as a leader of the Bogomil heresy in 1110 and burnt at the stake eight years later after every attempt by the Byzantine Emperor Alexius I Comnenus to persuade him to recant had failed. Bogomilism had grown in strength since its foundation a century earlier, and was spreading rapidly across Europe arousing great fears, and savage persecution, for its denunciation of the Church's aloof hierarchy and its close association with the political elite and rigid feudal stratification in each country. They believed the world was inherently evil and sought a return to early Christianity, autonomous local churches and equality among worshippers.

Two stamps celebrated medieval Bulgaria and the great empire wrestled after forty-five years of Byzantine control, and defended against repeated Hungarian attacks, by Ivan Asen II (reigned 1186–96) and Ivan Asen II (reigned 1218–41). The role of strolling minstrels in keeping alive the stories of ancient heroes was celebrated, and so were the courageous efforts of Evtimii, the fourteenth-century Patriarch of Bulgaria, to encourage resistance to the Turkish invaders, not least by the story that a miraculous force stopped the hand of a headsman completing his execution. The final two stamps moved the stories on to more modern times. One commemorated the Slav–Bulgarian *History* of Father Paissi (1722–73) that kept national culture alive during the Ottoman oppression and became part of the popular patriotic gospel which stirred up the 1876 uprising. The other pictured the dramatic Shipka Pass Memorial marking the place where a vastly outnumbered Bulgarian Corps of Volunteers held the captured pass against repeated Turkish attacks in July 1877 to enable the Russian Army to advance through it to the final victory against the Ottoman Army in January 1878.

1944, though, saw the collapse of all Bulgarian aspirations. A severe drought, the need to provision the army, the vast exports to Germany, the endless stream of casualties and the internal instability as hopes of an Axis victory turned to dust, all contributed to the malaise. In February a mourning issue lamented the passing of Boris III who remained popular until his death the previous year, and in June his definitive stamps started to be replaced by those of the young King Simeon II (Fig. 21.12). But there were no leaders similar to those portrayed in the recent set of historic heroes. In May and June 1943 Bulgarian and German forces were occupied in fighting partisans near the Sutjeska River in south-east Bosnia, and in December they were engaged in an equally vicious and frustrating campaign in eastern Croatia.

As the summer of 1944 drew near so did the Soviet armies pushing Axis forces out of the Ukraine. In August Romania changed sides and allowed Soviet troops to cross the country and approach Bulgaria. The reinvigorated Bulgarian Fatherland Front orchestrated widespread opposition to the pro-Nazi government of the Regent Prince Kyril, but failed to seize power until after the Soviet Union had declared war on Bulgaria on 5 September and quickly overran the northeast. Macedonia, though, was occupied by German troops and declared its longed-for but short-lived independence. Bulgarian stamps were issued overprinted 'Macedonia 8.IX.1944' and Greek values. (See Fig. 21.13 in colour section). On 9 September a

Fig. 21.12

pro-communist Fatherland Front government backed up by partisan brigades took control, and Bulgaria changed sides.

In October and November 1944 Bulgarian, Albanian and Soviet forces drove the Germans and their collaborators out of Kosovo, and later took Belgrade. In March 1945 Bulgarian and Soviet armies drove German and Hungarian troops from the oil fields around Lake Balaton and then took Budapest. In early 1945 the new allies steadily advanced towards Austria and successfully besieged Vienna in April. In all these campaigns the fighting was fierce and casualties on both sides were high. The new Bulgarian government was dedicated to Allied, and primarily Soviet, victory. Parcel post stamps were issued for general use overprinted 'All For The Front' and in March 1945 the domestic situation was dire enough for the remaining stocks of Boris III definitive stamps to be reissued with several over-prints – 'Collect All Rags', 'Collect Old Iron' and 'Collect Wastepaper' (Fig. 21.14).

With victory complete, the communist-led government merely stayed in power, and continued to purge the country of its opponents. A republic was voted for in a rigged election in September 1946, the monarchy was abolished and Simeon went into exile. On 1 September 1945 two small and relatively insignificant stamps marked Victory in Europe Day with the number '9' a central feature on each of them (Fig. 21.15). Soon afterwards, on 7 September, seven far larger stamps marked the first anniversary of the Fatherland Front Coalition with the whole designs centred on the number '9' – the day in September 1944 when the Fatherland Front seized power (Fig. 21.16).

When Southern Dobrudja was incorporated into Bulgaria under the terms of the Paris Peace Treaties of 1947 it became the only ally of Germany to increase its post-war boundaries.

Fig. 21.15

Fig. 21.14

Fig. 21.16

Illustrations

Fig. 21.1 Celebratory cover with the Recovery of Dobrudja set (20 September 1940) and a Tsar Boris definitive stamp with commemorative cachet and postmarks from Toutrakan, Dobritch, Karapelit and the fashionable Black Sea resort of Baltchik, all in South Dobrudja.

Fig. 21.2 10*st* Grapes and 30*st* Ploughing from the definitive stamps (1940–42).

Fig. 21.3 30*st* Beekeeper and 3*l* Shepherd from the Agriculture set (1940–44).

Fig. 21.4 2*l* King Boris and Map from the Reacquisition of Macedonia set (3 October 1941).

Fig. 21.5 1*l* Petko Slaveykov, 2*l* Bishop Sophronius and 10*l* Kolyu Ficheto from the National Relief Fund set (23 November 1940).

Fig. 21.6 1*l* Johannes Gutenberg and 2*l* Nikola Karastoyanov from the Invention and Introduction of Printing set (16 December 1940).

Fig. 21.7 1*l* Botev, 2*l* Bortev in Koslodui and 3*l* Botev Memorial Cross from the Hristo Botev set (3 May 1941).

Fig. 21.8 6*l* Motorcycle delivery and 9*l* Loading railway train from the Parcel Post sets (7 January 1942) and 20*l* Workers' Hospital from the Modern Buildings set (June 1941–March 1943).

Fig. 21.9 1*l* Girls making music and 7*l* Camp and bugler from the Work and Joy set (1 June 1942).

Fig. 21.10 20*l* Queen Giovanna visiting the wounded from the War Invalids set (7 September 1942).

Fig. 21.11 50*st* Baptism of Boris I, 1*l* St Naum's School and 4*l* Bogomil Vasili's trial from the Historic Series set (1942–43).

Fig. 21.12 5*l* Portrait from the Tsar Boris Mourning Issue set (28 February 1944) and 3*l* Portrait from the Tsar Simeon II set (12 June 1944).

Fig. 21.13 Examples (3) of Bulgarian stamps overprinted by liberated Macedonia.

Fig. 21.14 7*l* Parcel post stamp overprinted 'All For The Front' (25 January 1944) and 4*l* Boris III definitive stamp overprinted 'Collect All Rags', and 2*l* overprinted 'Collect Old Iron' (March 1945).

Fig. 21.15 50*l* from the VE Day set (1 September 1945).

Fig. 21.16 20*l* stamp from First Anniversary of the Fatherland Front Coalition set (7 September 1945).

22

CONCLUSION

VE Day – Victory in Europe Day – was celebrated on 8 May 1945. It was also the start of the Cold War. Much of western and eastern Europe was a wasteland, peopled by millions of families made homeless by the devastation or ejected by the restored rulers of the countries in which they had settled. Economic chaos haunted many countries along with the legal, social, political and psychological problems associated with dealing with the numerous citizens who cooperated with and sometimes fought for the enemy. France in particular experienced long-lasting difficulty in coming to terms with its humiliating surrender and the policies and practices of its pro-Axis Vichy state. Bulgaria, Romania, Hungary and the Baltic States had fallen under communist and Soviet Union domination by the end of 1945, and Czechoslovakia and Poland soon followed. Yugoslavia and Albania formed their own more independent versions of communist states. Greece and Italy survived strong internal communist threats to become, respectively, a brittle monarchy and republic. Germany lay prostrate at the feet of the Allies, with Great Britain, the USA, France and the Soviet Union administering various parts – the precursor to the creation of the separate West and East German states. Austria somehow ensured its independence through the Allies' willingness to believe it had been forced to unite with Germany in 1938. In 1946 Austria sought to impress the Allied Control Commission with a particularly lurid set of allegorical stamps showing Nazi daggers piercing a map of Austria and then Austria strangling a Nazi snake, sweeping away Nazi images and smashing Nazi pillars (Fig. 22.1). Finland, too, benefited from the Allies, especially the Soviet Union, tacitly agreeing that President Ryti's imprisonment for collaboration was sufficient retribution for fighting Soviet armies at the same time as Hitler.

Fig. 22.1

Liberation was a widely used term by the Allies and by occupied countries as Axis forces retreated, but it meant different things in Western nations such as Norway, Denmark, Belgium, the Netherlands, Luxembourg and France, where constitutional monarchies and freely elected republics were restored, and Eastern countries such as Poland, Czechoslovakia, Romania, Bulgaria and Hungary where Soviet pressure for a single party state obedient to dictates from Moscow was proving irresistible – although of course the internal wartime support for communism had been considerable, not least as it seemed to represent the antithesis of Nazi Germany and Fascist Italy.

Throughout the later 1940s and into the 1950s – and indeed intermittently up to the present day – both Western and Eastern European nations issued stamps celebrating their liberation and commemorating particular wartime events. Thus was born the various interpretations of this cataclysmic war according to the victors, and their understandable desire to place their role in the best possible light.

Early post war stamp issues show the different public responses. The Soviet Union emphasised both the heroism of its armed forces alongside numerous issues reinforcing the Marxist legacy and, thereby, its ideological stimulus to wartime efforts and, now, peacetime reconstruction (Fig. 22.2). There were no more images of Tsarist generals and admirals. In the new Eastern European satellite countries intermittent issues highlighted the horrors of Nazi occupation, such as the massacre at Lidice in Bohemia–Moravia, the ill-fated Warsaw and Slovak insurrections, and locally situated concentration camps. They sought to promote the idea that it was the devoted communists within these countries who had been entirely responsible for their liberation

Fig. 22.2

Fig. 22.3

Fig. 22.5

Fig. 22.4

Fig. 22.6

– alongside the sympathetic comrades they had cried out for from the Soviet Union (Fig. 22.3). The idea contained a great deal of truth, but not surprisingly overlooked both the contribution of non-communist partisans, and all those, including communist sympathisers, who sought autonomy for those countries. It was as though everyone who fought the Nazis was by definition fighting for Soviet-style communism. Numerous Bulgarian, Romanian, Hungarian, Polish and Czechoslovakian stamps appeared celebrating each country's long standing Communist Party and friendship with the Soviet Union, and Soviet Union stamps responded in similar vein (Fig. 22.4).

Western European countries were less exuberant in their issues. Liberation issues were usually limited to single stamps, not sets, and few subsequent issues looked back to the war (Fig. 22.5). Great Britain waited until 11 June 1946 to issue two stamps that some souvenir covers claimed to be a 'Victory' set, although others looked more closely at the stamps and noted the images were about 'Peace and Reconstruction' (Fig. 22.6). The Channel Islands waited until 10 May 1948 for two innocuous stamps picturing seaweed gathering that needed cachets on souvenir covers to explain they were marking the third anniversary of liberation.

France was different. Its traumatic collapse and extensive Vichy collaboration proved difficult for the country to come to terms with for decades after the war. There were many years without relevant stamp issues and then sudden outpourings of images that seemed to reveal the country's agonising process of self-rehabilitation. In November 1945 France decided to emphasise the damage the Allies had wrought upon Dunkirk, Rouen, Caen and St Malo, largely after the D-Day landings. In 1945 stamps celebrated liberated Metz and Strasbourg and Alsace-Lorraine in the east, but the D-Day landings had to wait until the tenth anniversary in 1954. In 1947 a stamp acknowledged the courageous British raid on St Nazaire docks, and in 1952 others commemorated the involvement of Free French forces in the battles at Narvik and Bir Hakeim. The resistance movement merited a stamp in 1947, the deportees to concentration camps in 1955, and then between 1957 and 1961 a series of five sets reinforced memories of both the heroism and the lingering scars of occupation and the ensuing collaboration with portraits of twenty-five men and women who died fighting the Nazis (Fig. 22.7a & 22.7b).

Fig. 22.7a

However, the fuller stories of Europe's immediate post-war issues as a radically different continent painfully emerged from its unprecedented traumas are really another book.

LES HÉROS DE LA RÉSISTANCE

———

Honoré d'ESTIENNE-d'ORVES

1901-1941

Officier de Marine Français

*rejoint les F F L l'été 1940
parachuté en France, capturé
tomba sous les balles ennemies
le 29 Août 1941*

MÉDAILLE DE LA LIBÉRATION

**PREMIER JOUR
D'EMISSION**
FIRST DAY COVER

M. J. BONITHON
6, Passage Sarget
BORDEAUX
(Gironde)

Fig. 22.7b

Illustrations

Fig. 22.1 Austria: 5*g*+3*g* Nazi dagger piercing Austria and 6*g*+4*g* Sweeping the swastika away from the Anti-Fascist Exhibition set (16 September 1946).

Fig. 22.2 Soviet Union: 60*k* grey-green Victory Medal featuring Stalin and 60*k* slate and red Soldier and Stalin banner from the Victory sets (1946) and 30*k* Tank and banner from the Tank Heroes set (1946).

Fig. 22.3 Czechoslovakia: 1.20*k* Fifth Anniversary of the Massacre at Lidice (10 June 1947). Poland: 15*z* Fifth Anniversary of the Warsaw Uprising (19 April 1948) and 1*z* Comrades in Arms (24 August 1954). Romania: 11*l* Communist Resistance fighter Filimon Sarbu (1954). Bulgaria: 30*l* Resistance fighters from the Resistance set (1946).

Fig. 22.4 Czechoslovakia: 3*k* First Anniversary of President Gottwald's Government (25 February 1949).

Fig. 22.5 Denmark: 20+5 Saboteurs from the Liberation Fund set (1947). Norway: 60+10 National Flags stamp from the Liberation Anniversary set (1965).

Fig. 22.6 Great Britain: First day cover with the Peace and Reconstruction set (11 June 1946).

Fig. 22.7 France: 5*f* 'Resistance' (10 November 1947) and 15*f* Tenth Anniversary of Liberation (5 June 1954) and first day cover (19 May 1957) of the Honoré d'Estienne-d'Orves stamp from the Heroes of the Resistance series issued between 1957 and 1961.

APPENDIX

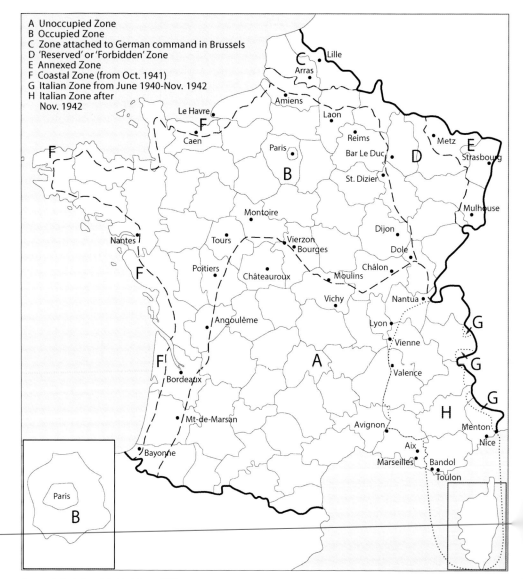

A Unoccupied Zone
B Occupied Zone
C Zone attached to German command in Brussels
D 'Reserved' or 'Forbidden' Zone
E Annexed Zone
F Coastal Zone (from Oct. 1941)
G Italian Zone from June 1940-Nov. 1942
H Italian Zone after
  Nov. 1942

France defeated and divided, June 1940

Poland under German and Soviet occupation, September 1939–June 1941

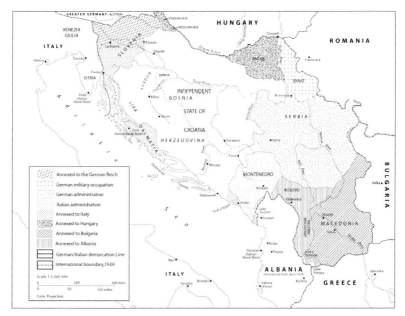

Division of Yugoslavia, April 1941

SELECT BIBLIOGRAPHY

Books

Bellamy, C., *Absolute War: Soviet Russia in the Second World War* (London: Pan Books, 2007).

Blom, J.C.H. and Lamberts, E. (eds), *History of the Low Countries* (New York and Oxford: Berghahn, 1999).

Bosworth, R.J.B., *Mussolini* (London: Hodder Education, 2002).

Botting, G., *In the Ruins of the Reich* (London: Methuen, 2005).

Burleigh, M., *Moral Combat: A History of World War II* (London: Harper Press, 2010).

Cornwell, J., *Hitler's Pope: The Secret History of Pius XII* (Harmondsworth: Penguin, 1999).

Crampton, R.J., *Eastern Europe in the Twentieth Century – and After* (London: Routledge, 1994).

Deighton, L., *Blood, Tears and Folly: An Objective Look at World War II* (London: Pimlico, 1993).

Duggan, C., *The Force of Destiny: A History of Italy since 1796* (London: Allen Lane, 2007).

Glenny, M., *The Balkans: Nationalism, War and the Great Powers 1804–1999* (Harmondsworth: Penguin, 2001).

Hastings, M., *Finest Years: Churchill as Warlord 1940–45* (London: Harper Press, 2009).

Hastings, M., *All Hell Let Loose: The World at War 1939–1945* (London: Harper Press, 2011).

Holland, J., *Italy's Sorrow: A Year of War 1944–45* (London: HarperCollins, 2009).

Jackson, J., *France: The Dark Years 1940–1944* (Oxford: Oxford University Press, 2001).

Kasekamp, A., *A History of the Baltic States* (London: Palgrave Macmillan, 2010).

Kershaw, I., *Hitler 1889–1936: Hubris* (Harmondsworth: Penguin, 1998).

Kershaw, I., *Hitler 1936–1945: Nemesis* (Harmondsworth: Penguin, 2000).

Kochanski, H., *The Eagle Unbowed: Poland and the Poles in the Second World War* (London: Penguin, 2012).

Lee, S., *Aspects of European History 1789–1980* (London: Routledge, 1982).

MacDonogh, G., *After the Reich: From the Liberation of Vienna to the Berlin Airlift* (London: John Murray, 2007).

Macmillan, M., *Peacemakers: Six Months that Changed the World* (London: John Murray, 2002).

Mazower, M., *Dark Continent: Europe's Twentieth Century* (Harmondsworth: Penguin, 1998).

Overy, R., *Russia's War* (Harmondsworth: Penguin, 1997).

Overy, R., with A. Wheatcroft, *The Road to War* (London: Vintage, 2009).

Roberts, A., *The Storm of War: A New History of the Second World War* (London: Harper, 2011).

Roberts, J.M., *A History of Europe* (Oxford: Helicon, 1996).

Sixsmith, M., *Russia: A 1,000-Year Chronicle of the Wild East* (London: BBC Books, 2011).

Stevenson, D., *1914–1918: The History of the First World War* (London: Penguin, 2004).

Taylor, A.J.P., *The Hapsburg Monarchy 1809–1918* (Harmondsworth: Pelican, 1981).

Trigg, J., *Hitler's Vikings: The History of the Scandinavian Waffen-SS* (Stroud: Spellmount/ The History Press, 2012).

Wheal, E.A. and Pope, S., *The Macmillan Dictionary of the Second World War*, 2nd edn (Basingstoke: Macmillan, 1995).

Zamoyski, A., *Poland: A History* (London: Harper, 2009).

Stamp Catalogues

Michel Deutschland-Spezial-Katalog Band 1: 1849 bis April 1945; Band 2: Ab May 1945.

Stanley Gibbons European Stamp Catalogues Nos 2, 3, 4, 5, 6, 7, 8, 10, 11.

INDEX

The
History
Press

The destination for history
www.thehistorypress.co.uk